THOR
LATVERIAN PROMETHEUS

WRITER: **KIERON GILLEN**
PENCILER: **BILLY TAN**
INKERS: **BATT** WITH **BILLY TAN**
COLORISTS: **CHRISTINA STRAIN, JOHN RAUCH**
& **PAUL MOUNTS** WITH **EMILY WARREN**
LETTERER: **VC'S JOE SABINO**
COVER ART: **BILLY TAN, BATT** & **JUSTIN PONSOR**
SPECIAL THANKS TO DON HO

"I AM THE LADY SIF"
WRITER: **KELLY SUE DECONNICK**
PENCILER: **RYAN STEGMAN**
INKERS: **TOM PALMER** WITH **VICTOR OLAZABA**
COLORIST: **JUAN DOE**
LETTERER: **VC'S JOE SABINO**
COVER ART: **TRAVEL FOREMAN** & **JUNE CHUNG**

"TO ASGARD! FOREVER!"
WRITER: **STAN LEE**
ARTIST: **DAVID AJA**
COLORIST: **MATT HOLLINGSWORTH**
LETTERER: **VC'S CHRIS ELIOPOULOS**

"WELCOME BACK, THOR"
WRITER & ARTIST: **CHRIS GIARRUSSO**

ASSISTANT EDITOR: **ALEJANDRO ARBONA**
EDITORS: **RALPH MACCHIO** & **WARREN SIMONS**

COLLECTION EDITOR: **JENNIFER GRÜNWALD**
ASSISTANT EDITOR: **ALEX STARBUCK**
ASSOCIATE EDITOR: **JOHN DENNING**
EDITOR, SPECIAL PROJECTS: **MARK D. BEAZLEY**
SENIOR EDITOR, SPECIAL PROJECTS: **JEFF YOUNGQUIST**
SENIOR VICE PRESIDENT OF SALES: **DAVID GABRIEL**

EDITOR IN CHIEF: **JOE QUESADA**
PUBLISHER: **DAN BUCKLEY**
EXECUTIVE PRODUCER: **ALAN FINE**

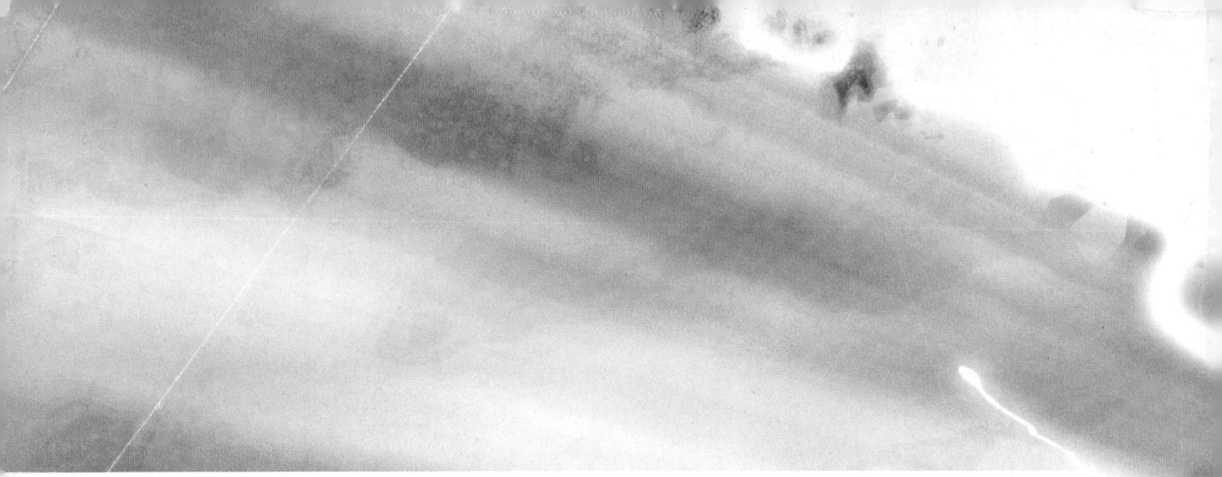

PREVIOUSLY:

FROM THE VERY FIRST DAY THAT THOR, THE GOD OF THUNDER, RESTORED TO EXISTENCE HIS PEOPLE AND THEIR HOME – ASGARD – HIS WICKED HALF-BROTHER LOKI HAS CONSPIRED AGAINST THEM.

THROUGH LOKI'S DIABOLICAL MANIPULATIONS, THOR WAS CAST INTO EXILE. IN HIS ABSENCE, THEIR BROTHER BALDER WAS PLACED ON THE THRONE. AND WITH LOKI WHISPERING POISON IN HIS EAR, BALDER ALLOWED MOST OF HIS POPULACE TO BE RELOCATED – FROM THE WELCOMING TOWN OF BROXTON, OKLAHOMA, SITE OF THEIR NEW SHINING CITY, TO A COLD AND REMOTE HOME...IN THE TYRANT DR. DOOM'S SOVEREIGN NATION OF LATVERIA.

WITH LOKI'S AID, DOOM BEGAN TO ABDUCT AND VIVISECT UNSUSPECTING ASGARDIANS...BUT NOT EVERYBODY WAS SO OBLIVIOUS. SUSPECTING TREACHERY, YOUNG BILL – THE MORTAL MAN WHOM THE IMMORTAL KELDA LOVED – PURSUED LOKI AND DISCOVERED DOOM'S PLAN.

IN A RAGE, LOKI SENT SINISTER WARRIORS AFTER BILL. THEY FOUGHT, AND BILL WAS MORTALLY STABBED. AS BILL LAY DYING, GOOD KING BALDER RODE TO THE SCENE. WITH HIS DYING BREATH, BILL WHISPERED IN BALDER'S EAR, TELLING HIM WHAT HE'D VALIANTLY PAID WITH HIS LIFE TO WITNESS. WHEN SHE LEARNED OF BILL'S DEATH, KELDA WAS INCONSOLABLE...

MEANWHILE, IN BROXTON, AN ATTACK FORCE OF LETHAL DOOMBOTS SWEPT DOWN ON THE UNSUSPECTING DR. DON BLAKE, THE HUMAN HOST TO THOR. AS THEY STRUCK, THE LADY SIF AND THE NOBLE WARRIORS THREE – THOR'S LOYAL COMPANIONS IN EXILE – JUMPED TO BLAKE'S SIDE AND SAVED HIS LIFE. BUT BLAKE DIDN'T ESCAPE UNSCATHED...HE WAS HIT BY A HIGH-POWERED ENERGY BLAST, AND LEFT WITH PERMANENT NERVE DAMAGE AND A LIMP...

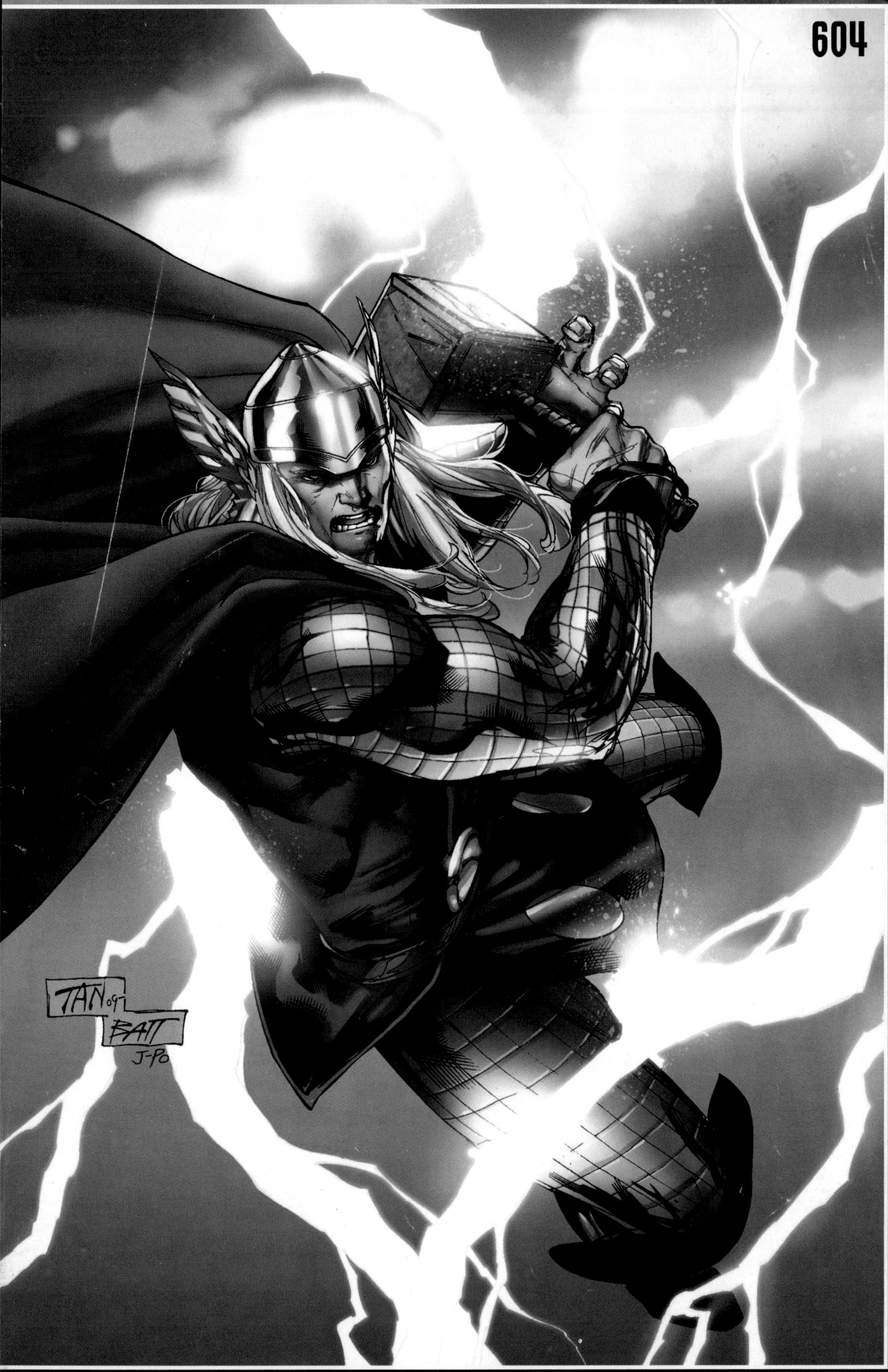
604
TAN 09
BATT
J-Po

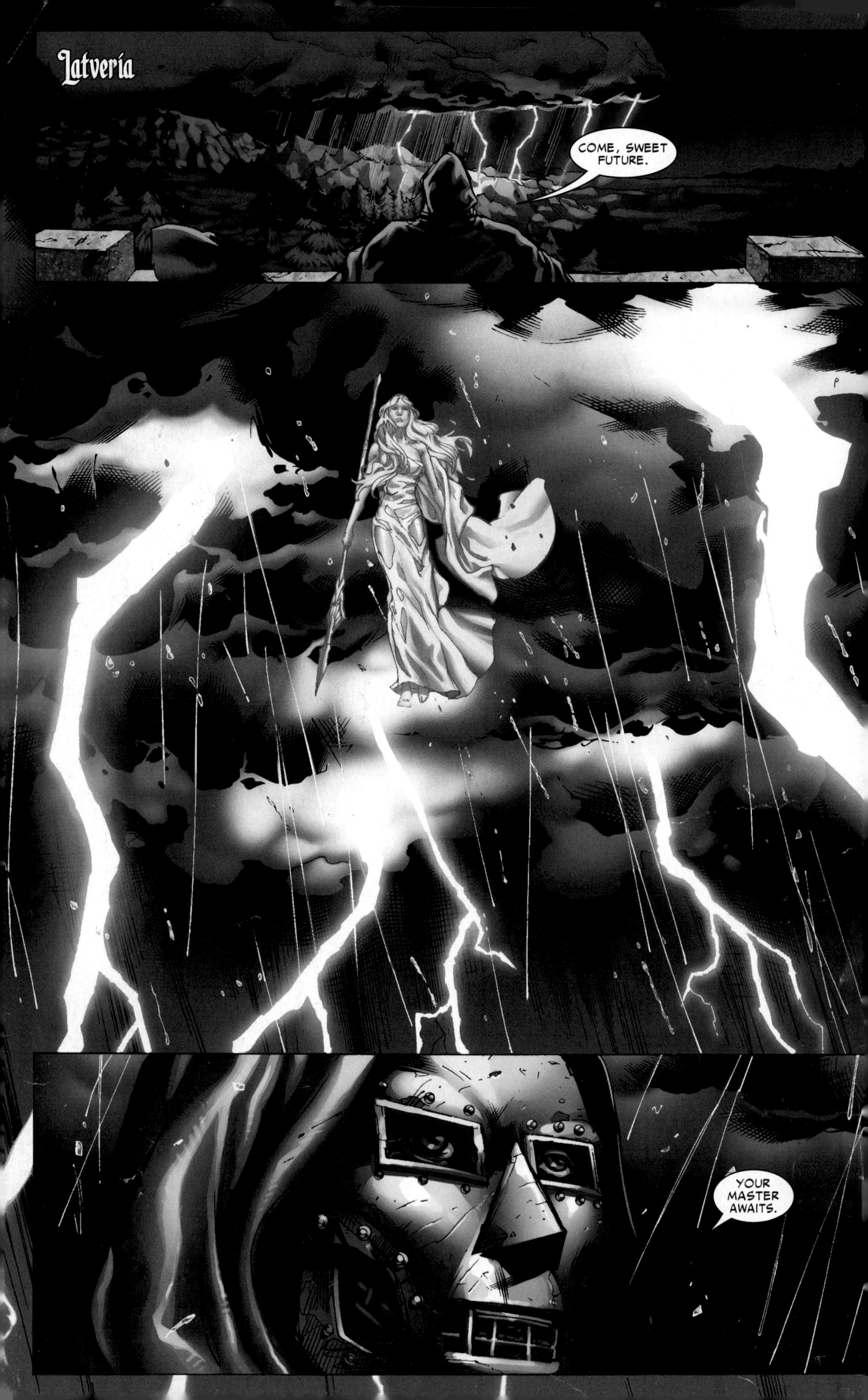
Latveria
COME, SWEET FUTURE.
YOUR MASTER AWAITS.

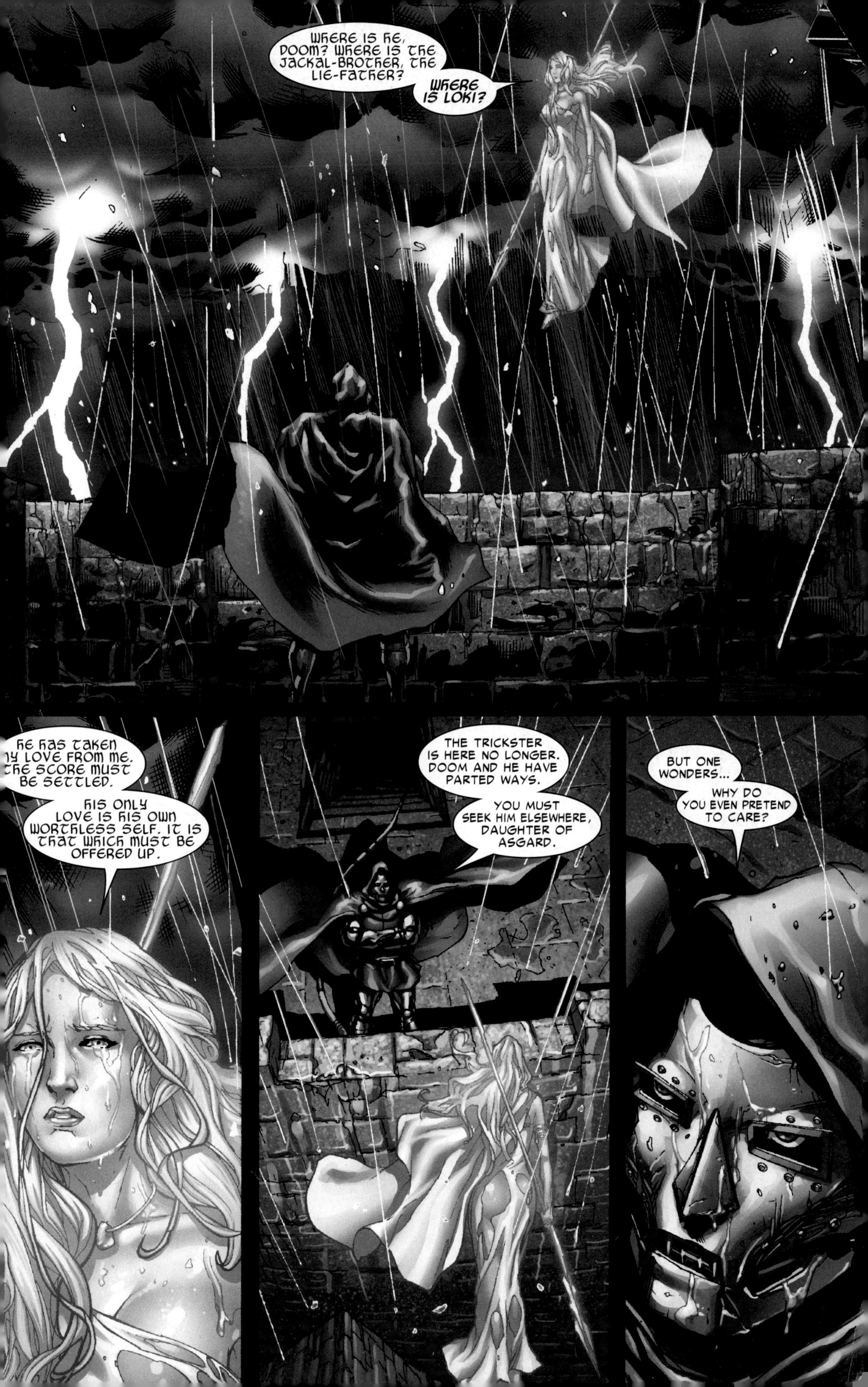
WHERE IS HE, DOOM? WHERE IS THE JACKAL-BROTHER, THE LIE-FATHER?
WHERE IS LOKI?
HE HAS TAKEN MY LOVE FROM ME. THE SCORE MUST BE SETTLED.
HIS ONLY LOVE IS HIS OWN WORTHLESS SELF. IT IS THAT WHICH MUST BE OFFERED UP.
THE TRICKSTER IS HERE NO LONGER. DOOM AND HE HAVE PARTED WAYS.
YOU MUST SEEK HIM ELSEWHERE, DAUGHTER OF ASGARD.
BUT ONE WONDERS...
WHY DO YOU EVEN PRETEND TO CARE?

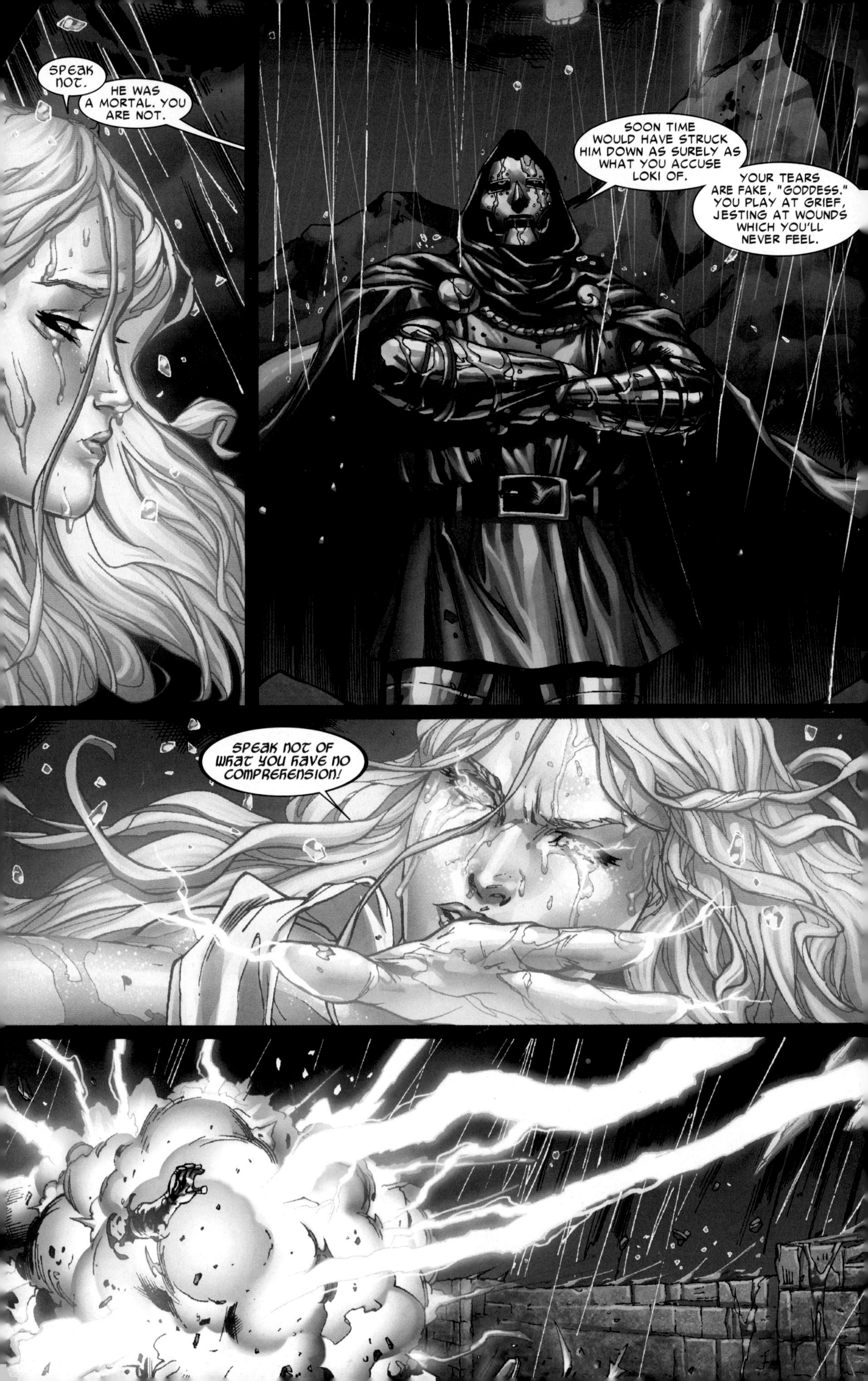
SPEAK NOT.
HE WAS A MORTAL. YOU ARE NOT.
SOON TIME WOULD HAVE STRUCK HIM DOWN AS SURELY AS WHAT YOU ACCUSE LOKI OF.
YOUR TEARS ARE FAKE, "GODDESS." YOU PLAY AT GRIEF, JESTING AT WOUNDS WHICH YOU'LL NEVER FEEL.
SPEAK NOT OF WHAT YOU HAVE NO COMPREHENSION!

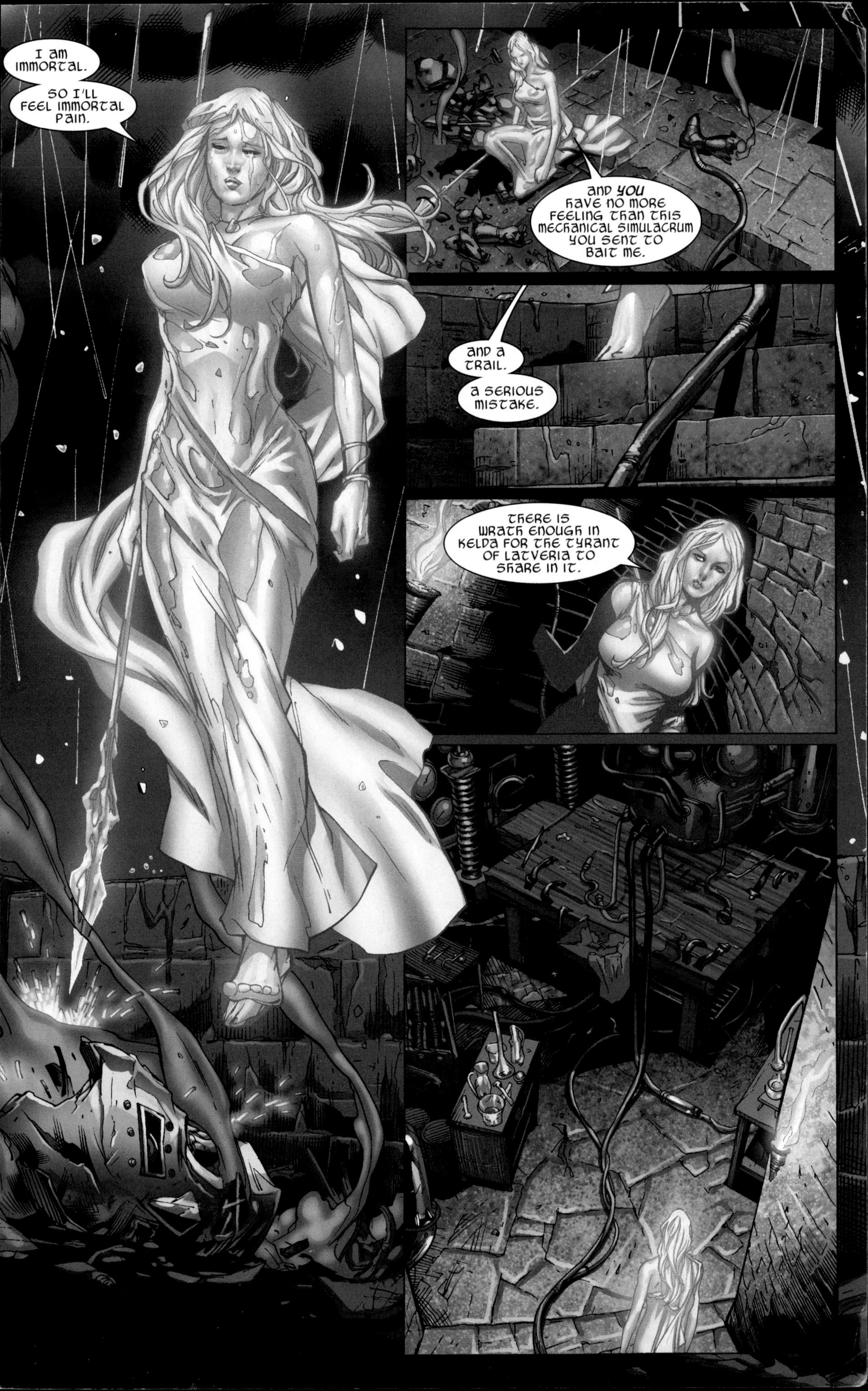
I AM IMMORTAL.
SO I'LL FEEL IMMORTAL PAIN.
AND YOU HAVE NO MORE FEELING THAN THIS MECHANICAL SIMULACRUM YOU SENT TO BAIT ME.
AND A TRAIL.
A SERIOUS MISTAKE.
THERE IS WRATH ENOUGH IN KELDA FOR THE TYRANT OF LATVERIA TO SHARE IN IT.

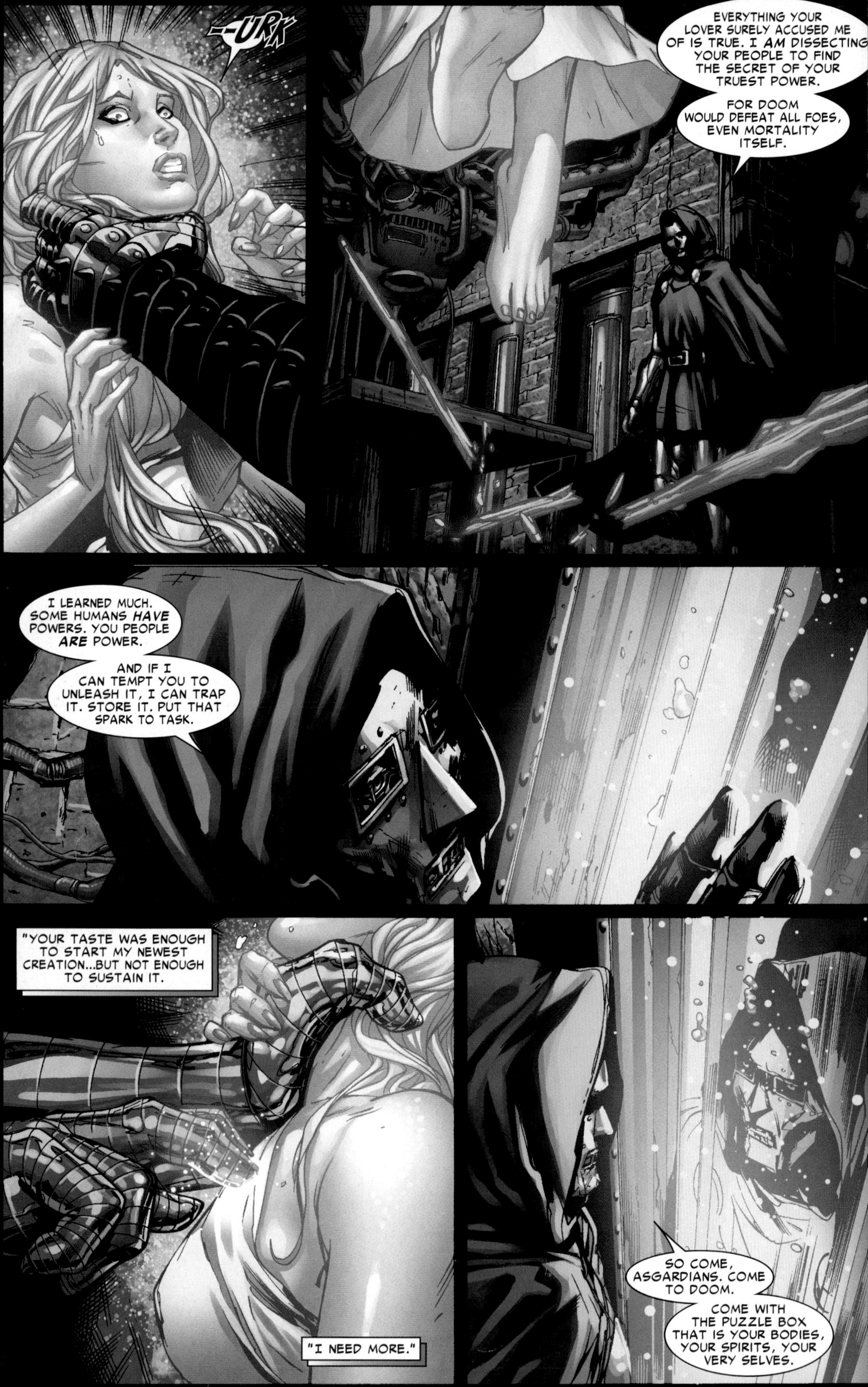

-URK
EVERYTHING YOUR LOVER SURELY ACCUSED ME OF IS TRUE. I AM DISSECTING YOUR PEOPLE TO FIND THE SECRET OF YOUR TRUEST POWER.
FOR DOOM WOULD DEFEAT ALL FOES, EVEN MORTALITY ITSELF.
I LEARNED MUCH. SOME HUMANS HAVE POWERS. YOU PEOPLE ARE POWER.
AND IF I CAN TEMPT YOU TO UNLEASH IT, I CAN TRAP IT. STORE IT. PUT THAT SPARK TO TASK.
"YOUR TASTE WAS ENOUGH TO START MY NEWEST CREATION...BUT NOT ENOUGH TO SUSTAIN IT.
"I NEED MORE."
SO COME, ASGARDIANS. COME TO DOOM.
COME WITH THE PUZZLE BOX THAT IS YOUR BODIES, YOUR SPIRITS, YOUR VERY SELVES.

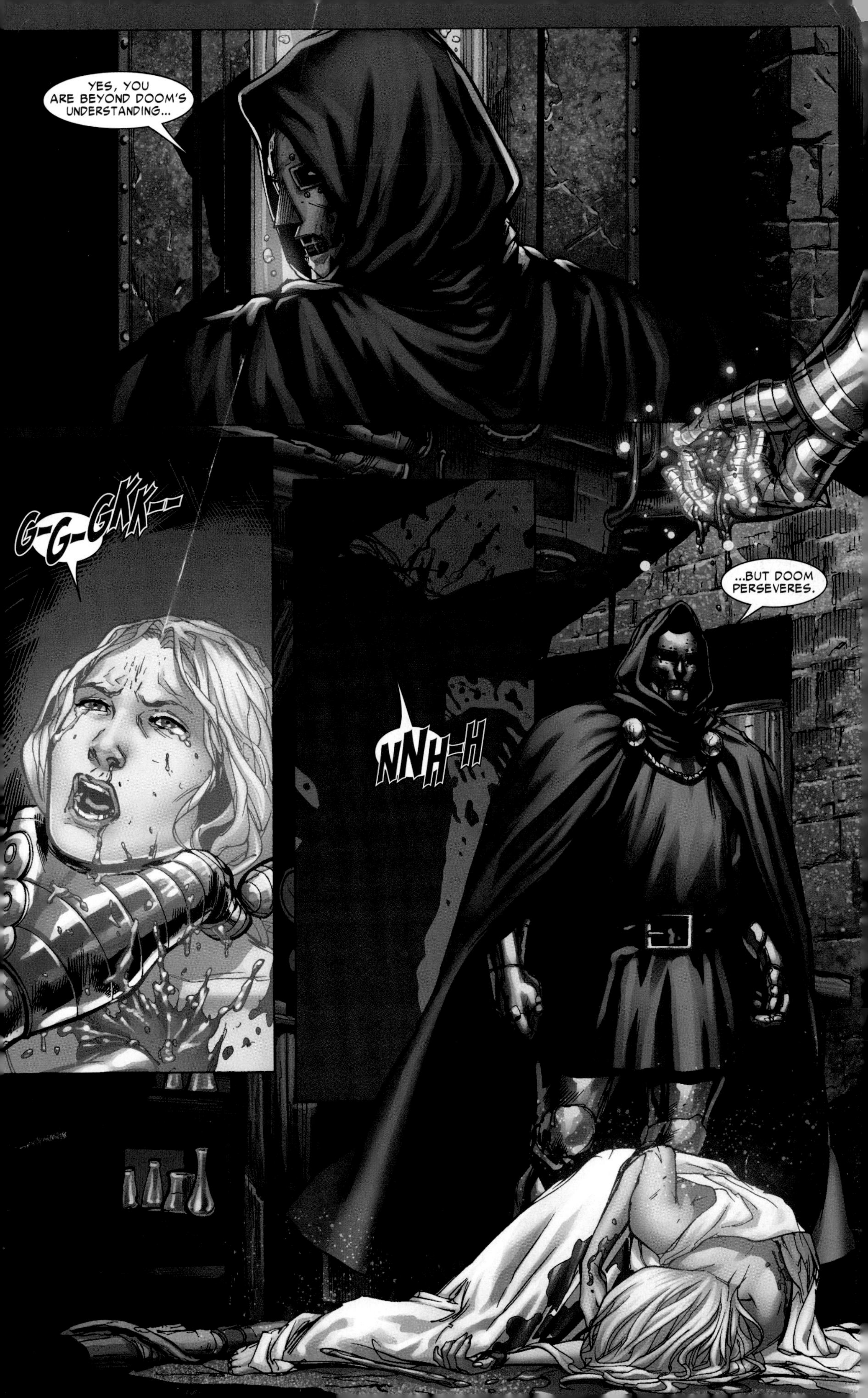
YES, YOU ARE BEYOND DOOM'S UNDERSTANDING...
G-G-GKK--
NNH-H
...BUT DOOM PERSEVERES.

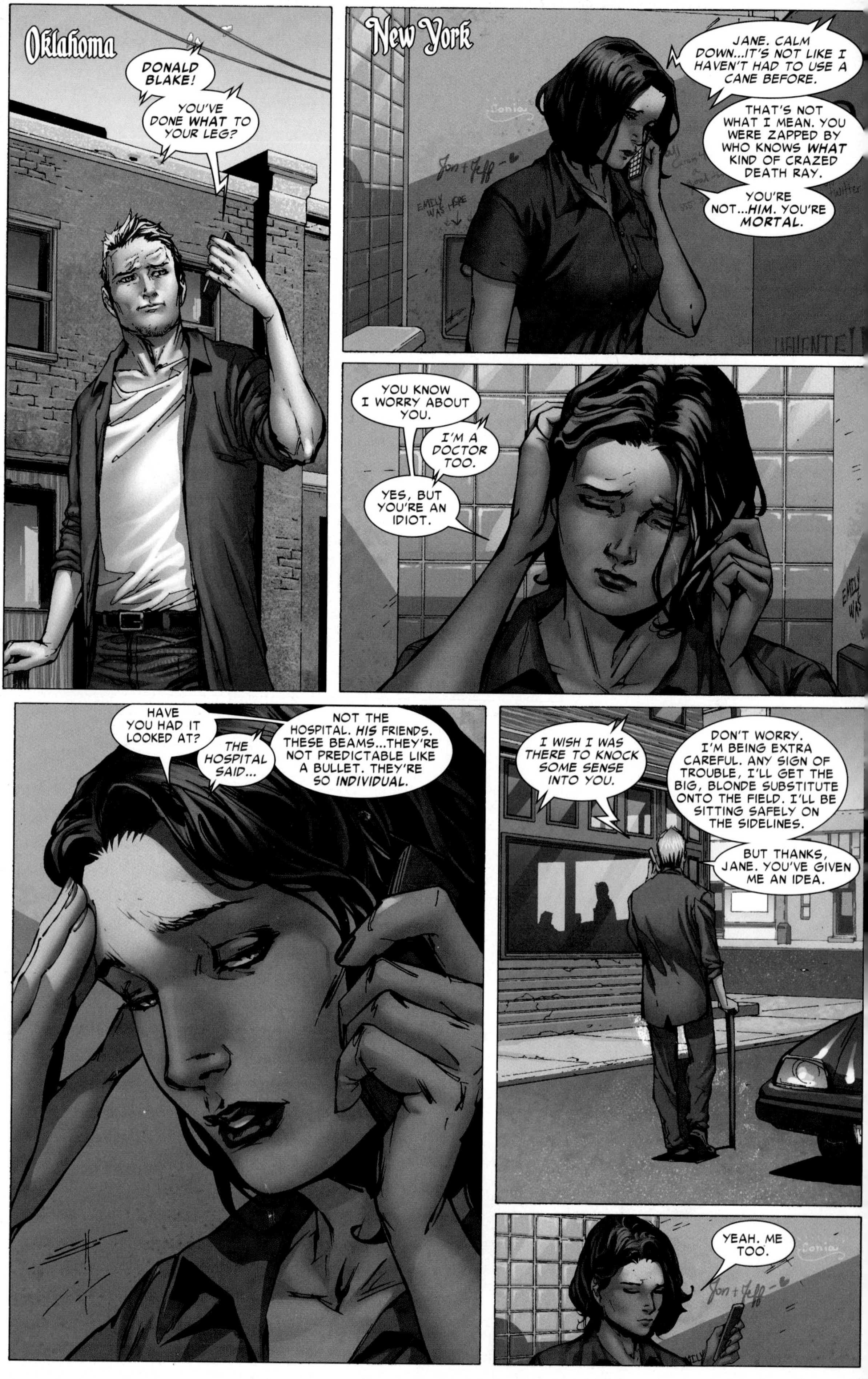
Oklahoma
DONALD BLAKE!
YOU'VE DONE WHAT TO YOUR LEG?
New York
JANE. CALM DOWN...IT'S NOT LIKE I HAVEN'T HAD TO USE A CANE BEFORE.
THAT'S NOT WHAT I MEAN. YOU WERE ZAPPED BY WHO KNOWS WHAT KIND OF CRAZED DEATH RAY.
YOU'RE NOT...HIM. YOU'RE MORTAL.
YOU KNOW I WORRY ABOUT YOU.
I'M A DOCTOR TOO.
YES, BUT YOU'RE AN IDIOT.
HAVE YOU HAD IT LOOKED AT?
THE HOSPITAL SAID...
NOT THE HOSPITAL. HIS FRIENDS. THESE BEAMS...THEY'RE NOT PREDICTABLE LIKE A BULLET. THEY'RE SO INDIVIDUAL.
I WISH I WAS THERE TO KNOCK SOME SENSE INTO YOU.
DON'T WORRY. I'M BEING EXTRA CAREFUL. ANY SIGN OF TROUBLE, I'LL GET THE BIG, BLONDE SUBSTITUTE ONTO THE FIELD. I'LL BE SITTING SAFELY ON THE SIDELINES.
BUT THANKS, JANE. YOU'VE GIVEN ME AN IDEA.
YEAH. ME TOO.

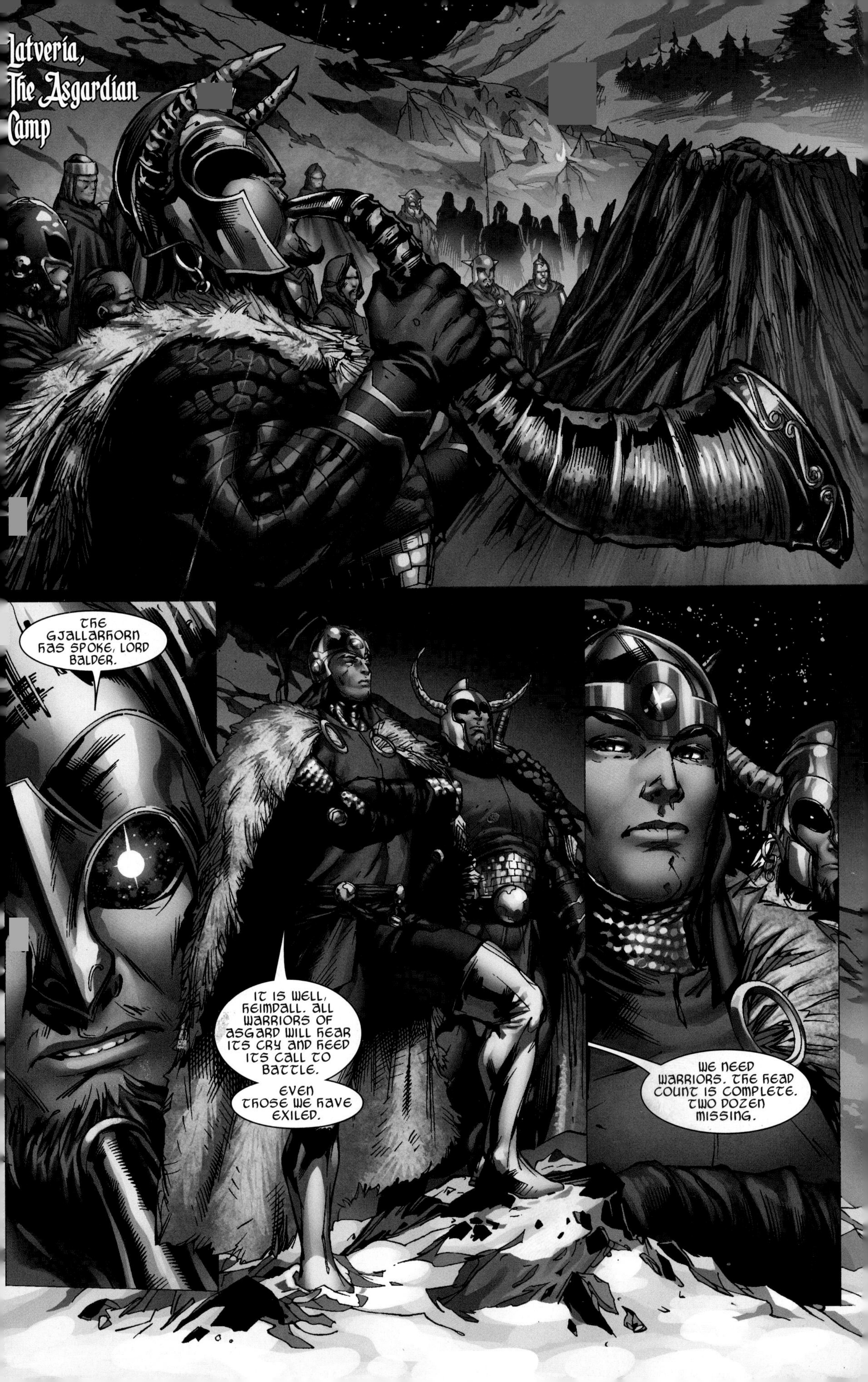
Latveria, The Asgardian Camp
THE GJALLARHORN HAS SPOKE, LORD BALDER.
IT IS WELL, HEIMDALL. ALL WARRIORS OF ASGARD WILL HEAR ITS CRY AND HEED ITS CALL TO BATTLE.
EVEN THOSE WE HAVE EXILED.
WE NEED WARRIORS. THE HEAD COUNT IS COMPLETE. TWO DOZEN MISSING.

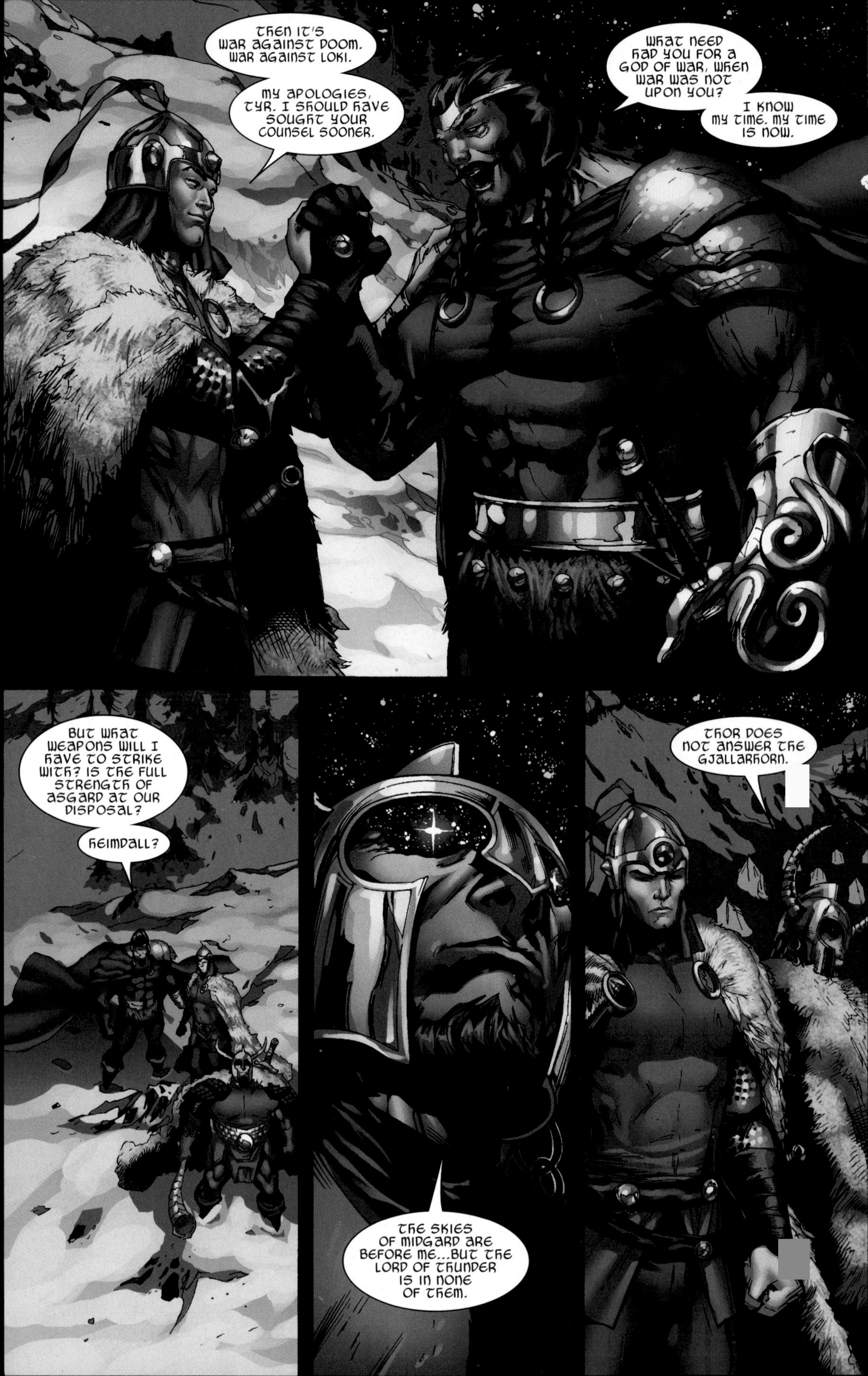
THEN IT'S WAR AGAINST DOOM. WAR AGAINST LOKI.
MY APOLOGIES, TYR. I SHOULD HAVE SOUGHT YOUR COUNSEL SOONER.
WHAT NEED HAD YOU FOR A GOD OF WAR, WHEN WAR WAS NOT UPON YOU?
I KNOW MY TIME. MY TIME IS NOW.
BUT WHAT WEAPONS WILL I HAVE TO STRIKE WITH? IS THE FULL STRENGTH OF ASGARD AT OUR DISPOSAL?
HEIMDALL?
THE SKIES OF MIDGARD ARE BEFORE ME...BUT THE LORD OF THUNDER IS IN NONE OF THEM.
THOR DOES NOT ANSWER THE GJALLARHORN.

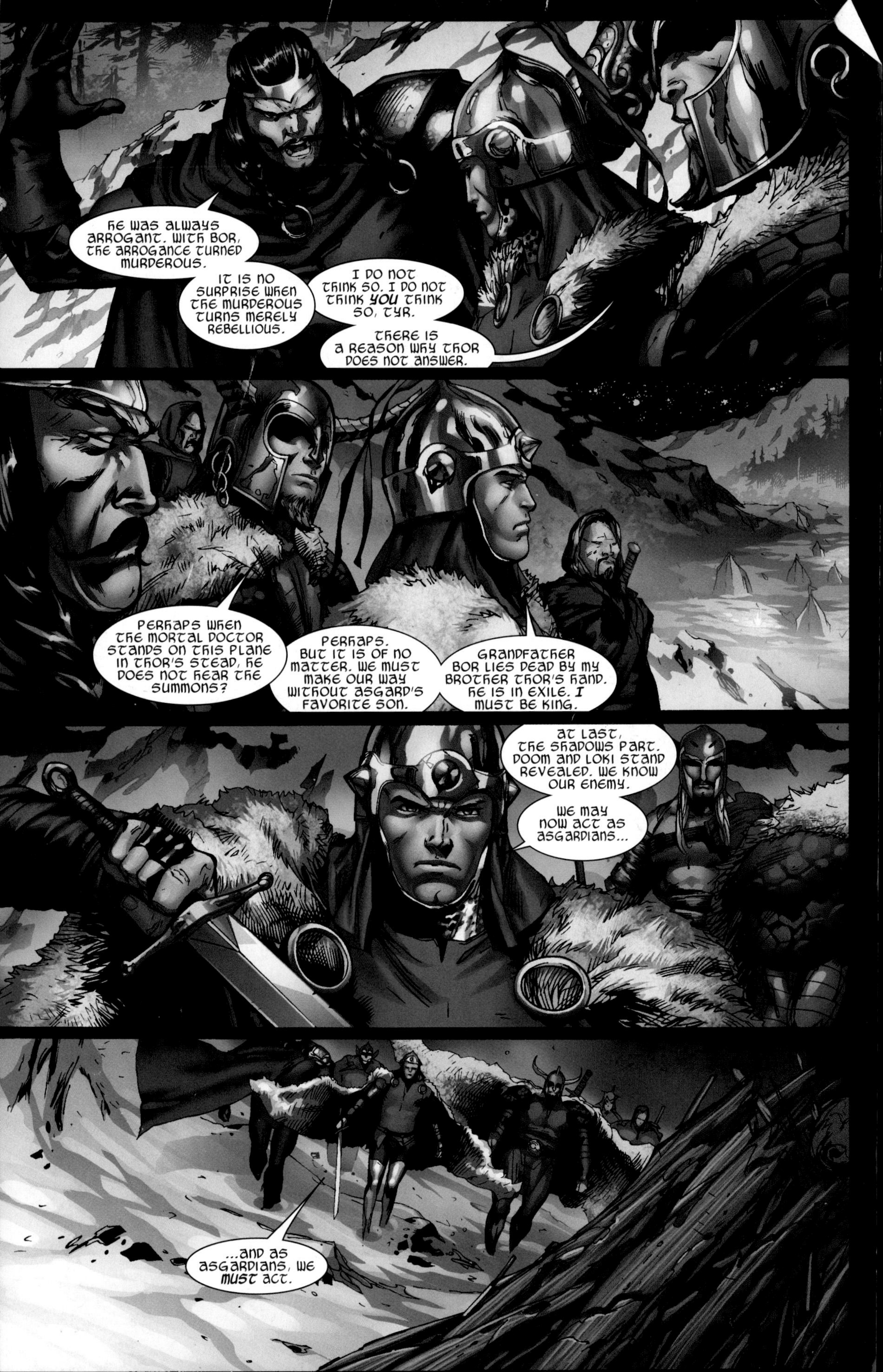
HE WAS ALWAYS ARROGANT. WITH BOR, THE ARROGANCE TURNED MURDEROUS.
IT IS NO SURPRISE WHEN THE MURDEROUS TURNS MERELY REBELLIOUS.
I DO NOT THINK SO. I DO NOT THINK YOU THINK SO, TYR.
THERE IS A REASON WHY THOR DOES NOT ANSWER.
PERHAPS WHEN THE MORTAL DOCTOR STANDS ON THIS PLANE IN THOR'S STEAD, HE DOES NOT HEAR THE SUMMONS?
PERHAPS. BUT IT IS OF NO MATTER. WE MUST MAKE OUR WAY WITHOUT ASGARD'S FAVORITE SON.
GRANDFATHER BOR LIES DEAD BY MY BROTHER THOR'S HAND. HE IS IN EXILE. I MUST BE KING.
AT LAST, THE SHADOWS PART. DOOM AND LOKI STAND REVEALED. WE KNOW OUR ENEMY.
WE MAY NOW ACT AS ASGARDIANS...
...AND AS ASGARDIANS, WE MUST ACT.

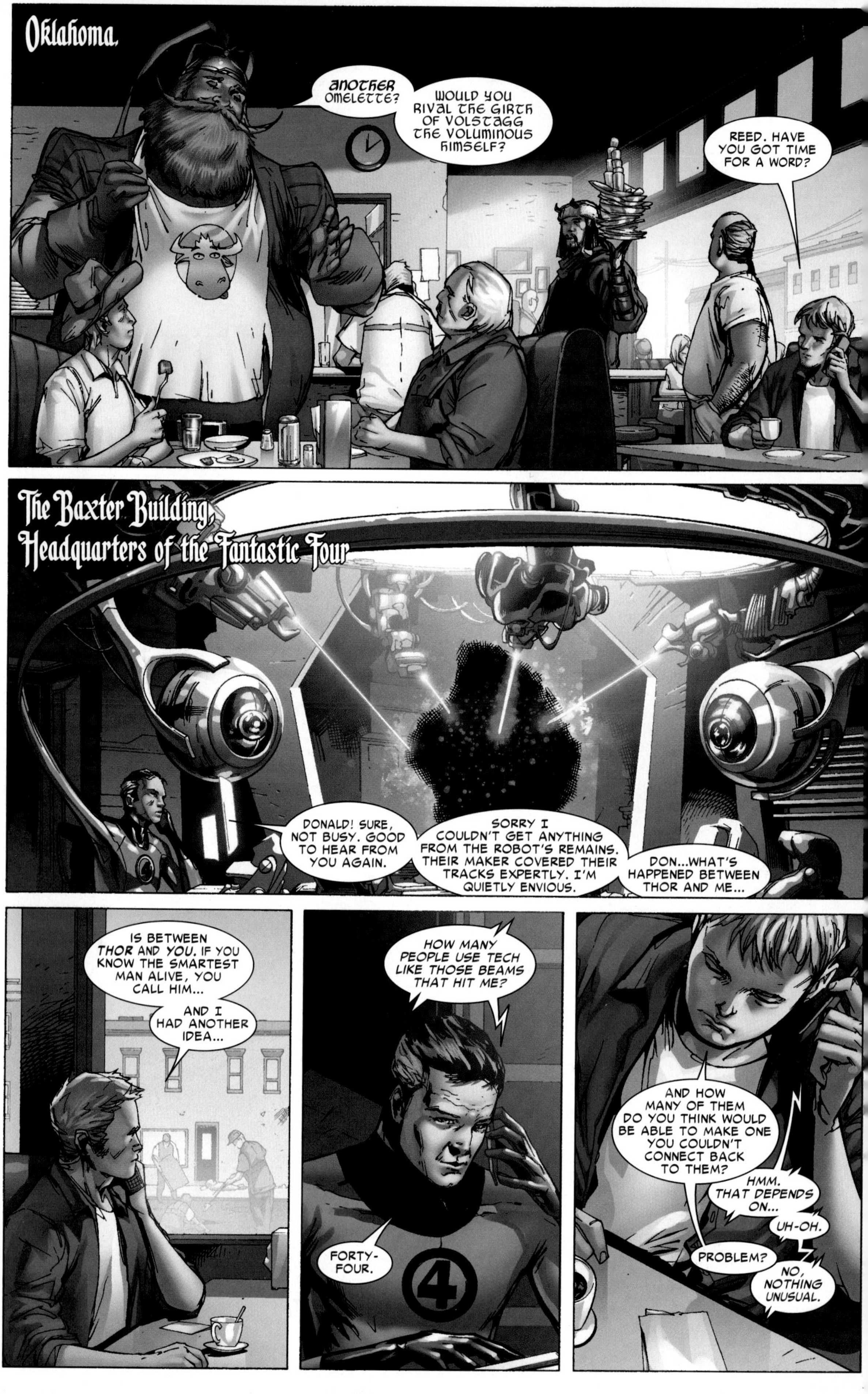
Oklahoma.
ANOTHER OMELETTE?
WOULD YOU RIVAL THE GIRTH OF VOLSTAGG THE VOLUMINOUS HIMSELF?
REED. HAVE YOU GOT TIME FOR A WORD?
The Baxter Building, Headquarters of the Fantastic Four
DONALD! SURE, NOT BUSY. GOOD TO HEAR FROM YOU AGAIN.
SORRY I COULDN'T GET ANYTHING FROM THE ROBOT'S REMAINS. THEIR MAKER COVERED THEIR TRACKS EXPERTLY. I'M QUIETLY ENVIOUS.
DON...WHAT'S HAPPENED BETWEEN THOR AND ME...
IS BETWEEN THOR AND YOU. IF YOU KNOW THE SMARTEST MAN ALIVE, YOU CALL HIM...
AND I HAD ANOTHER IDEA...
HOW MANY PEOPLE USE TECH LIKE THOSE BEAMS THAT HIT ME?
FORTY-FOUR.
AND HOW MANY OF THEM DO YOU THINK WOULD BE ABLE TO MAKE ONE YOU COULDN'T CONNECT BACK TO THEM?
HMM. THAT DEPENDS ON...
UH-OH.
PROBLEM?
NO, NOTHING UNUSUAL.

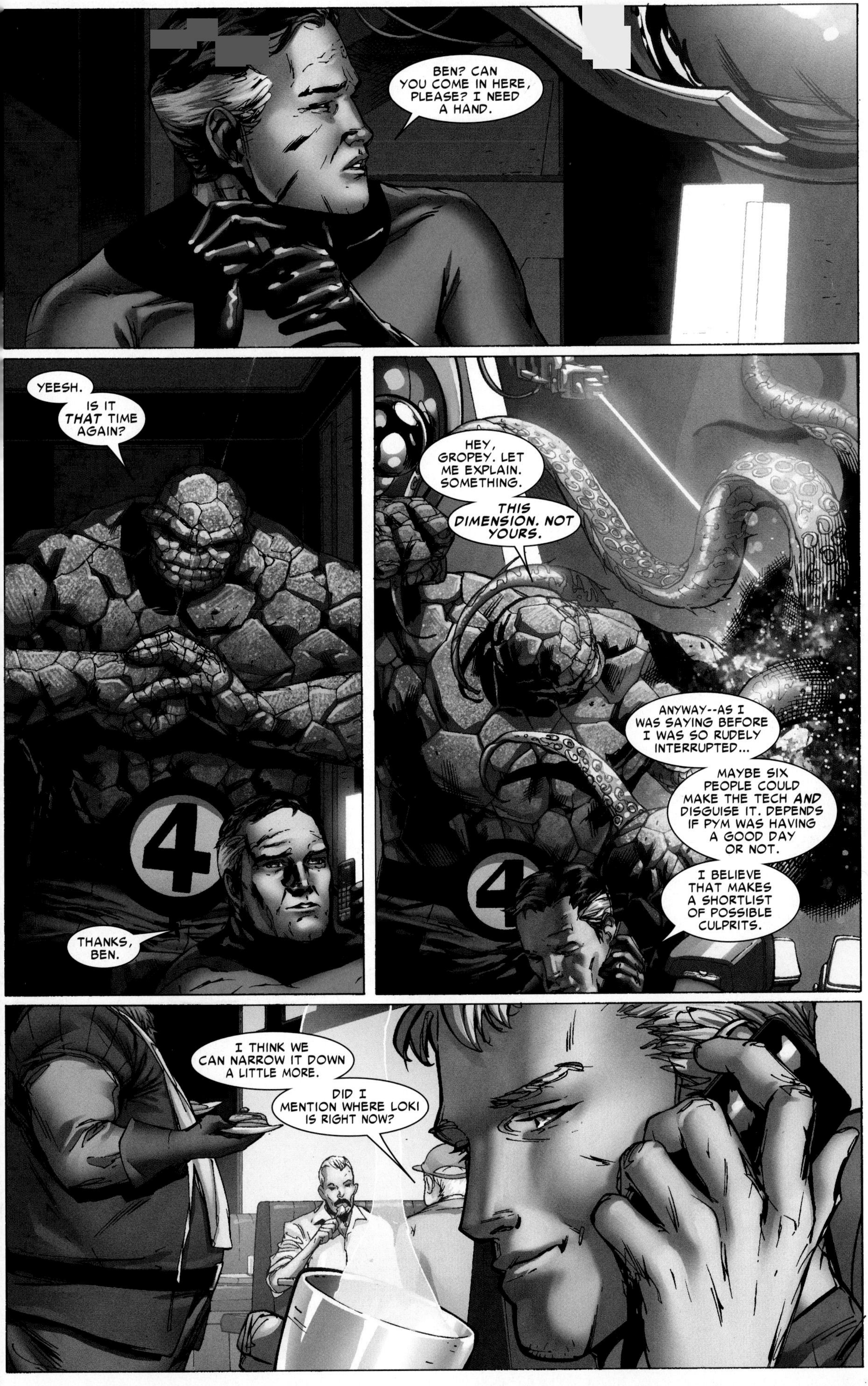
BEN? CAN YOU COME IN HERE, PLEASE? I NEED A HAND.
YEESH.
IS IT *THAT* TIME AGAIN?
THANKS, BEN.
HEY, GROPEY. LET ME EXPLAIN. SOMETHING.
THIS DIMENSION. NOT YOURS.
ANYWAY--AS I WAS SAYING BEFORE I WAS SO RUDELY INTERRUPTED...
MAYBE SIX PEOPLE COULD MAKE THE TECH *AND* DISGUISE IT. DEPENDS IF PYM WAS HAVING A GOOD DAY OR NOT.
I BELIEVE THAT MAKES A SHORTLIST OF POSSIBLE CULPRITS.
I THINK WE CAN NARROW IT DOWN A LITTLE MORE.
DID I MENTION WHERE LOKI IS RIGHT NOW?

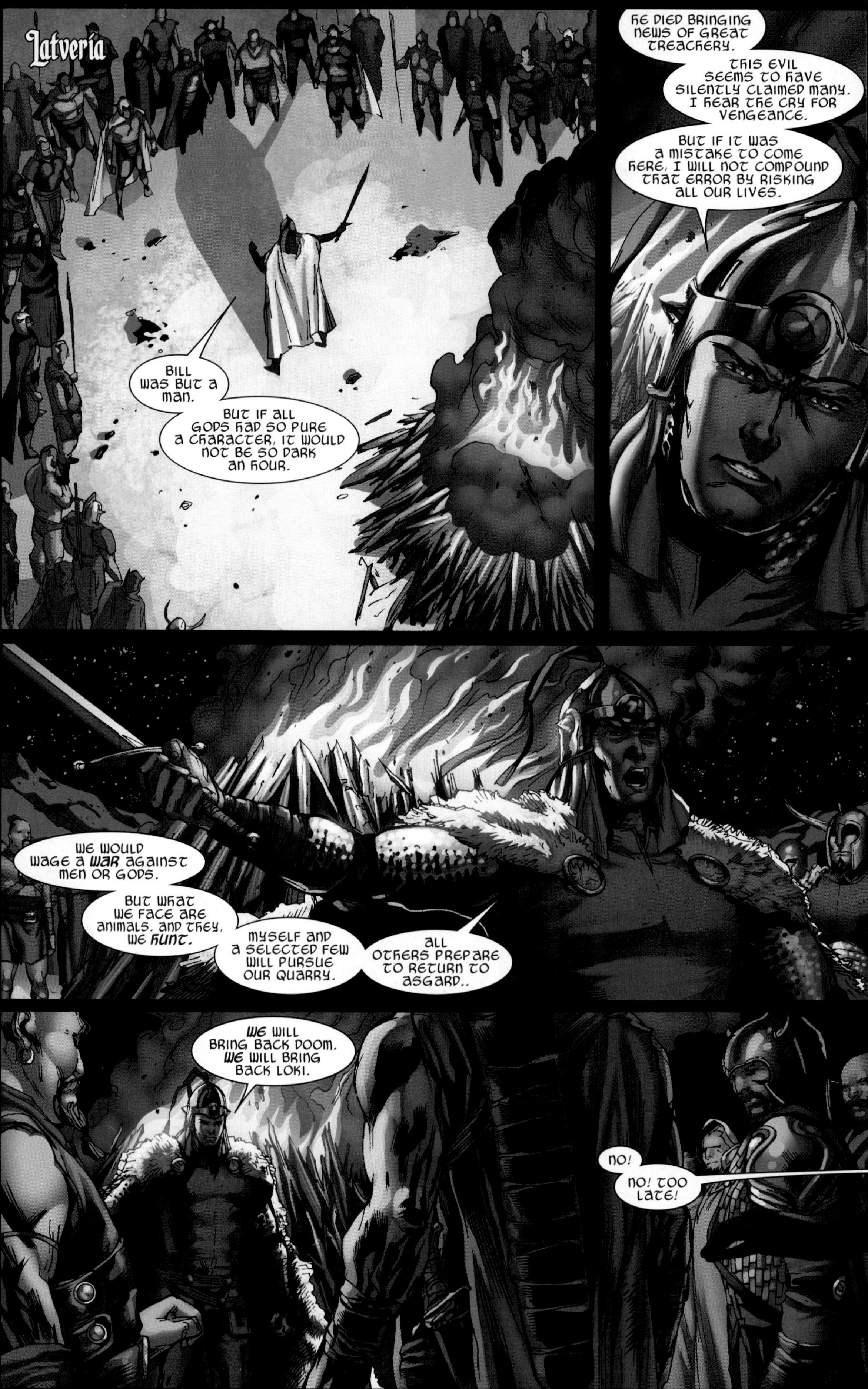
Latveria
BILL WAS BUT A MAN.
BUT IF ALL GODS HAD SO PURE A CHARACTER, IT WOULD NOT BE SO DARK AN HOUR.
HE DIED BRINGING NEWS OF GREAT TREACHERY.
THIS EVIL SEEMS TO HAVE SILENTLY CLAIMED MANY. I HEAR THE CRY FOR VENGEANCE.
BUT IF IT WAS A MISTAKE TO COME HERE, I WILL NOT COMPOUND THAT ERROR BY RISKING ALL OUR LIVES.
WE WOULD WAGE A **WAR** AGAINST MEN OR GODS.
BUT WHAT WE FACE ARE ANIMALS. AND THEY, WE **HUNT.**
MYSELF AND A SELECTED FEW WILL PURSUE OUR QUARRY.
ALL OTHERS PREPARE TO RETURN TO ASGARD..
WE WILL BRING BACK DOOM. **WE** WILL BRING BACK LOKI.
NO!
NO! TOO LATE!

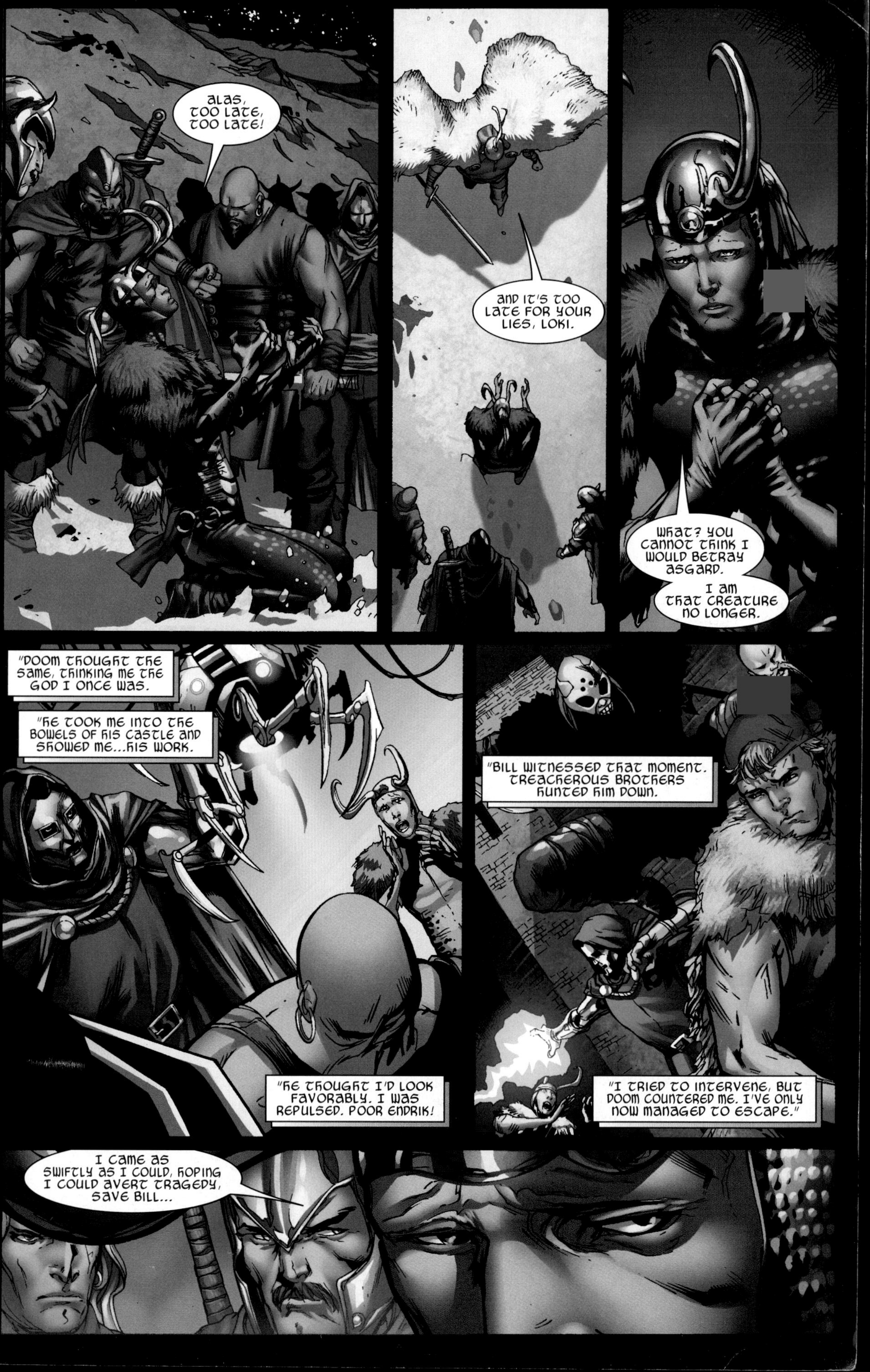
ALAS, TOO LATE, TOO LATE!
AND IT'S TOO LATE FOR YOUR LIES, LOKI.
WHAT? YOU CANNOT THINK I WOULD BETRAY ASGARD.
I AM THAT CREATURE NO LONGER.
"DOOM THOUGHT THE SAME, THINKING ME THE GOD I ONCE WAS.
"HE TOOK ME INTO THE BOWELS OF HIS CASTLE AND SHOWED ME...HIS WORK.
"HE THOUGHT I'D LOOK FAVORABLY. I WAS REPULSED. POOR ENDRIK!
"BILL WITNESSED THAT MOMENT. TREACHEROUS BROTHERS HUNTED HIM DOWN.
"I TRIED TO INTERVENE, BUT DOOM COUNTERED ME. I'VE ONLY NOW MANAGED TO ESCAPE."
I CAME AS SWIFTLY AS I COULD, HOPING I COULD AVERT TRAGEDY, SAVE BILL...

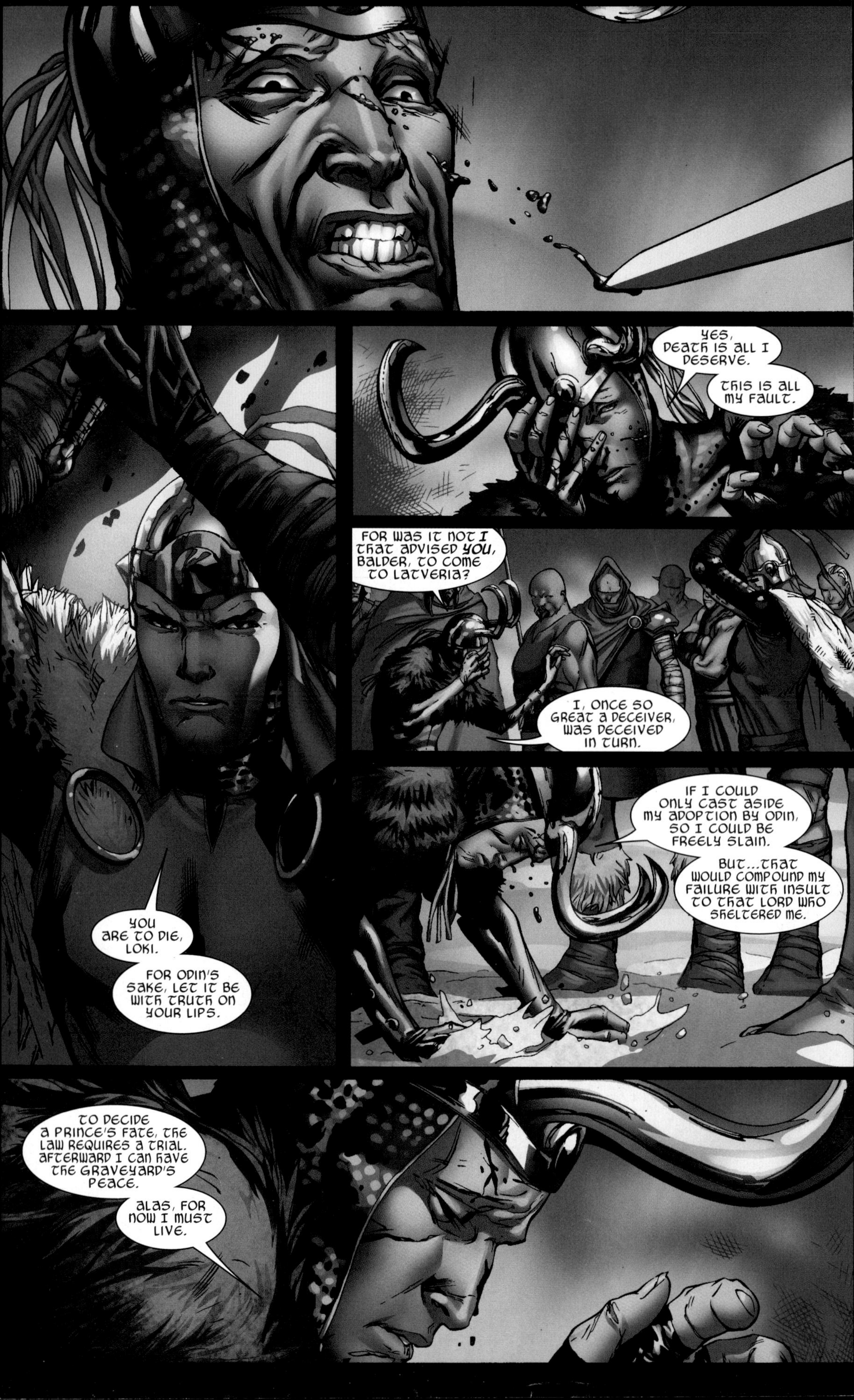
YES, DEATH IS ALL I DESERVE.
THIS IS ALL MY FAULT.
FOR WAS IT NOT I THAT ADVISED YOU, BALDER, TO COME TO LATVERIA?
I, ONCE SO GREAT A DECEIVER, WAS DECEIVED IN TURN.
YOU ARE TO DIE, LOKI.
FOR ODIN'S SAKE, LET IT BE WITH TRUTH ON YOUR LIPS.
IF I COULD ONLY CAST ASIDE MY ADOPTION BY ODIN, SO I COULD BE FREELY SLAIN.
BUT...THAT WOULD COMPOUND MY FAILURE WITH INSULT TO THAT LORD WHO SHELTERED ME.
TO DECIDE A PRINCE'S FATE, THE LAW REQUIRES A TRIAL. AFTERWARD I CAN HAVE THE GRAVEYARD'S PEACE.
ALAS, FOR NOW I MUST LIVE.

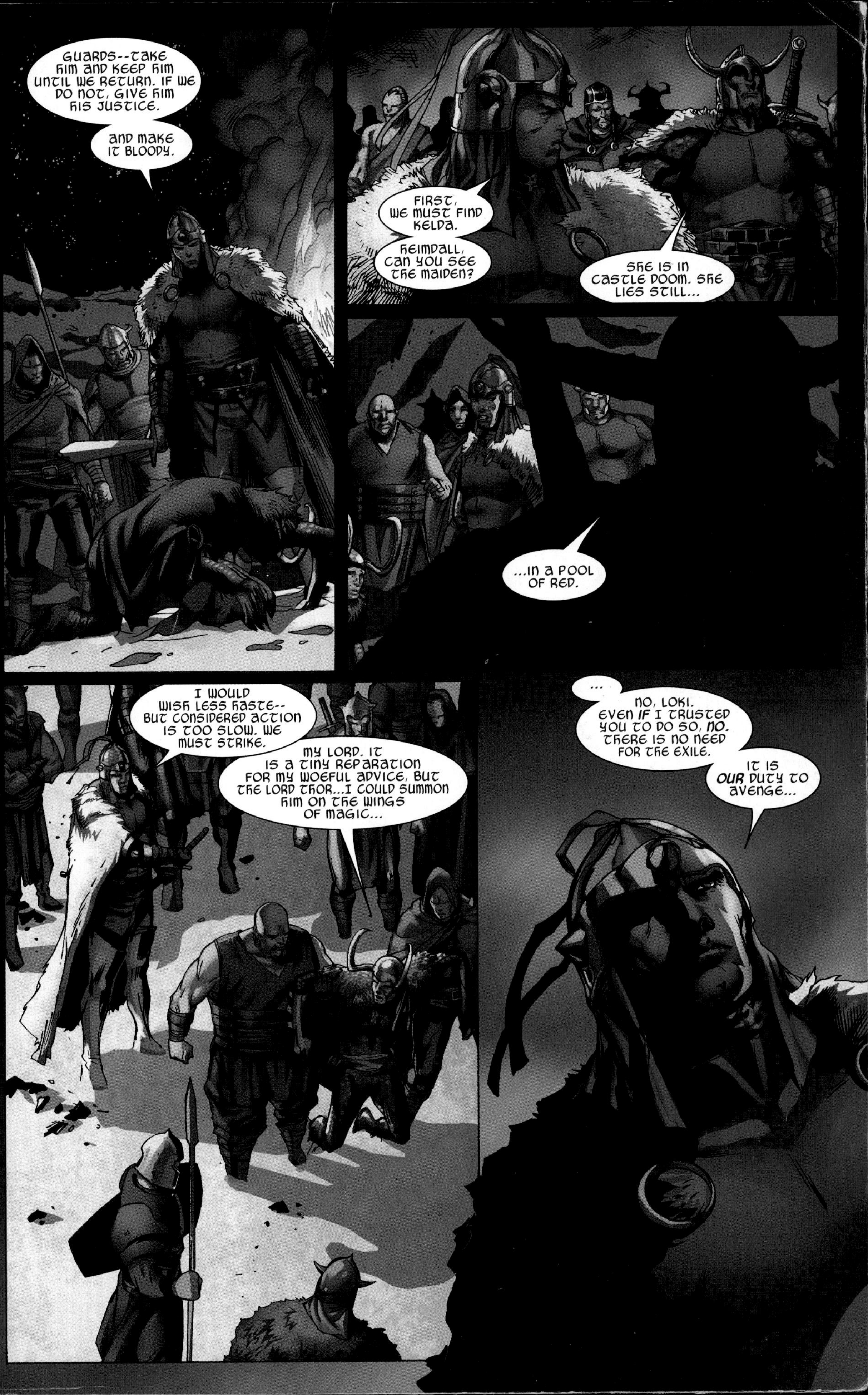
GUARDS--TAKE HIM AND KEEP HIM UNTIL WE RETURN. IF WE DO NOT, GIVE HIM HIS JUSTICE.
AND MAKE IT BLOODY.
FIRST, WE MUST FIND KELDA.
HEIMDALL, CAN YOU SEE THE MAIDEN?
SHE IS IN CASTLE DOOM. SHE LIES STILL...
...IN A POOL OF RED.
I WOULD WISH LESS HASTE-- BUT CONSIDERED ACTION IS TOO SLOW. WE MUST STRIKE.
MY LORD. IT IS A TINY REPARATION FOR MY WOEFUL ADVICE, BUT THE LORD THOR...I COULD SUMMON HIM ON THE WINGS OF MAGIC...
...
NO, LOKI. EVEN IF I TRUSTED YOU TO DO SO, NO. THERE IS NO NEED FOR THE EXILE.
IT IS OUR DUTY TO AVENGE...

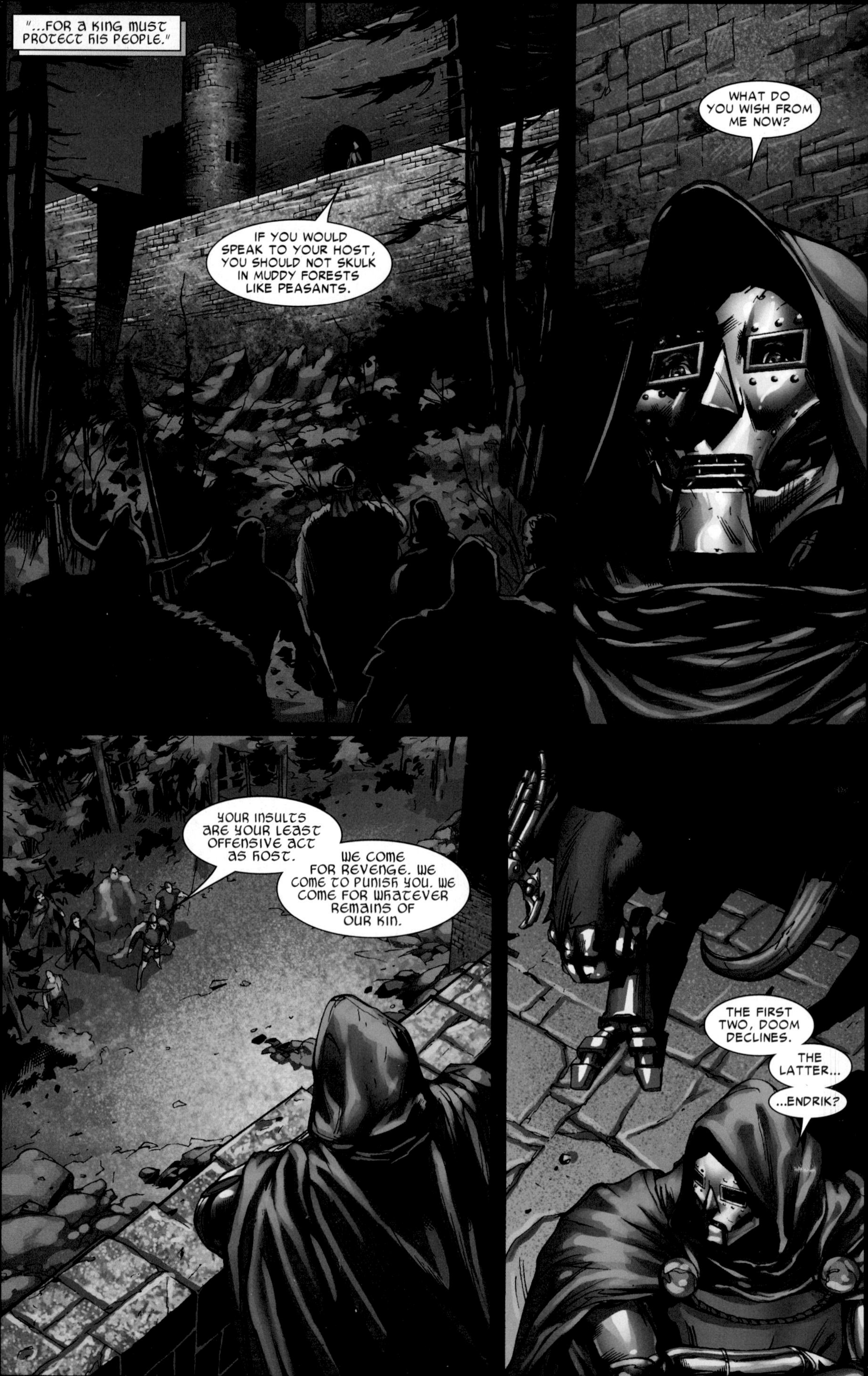
"...FOR A KING MUST PROTECT HIS PEOPLE."
WHAT DO YOU WISH FROM ME NOW?
IF YOU WOULD SPEAK TO YOUR HOST, YOU SHOULD NOT SKULK IN MUDDY FORESTS LIKE PEASANTS.
YOUR INSULTS ARE YOUR LEAST OFFENSIVE ACT AS HOST.
WE COME FOR REVENGE. WE COME TO PUNISH YOU. WE COME FOR WHATEVER REMAINS OF OUR KIN.
THE FIRST TWO, DOOM DECLINES.
THE LATTER...
...ENDRIK?

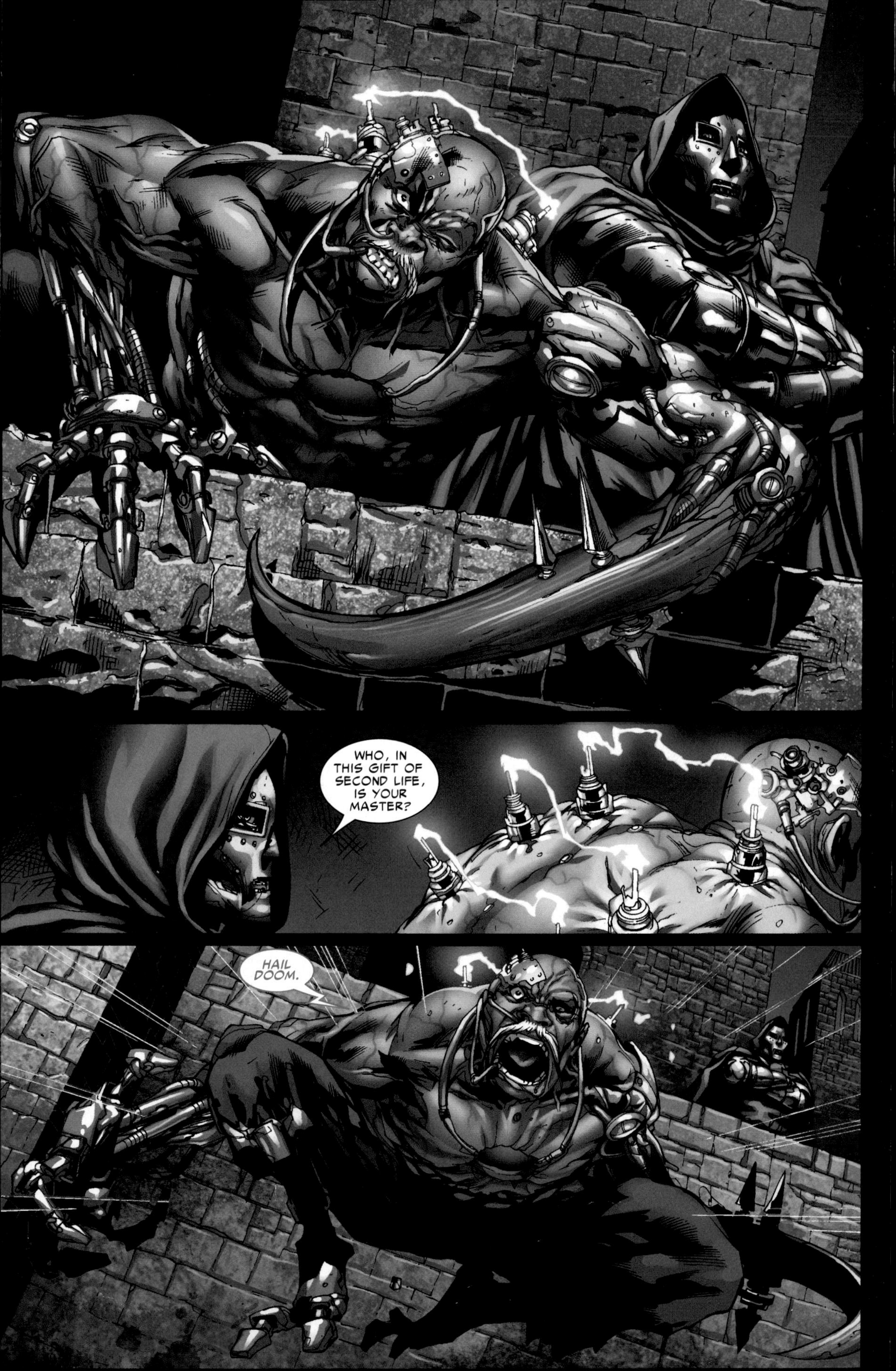
WHO, IN THIS GIFT OF SECOND LIFE, IS YOUR MASTER?
HAIL DOOM.

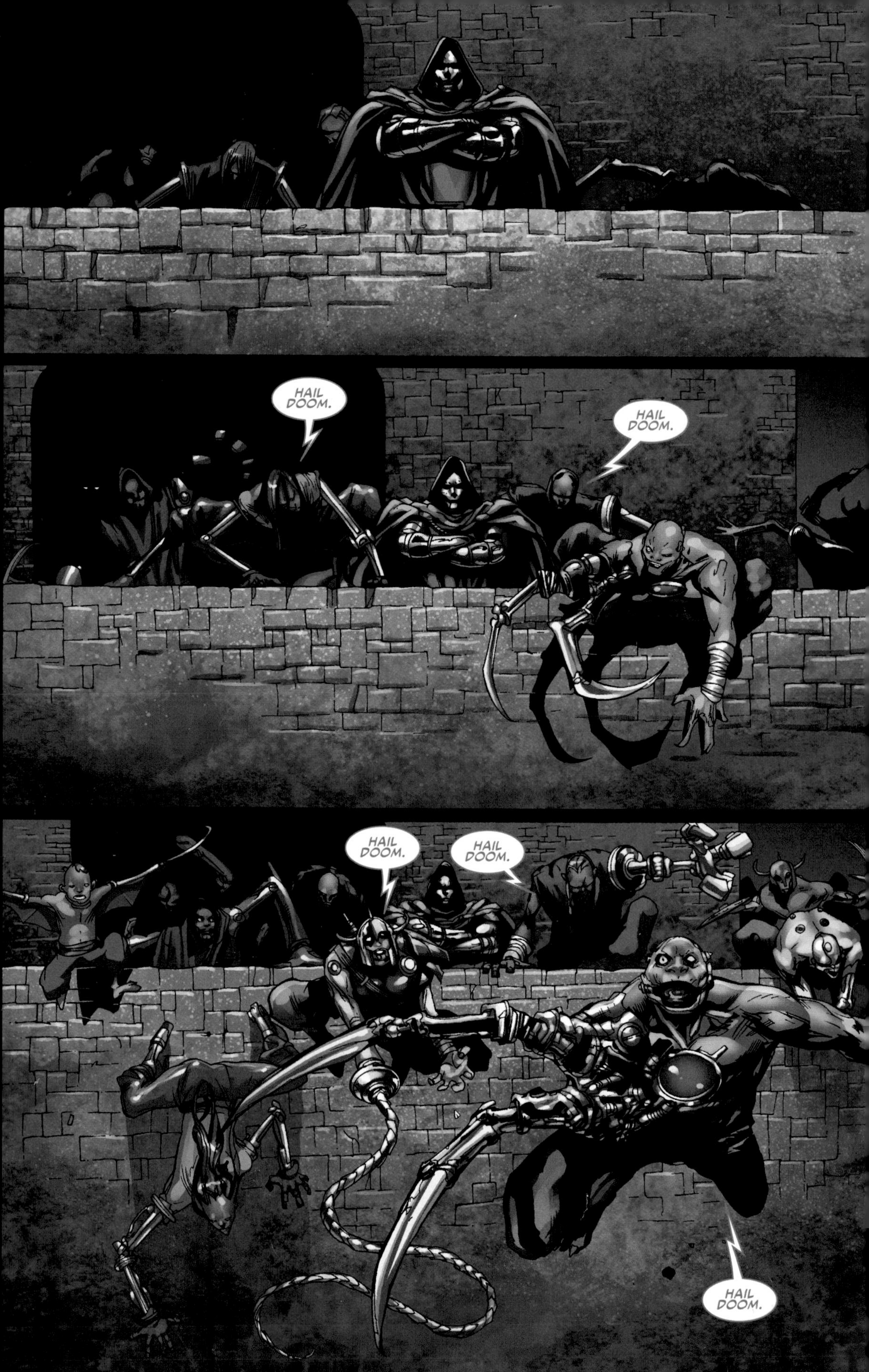
HAIL DOOM.
HAIL DOOM.
HAIL DOOM.
HAIL DOOM.
HAIL DOOM.

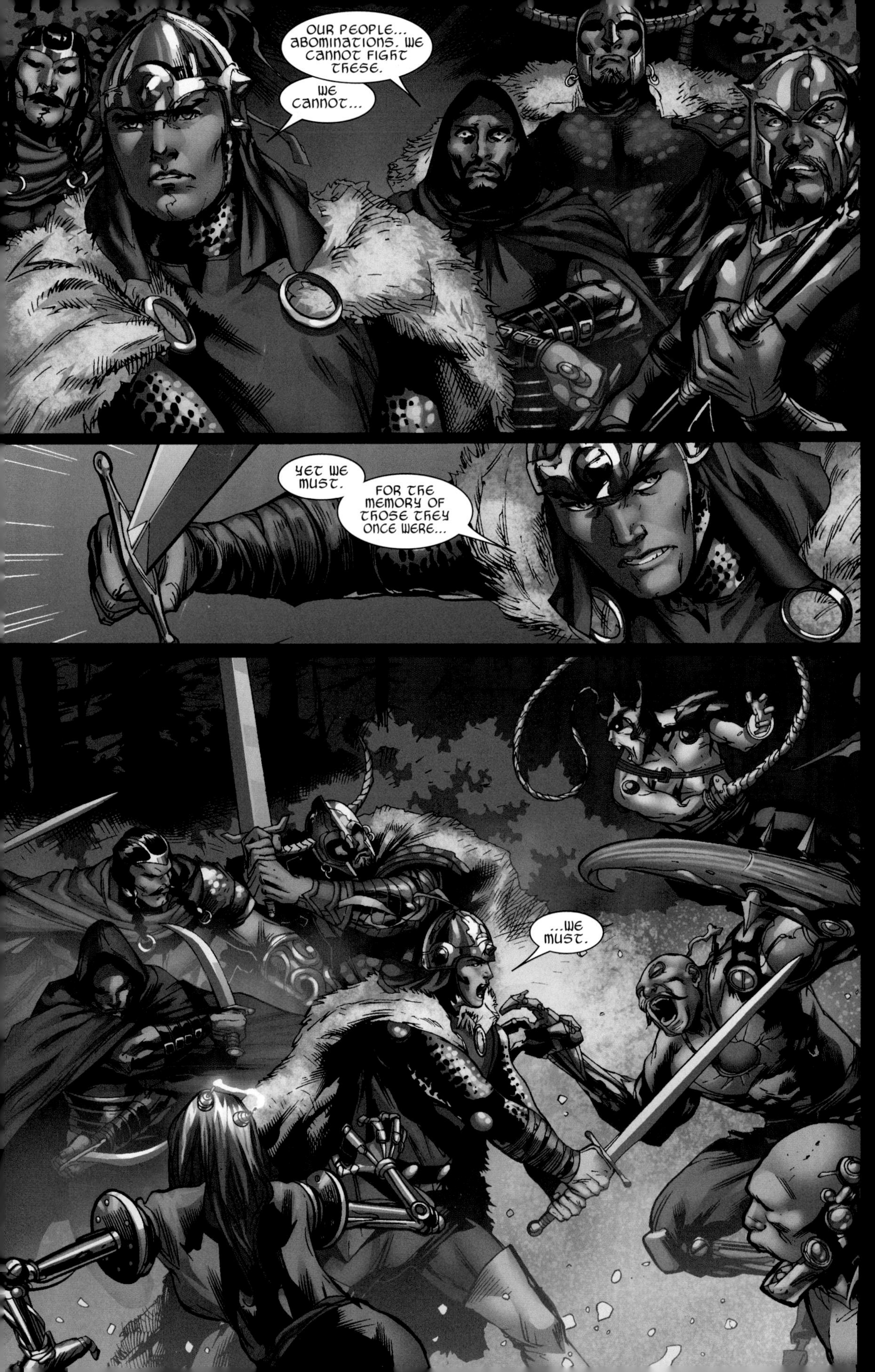
OUR PEOPLE... ABOMINATIONS. WE CANNOT FIGHT THESE.
WE CANNOT...
YET WE MUST.
FOR THE MEMORY OF THOSE THEY ONCE WERE...
...WE MUST.

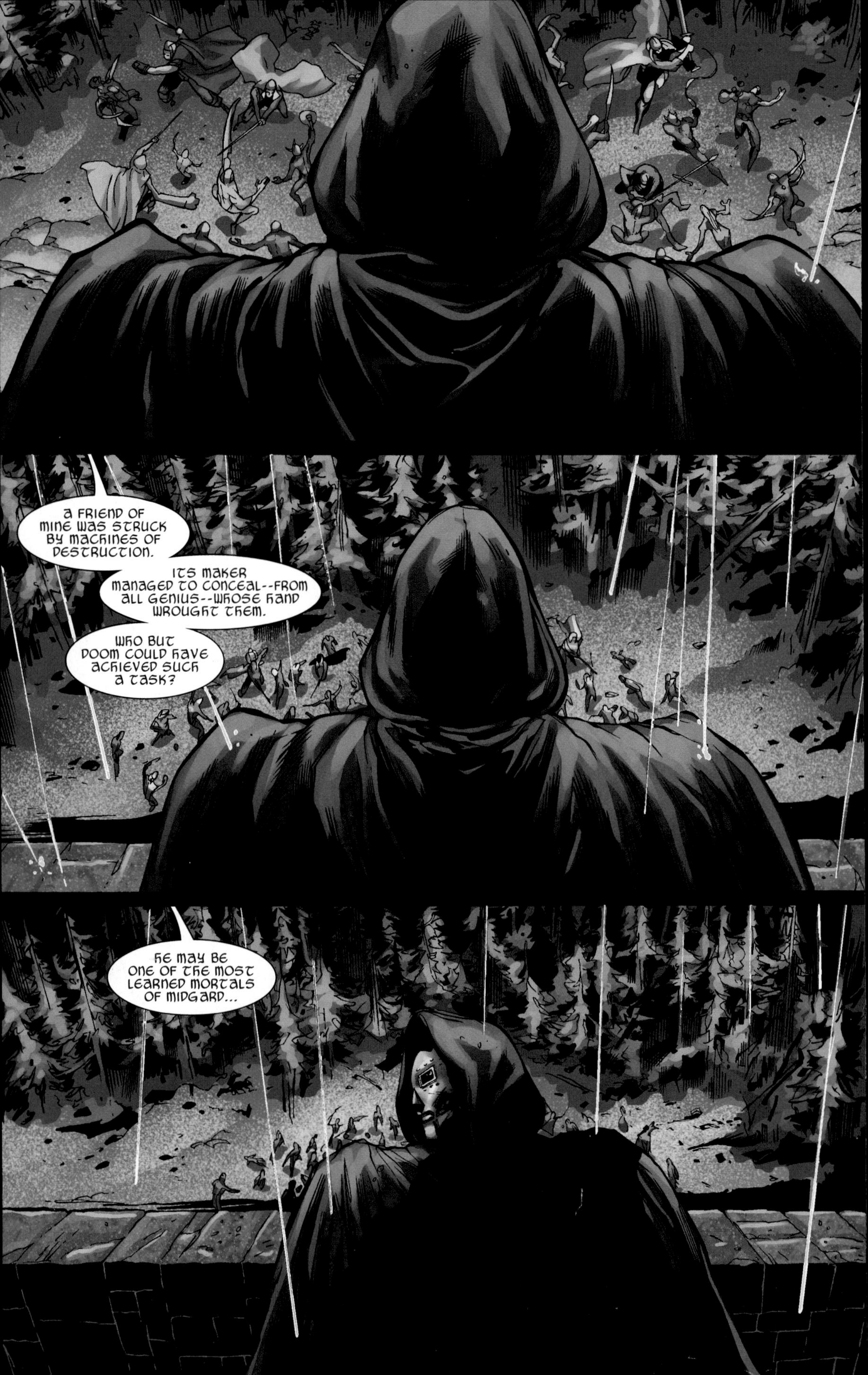
A FRIEND OF MINE WAS STRUCK BY MACHINES OF DESTRUCTION.
ITS MAKER MANAGED TO CONCEAL--FROM ALL GENIUS--WHOSE HAND WROUGHT THEM.
WHO BUT DOOM COULD HAVE ACHIEVED SUCH A TASK?
HE MAY BE ONE OF THE MOST LEARNED MORTALS OF MIDGARD...

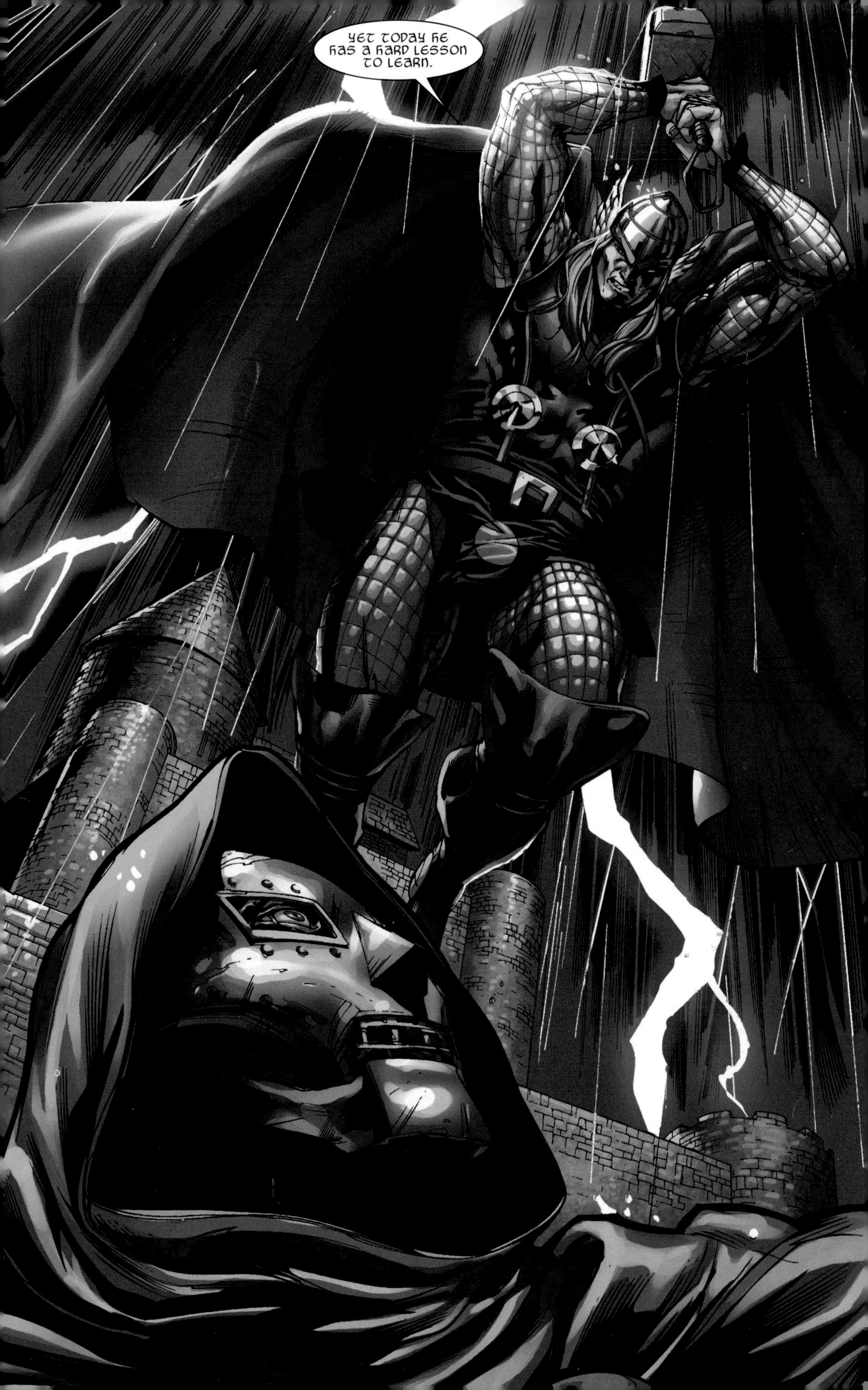
YET TODAY HE HAS A HARD LESSON TO LEARN.

605

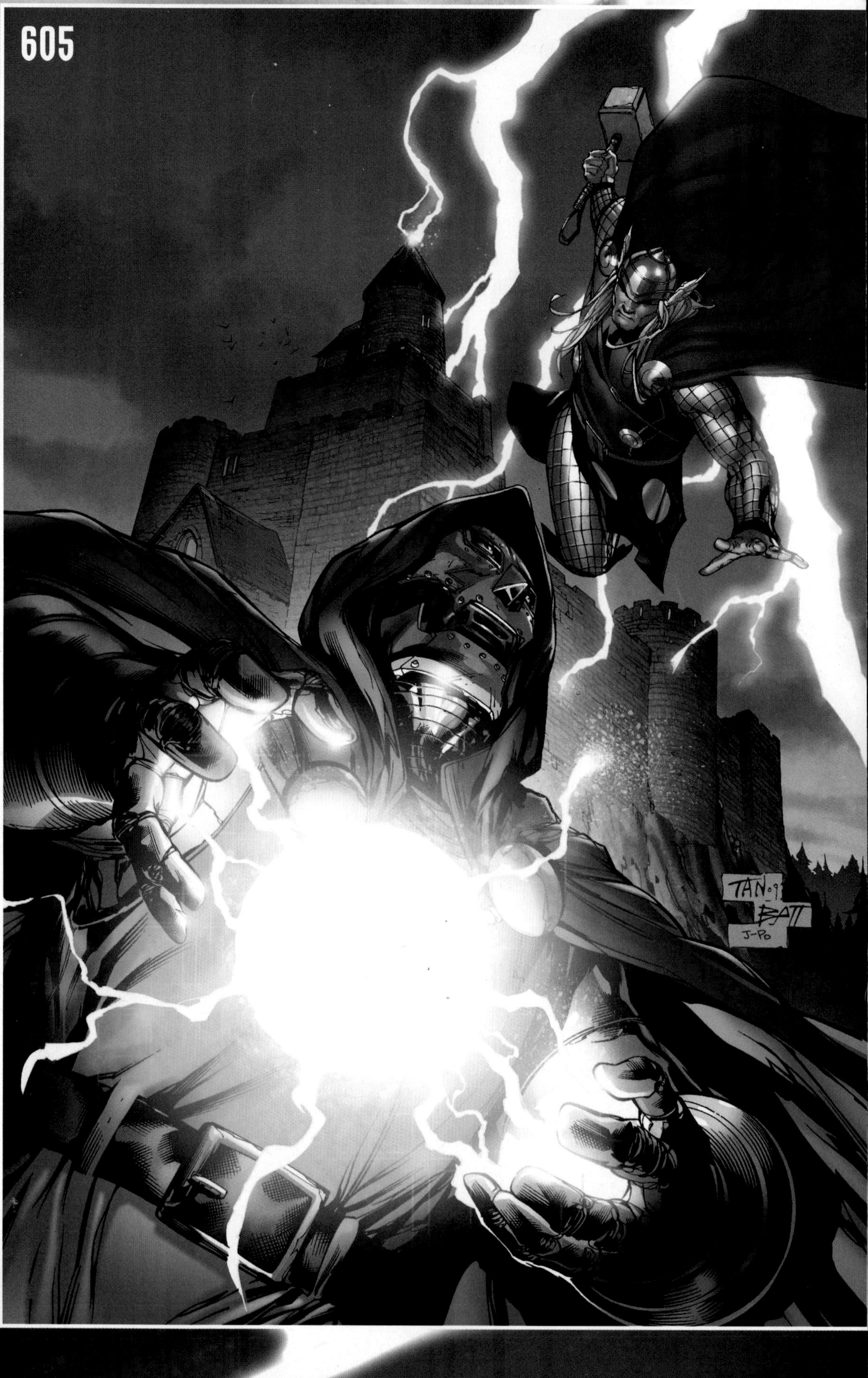
TAN 09
BATT
J-Po

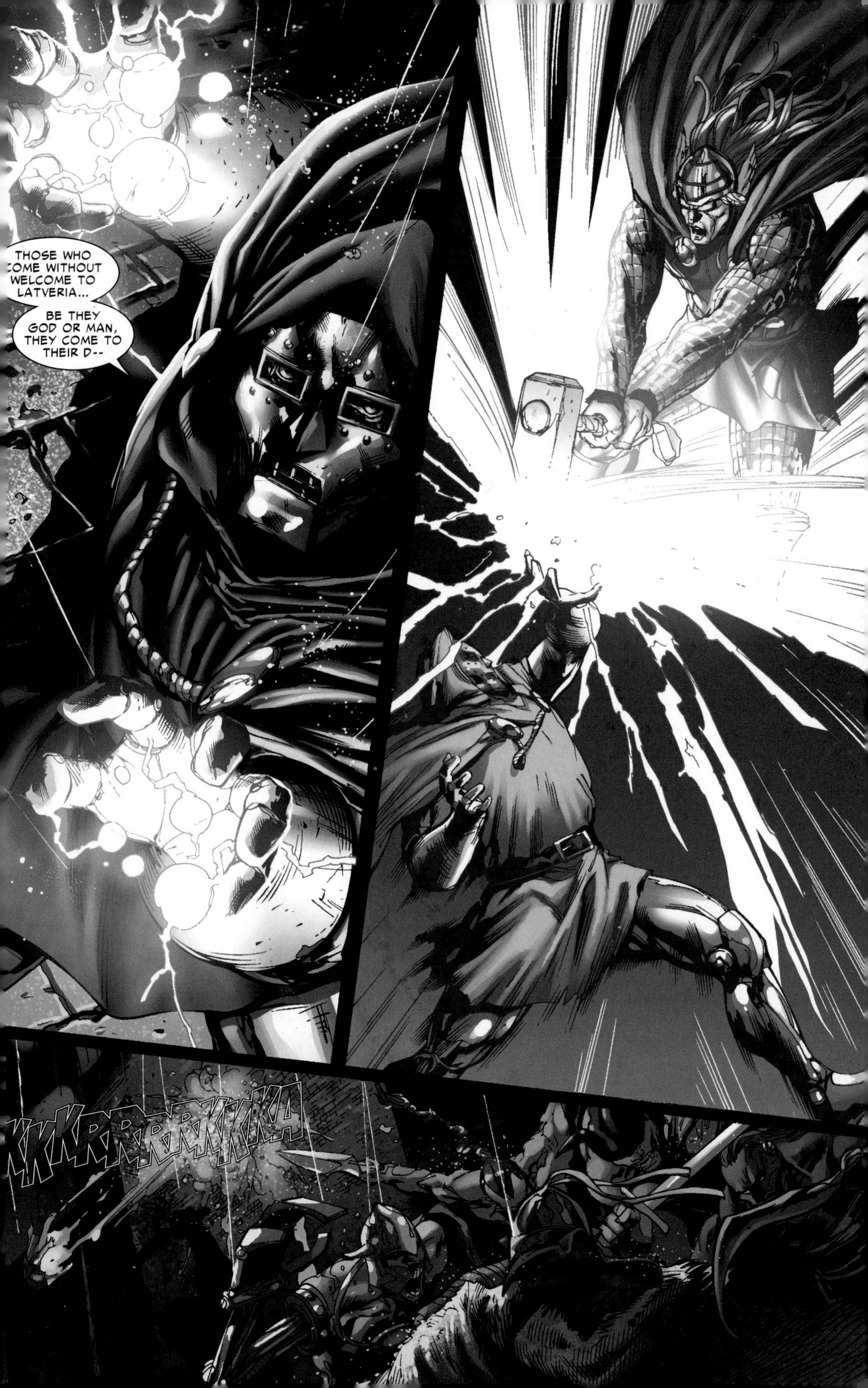
THOSE WHO COME WITHOUT WELCOME TO LATVERIA...
BE THEY GOD OR MAN, THEY COME TO THEIR D--
KKKRRRRKKKA

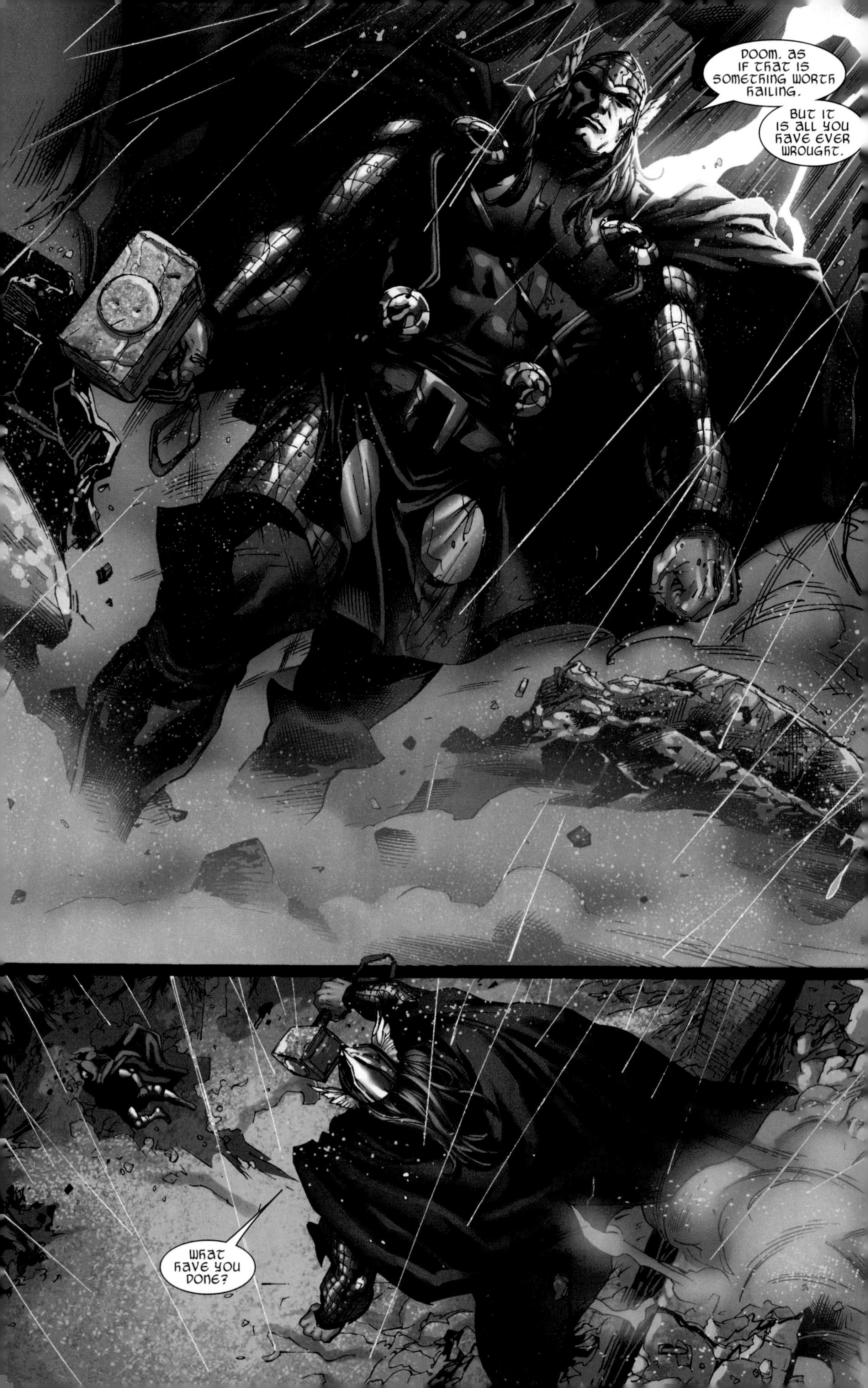
DOOM. AS IF THAT IS SOMETHING WORTH HAILING.
BUT IT IS ALL YOU HAVE EVER WROUGHT.
WHAT HAVE YOU DONE?

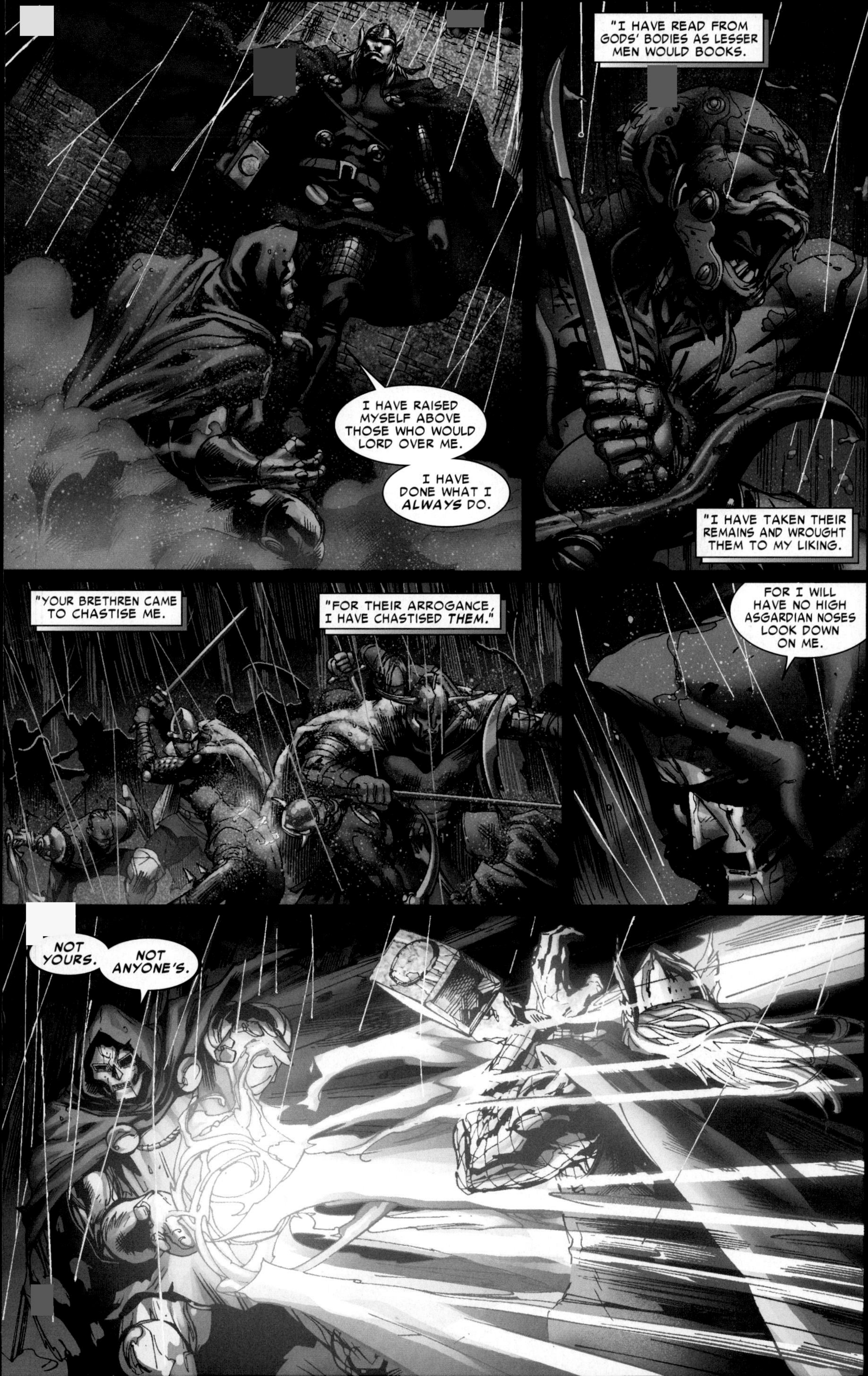
I HAVE RAISED MYSELF ABOVE THOSE WHO WOULD LORD OVER ME.
I HAVE DONE WHAT I *ALWAYS* DO.
"I HAVE READ FROM GODS' BODIES AS LESSER MEN WOULD BOOKS.
"I HAVE TAKEN THEIR REMAINS AND WROUGHT THEM TO MY LIKING.
"YOUR BRETHREN CAME TO CHASTISE ME.
"FOR THEIR ARROGANCE, I HAVE CHASTISED *THEM.*"
FOR I WILL HAVE NO HIGH ASGARDIAN NOSES LOOK DOWN ON ME.
NOT YOURS.
NOT ANYONE'S.

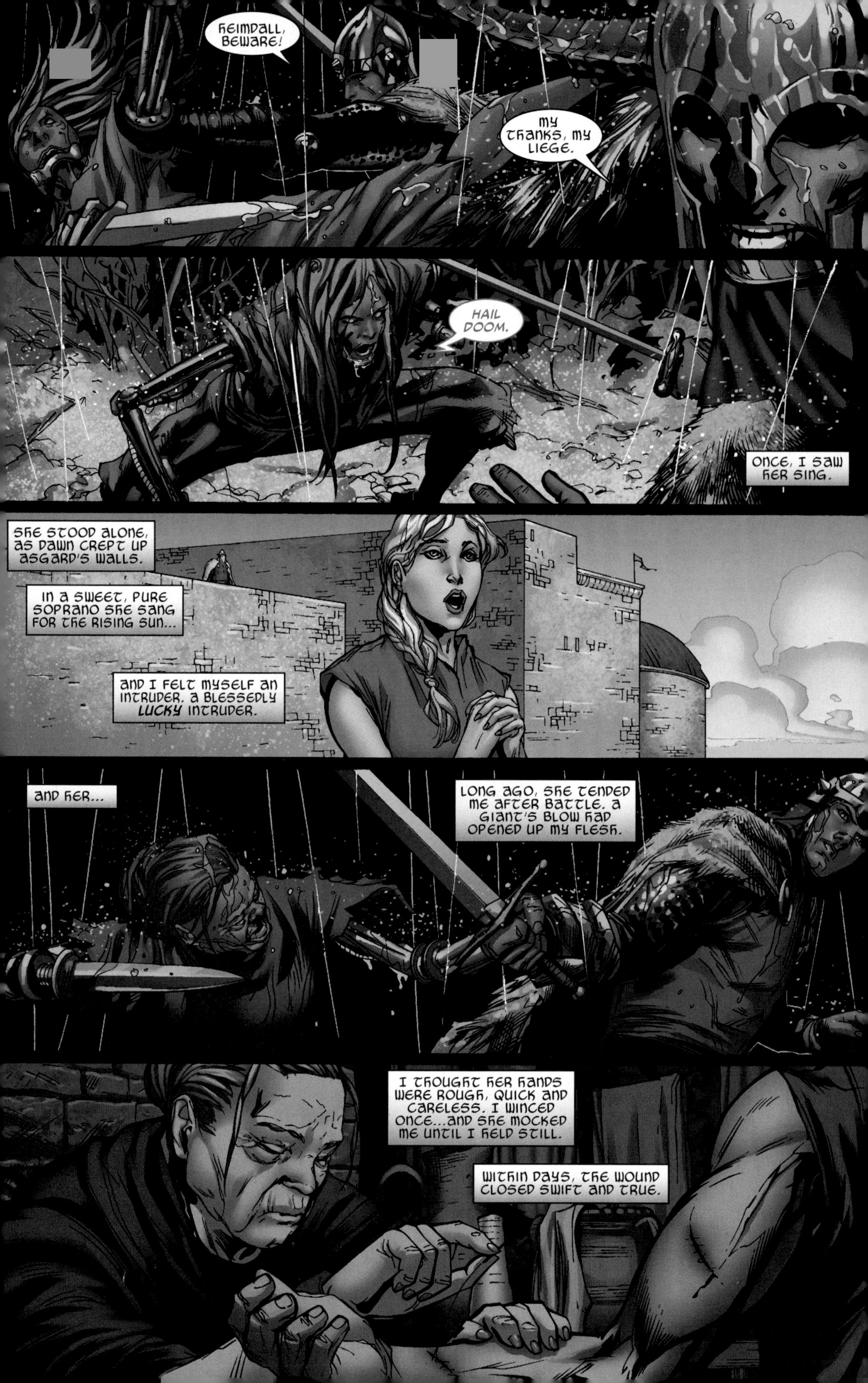
HEIMDALL, BEWARE!
MY THANKS, MY LIEGE.
HAIL DOOM.
ONCE, I SAW HER SING.
SHE STOOD ALONE, AS DAWN CREPT UP ASGARD'S WALLS.
IN A SWEET, PURE SOPRANO SHE SANG FOR THE RISING SUN...
AND I FELT MYSELF AN INTRUDER. A BLESSEDLY LUCKY INTRUDER.
AND HER...
LONG AGO, SHE TENDED ME AFTER BATTLE. A GIANT'S BLOW HAD OPENED UP MY FLESH.
I THOUGHT HER HANDS WERE ROUGH, QUICK AND CARELESS. I WINCED ONCE...AND SHE MOCKED ME UNTIL I HELD STILL.
WITHIN DAYS, THE WOUND CLOSED SWIFT AND TRUE.

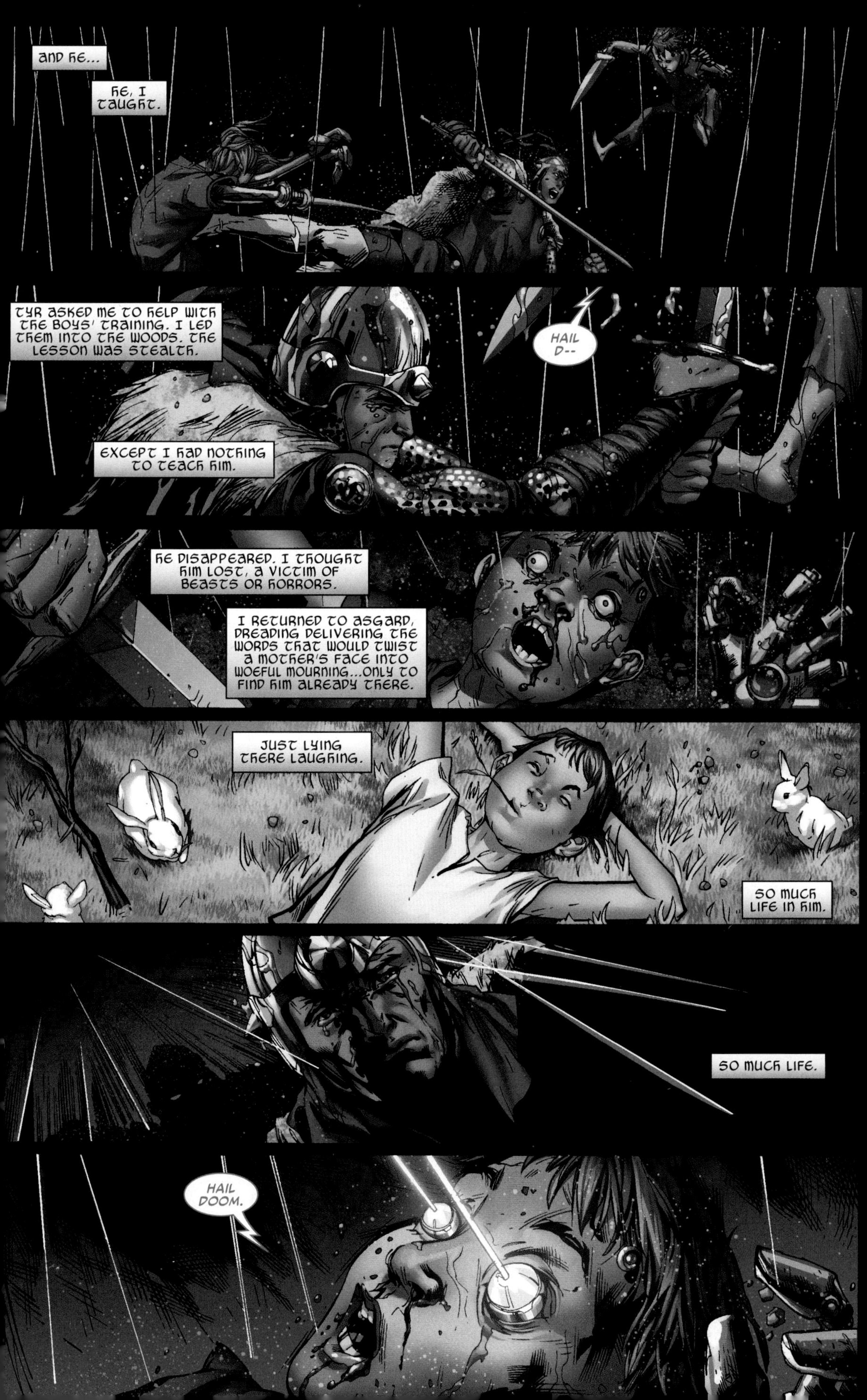

AND HE...
HE, I TAUGHT.
TYR ASKED ME TO HELP WITH THE BOYS' TRAINING. I LED THEM INTO THE WOODS. THE LESSON WAS STEALTH.
HAIL D--
EXCEPT I HAD NOTHING TO TEACH HIM.
HE DISAPPEARED. I THOUGHT HIM LOST, A VICTIM OF BEASTS OR HORRORS.
I RETURNED TO ASGARD, DREADING DELIVERING THE WORDS THAT WOULD TWIST A MOTHER'S FACE INTO WOEFUL MOURNING...ONLY TO FIND HIM ALREADY THERE.
JUST LYING THERE LAUGHING.
SO MUCH LIFE IN HIM.
SO MUCH LIFE.
HAIL DOOM.

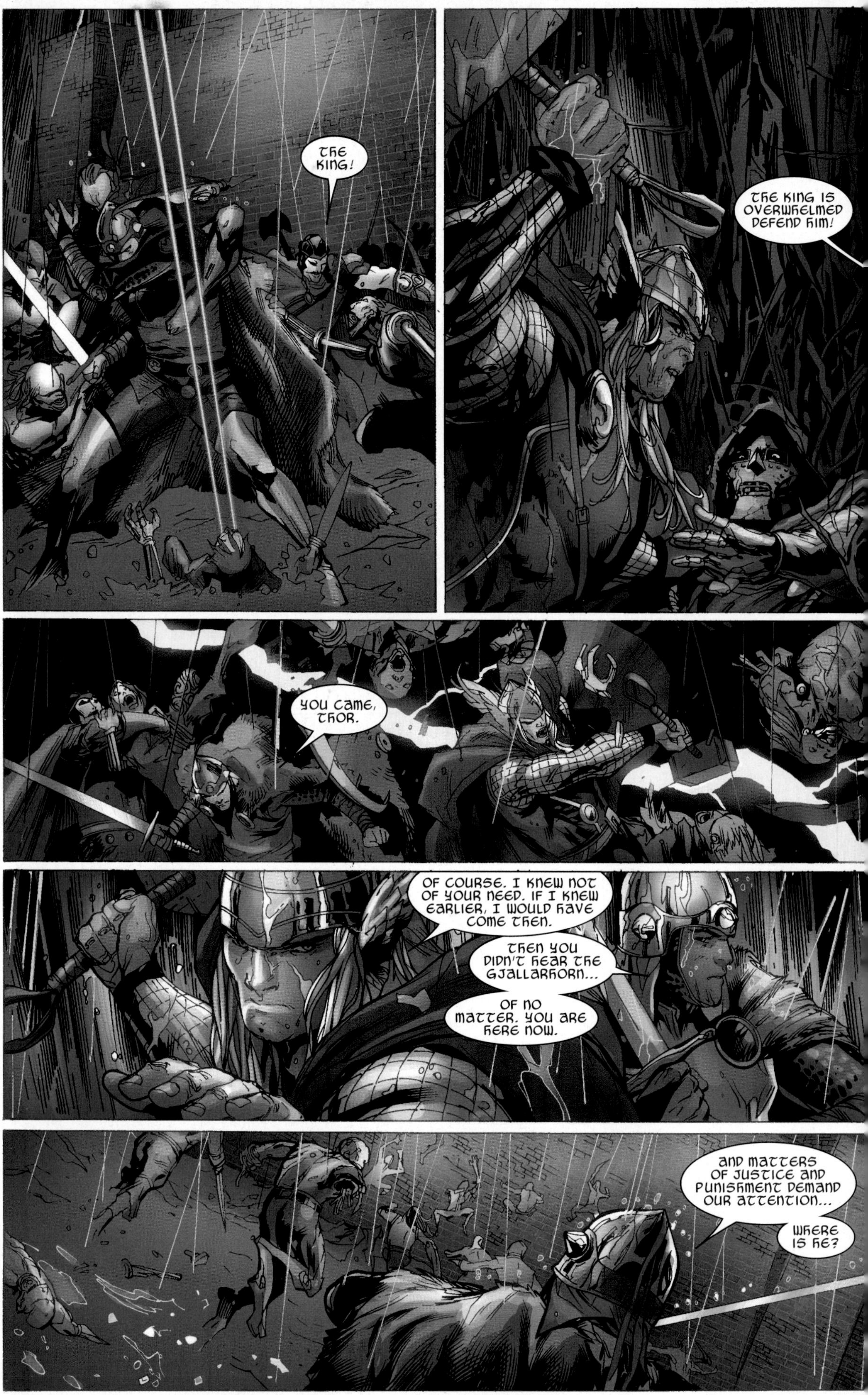
THE KING!
THE KING IS OVERWHELMED DEFEND HIM!
YOU CAME, THOR.
OF COURSE. I KNEW NOT OF YOUR NEED. IF I KNEW EARLIER, I WOULD HAVE COME THEN.
THEN YOU DIDN'T HEAR THE GJALLARHORN...
OF NO MATTER. YOU ARE HERE NOW.
AND MATTERS OF JUSTICE AND PUNISHMENT DEMAND OUR ATTENTION...
WHERE IS HE?

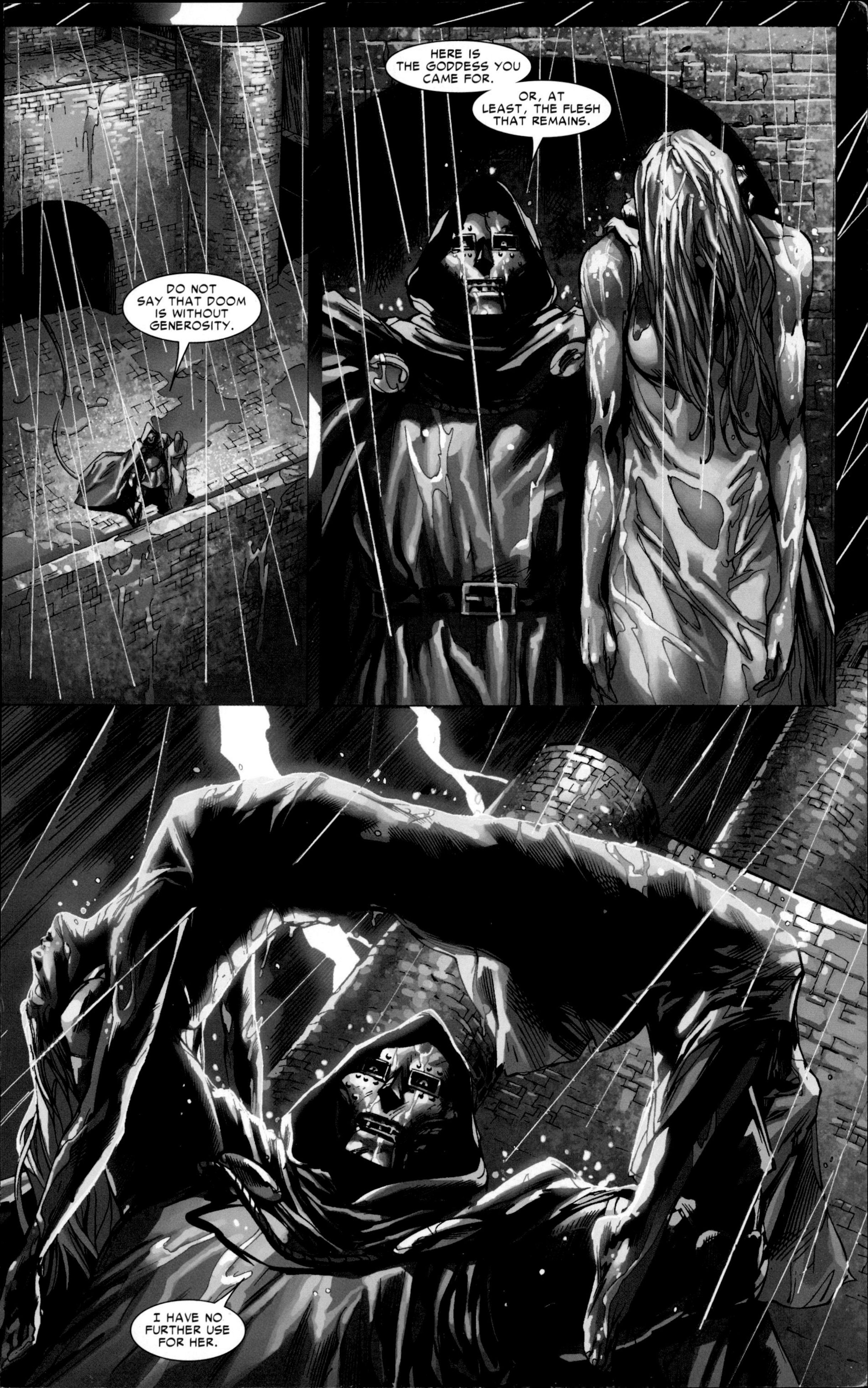

DO NOT SAY THAT DOOM IS WITHOUT GENEROSITY.
HERE IS THE GODDESS YOU CAME FOR.
OR, AT LEAST, THE FLESH THAT REMAINS.
I HAVE NO FURTHER USE FOR HER.

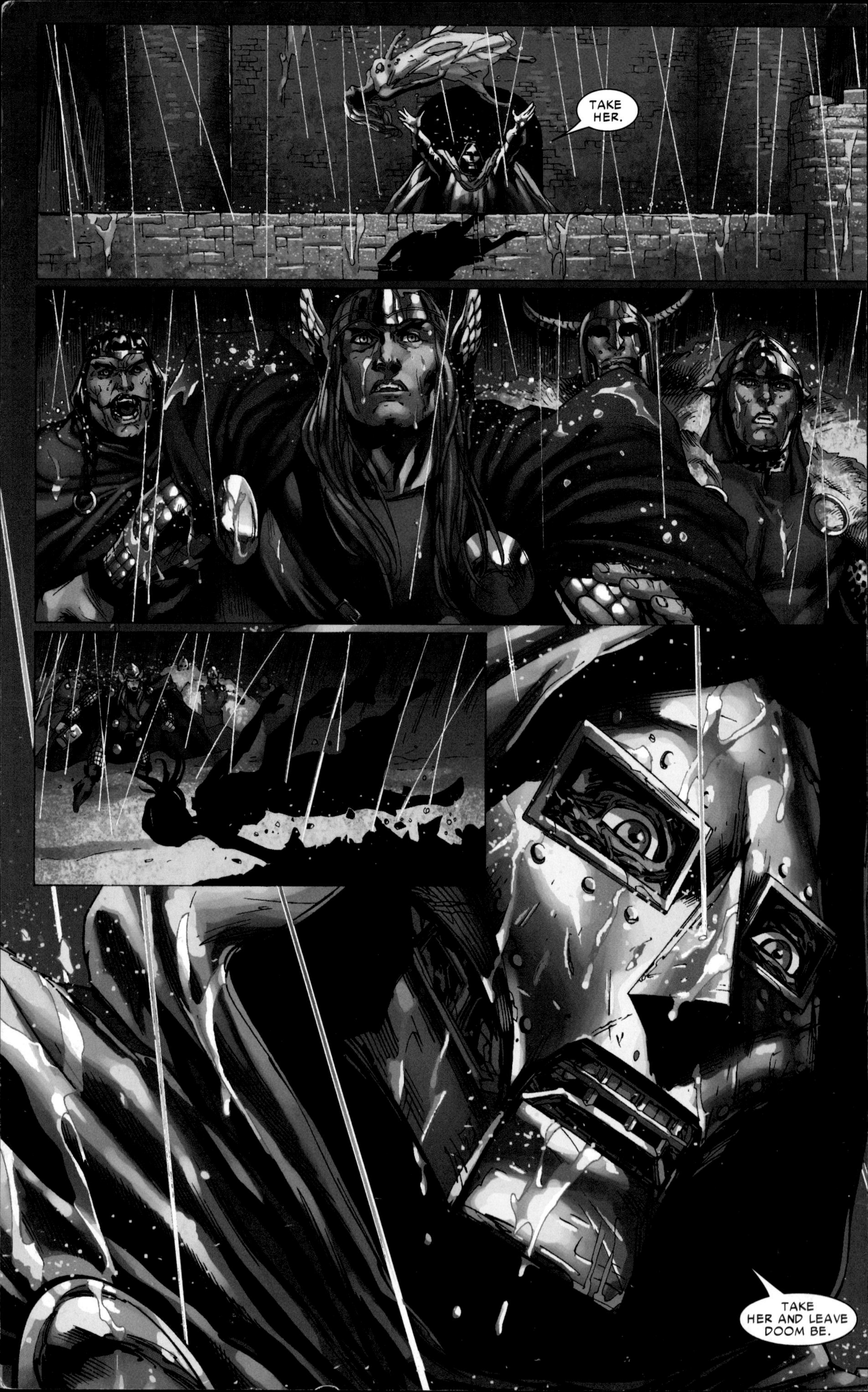
TAKE HER.
TAKE HER AND LEAVE DOOM BE.

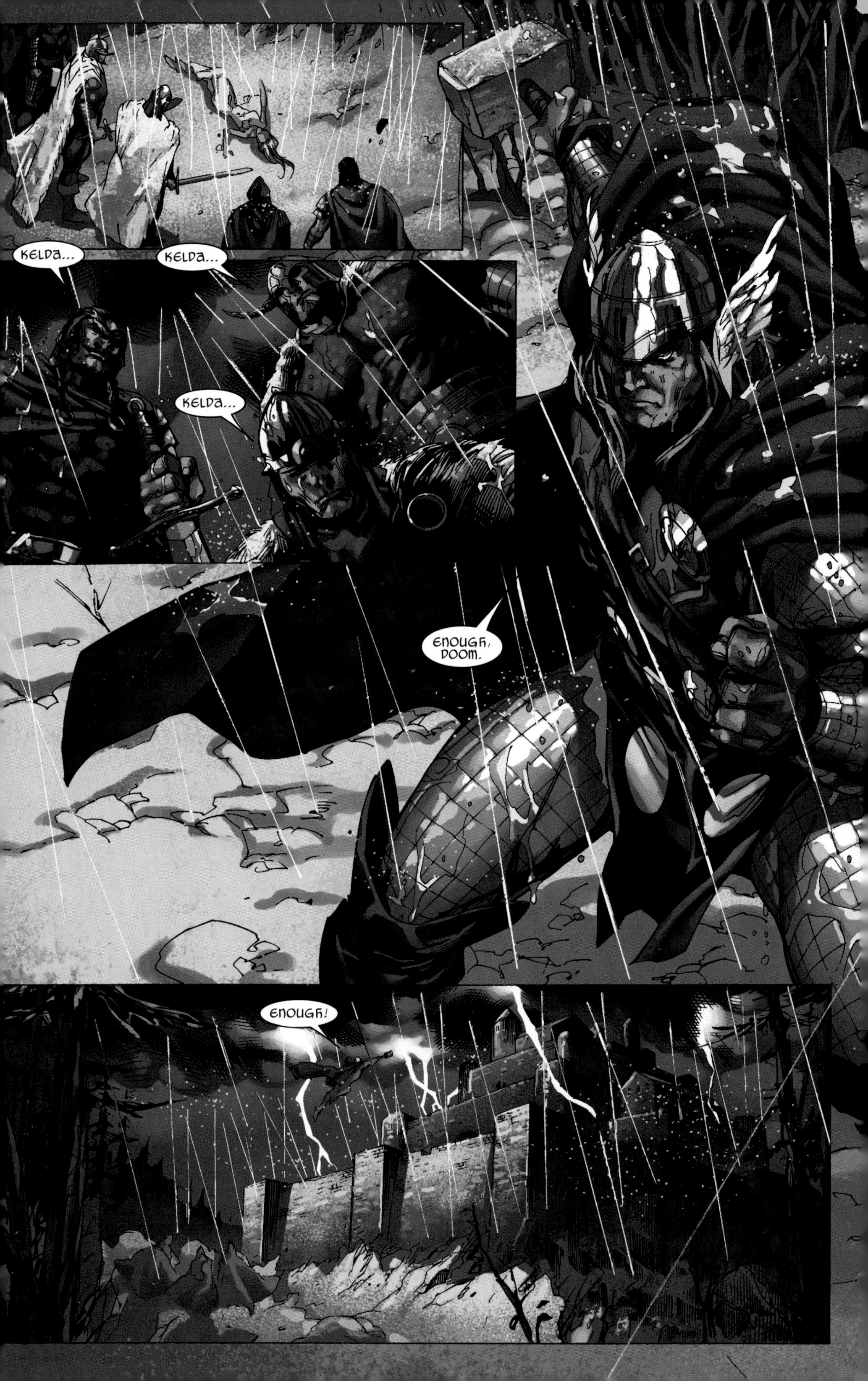
KELDA...
KELDA...
KELDA...
ENOUGH, DOOM.
ENOUGH!

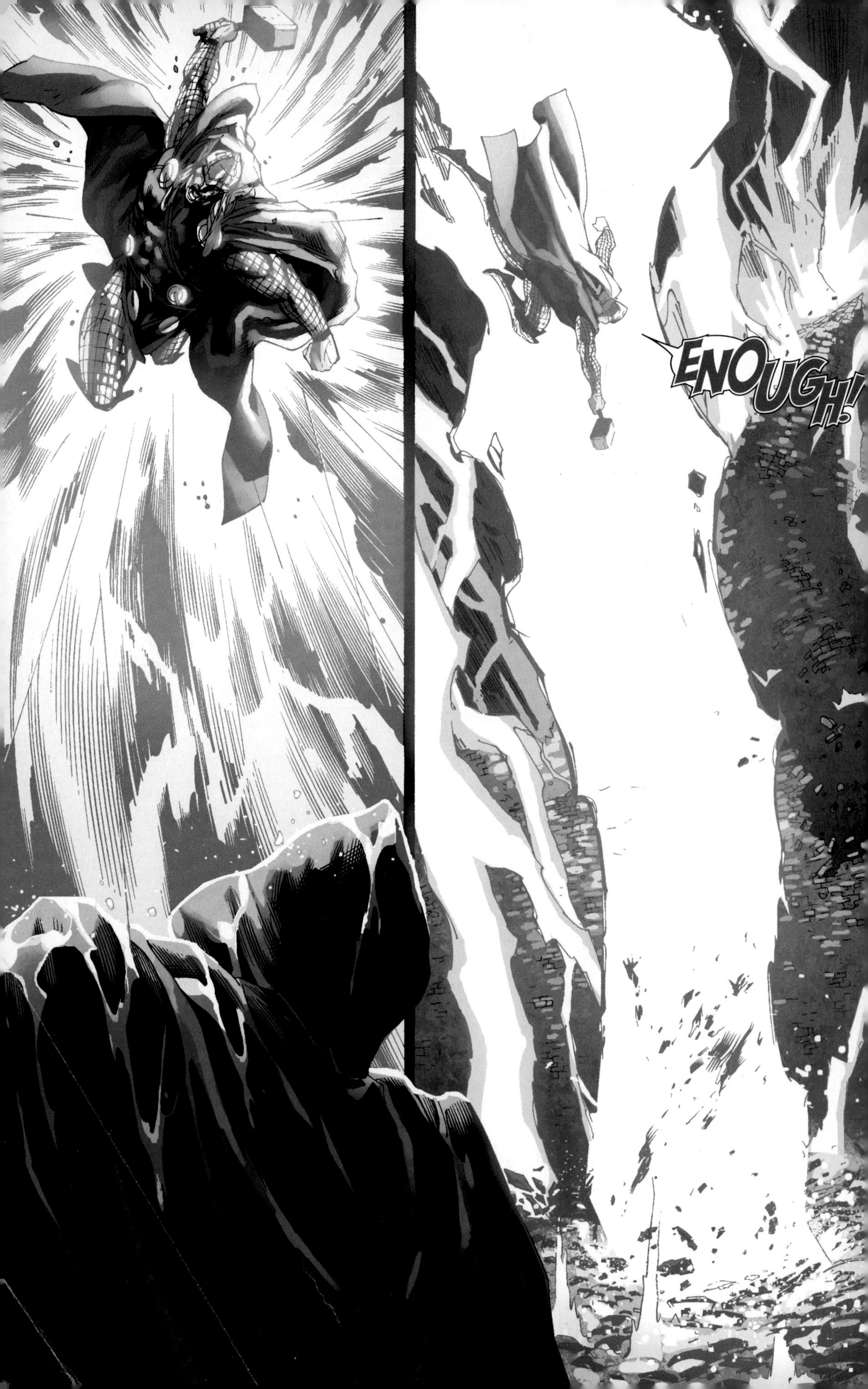
ENOUGH!

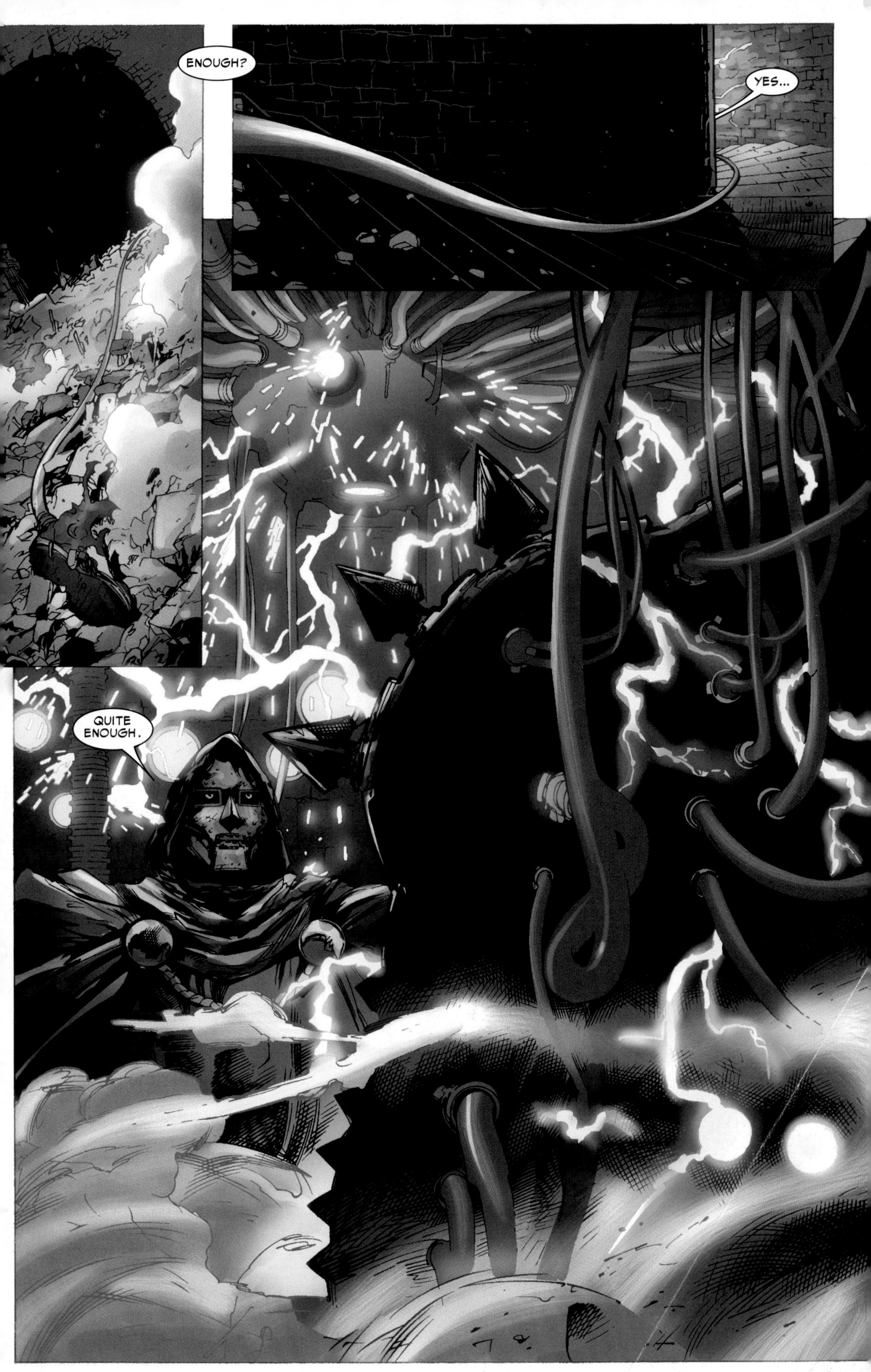
ENOUGH?
YES...
QUITE ENOUGH.

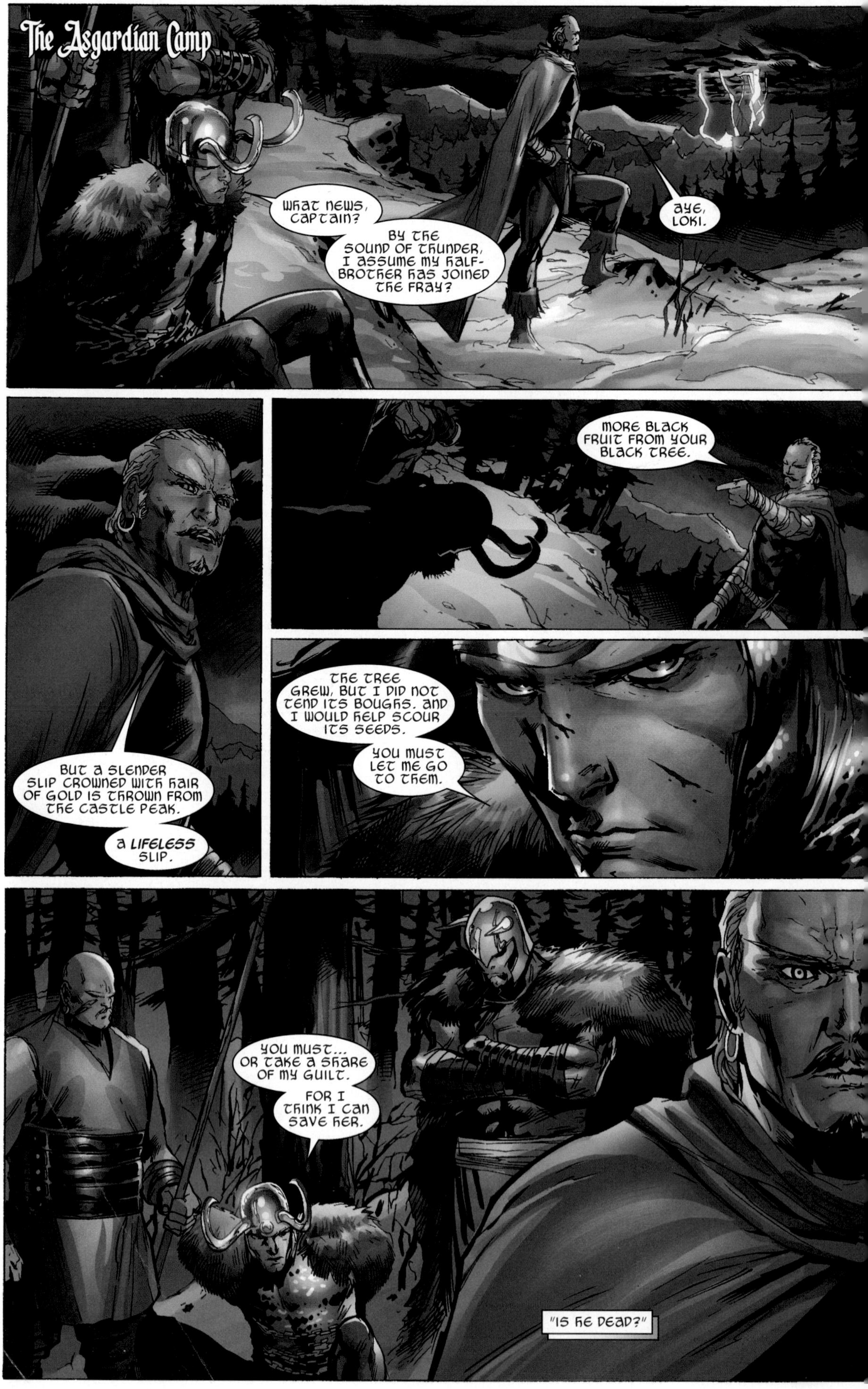
The Asgardian Camp
WHAT NEWS, CAPTAIN?
BY THE SOUND OF THUNDER, I ASSUME MY HALF-BROTHER HAS JOINED THE FRAY?
AYE, LOKI.
BUT A SLENDER SLIP CROWNED WITH HAIR OF GOLD IS THROWN FROM THE CASTLE PEAK.
A LIFELESS SLIP.
MORE BLACK FRUIT FROM YOUR BLACK TREE.
THE TREE GREW, BUT I DID NOT TEND ITS BOUGHS. AND I WOULD HELP SCOUR ITS SEEDS.
YOU MUST LET ME GO TO THEM.
YOU MUST... OR TAKE A SHARE OF MY GUILT.
FOR I THINK I CAN SAVE HER.
"IS HE DEAD?"

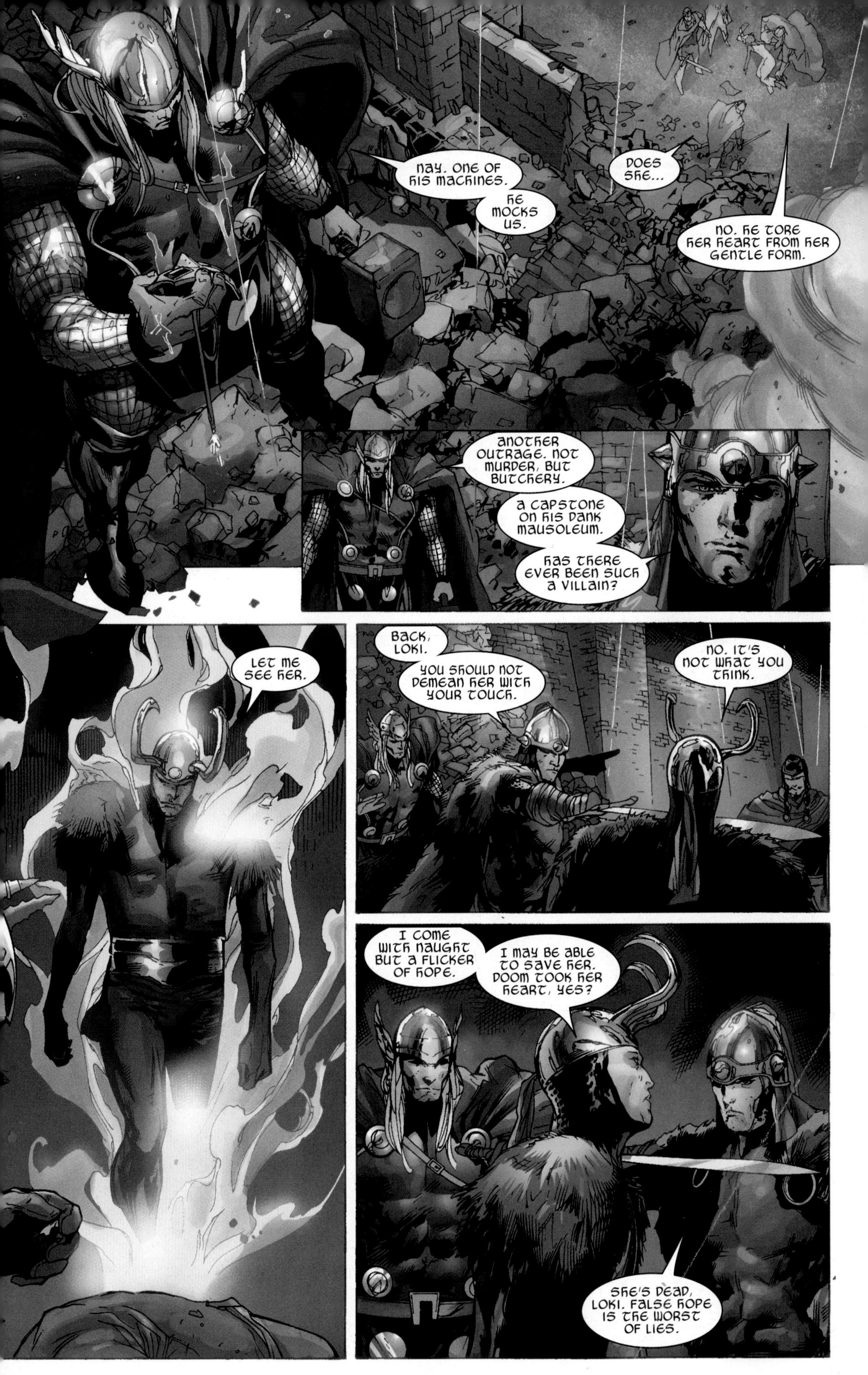
NAY. ONE OF HIS MACHINES.
HE MOCKS US.
DOES SHE...
NO. HE TORE HER HEART FROM HER GENTLE FORM.
ANOTHER OUTRAGE. NOT MURDER, BUT BUTCHERY.
A CAPSTONE ON HIS DANK MAUSOLEUM.
HAS THERE EVER BEEN SUCH A VILLAIN?
LET ME SEE HER.
BACK, LOKI.
YOU SHOULD NOT DEMEAN HER WITH YOUR TOUCH.
NO. IT'S NOT WHAT YOU THINK.
I COME WITH NAUGHT BUT A FLICKER OF HOPE.
I MAY BE ABLE TO SAVE HER. DOOM TOOK HER HEART, YES?
SHE'S DEAD, LOKI. FALSE HOPE IS THE WORST OF LIES.

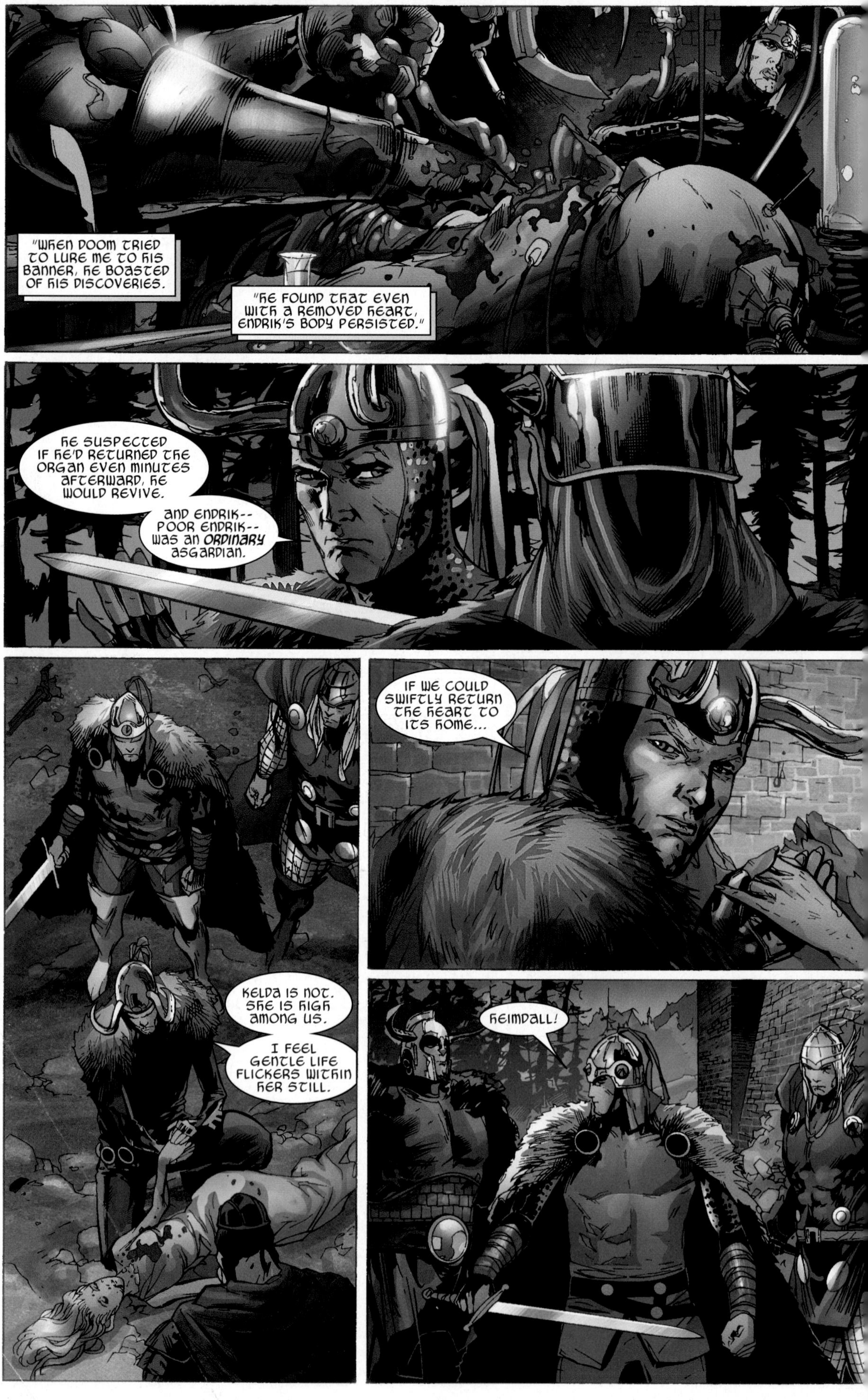
"WHEN DOOM TRIED TO LURE ME TO HIS BANNER, HE BOASTED OF HIS DISCOVERIES.
"HE FOUND THAT EVEN WITH A REMOVED HEART, ENDRIK'S BODY PERSISTED."
HE SUSPECTED IF HE'D RETURNED THE ORGAN EVEN MINUTES AFTERWARD, HE WOULD REVIVE.
AND ENDRIK-- POOR ENDRIK-- WAS AN ORDINARY ASGARDIAN.
IF WE COULD SWIFTLY RETURN THE HEART TO ITS HOME...
KELDA IS NOT. SHE IS HIGH AMONG US.
I FEEL GENTLE LIFE FLICKERS WITHIN HER STILL.
HEIMDALL!

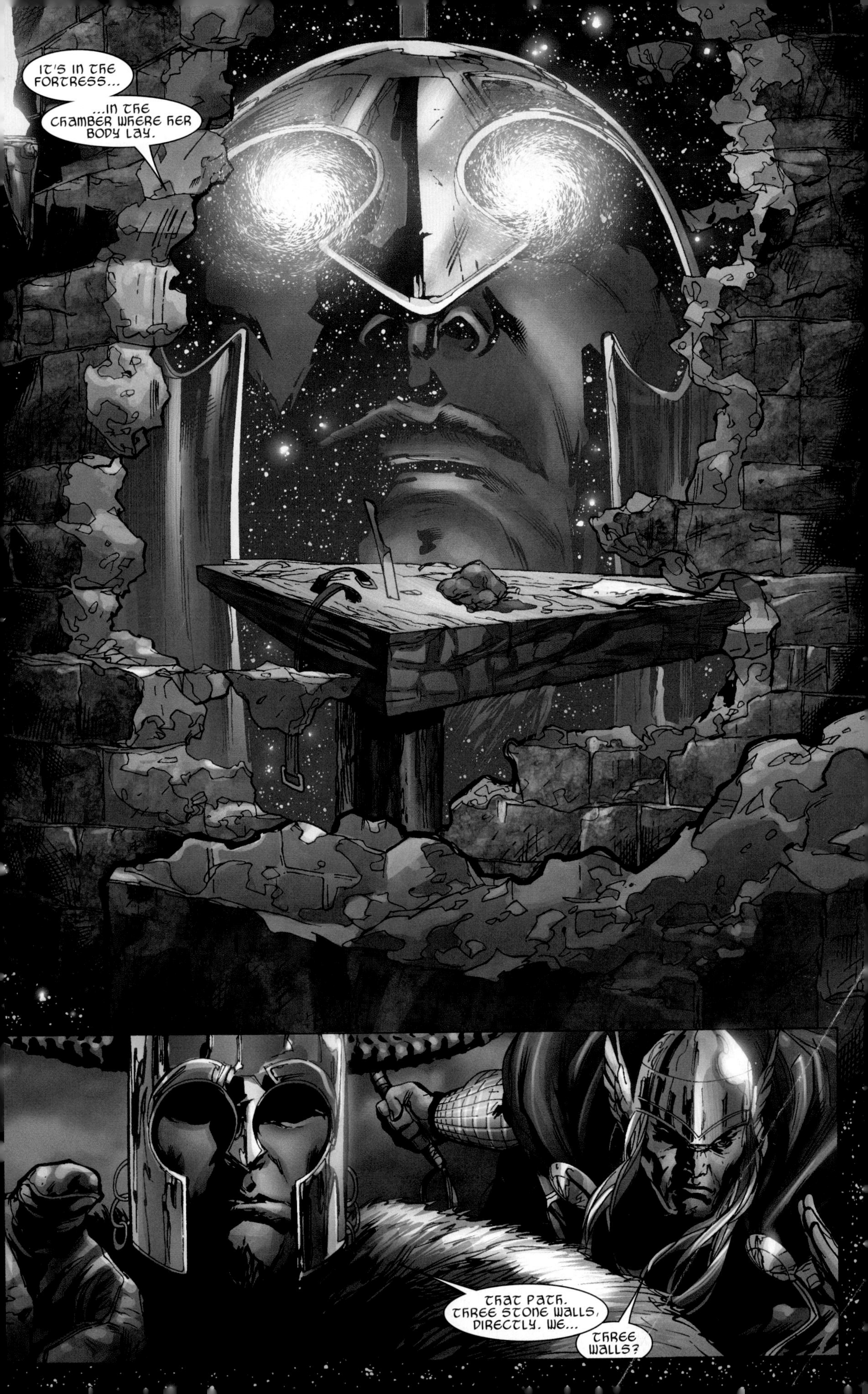
IT'S IN THE FORTRESS...
...IN THE CHAMBER WHERE HER BODY LAY.
THAT PATH. THREE STONE WALLS, DIRECTLY. WE...
THREE WALLS?

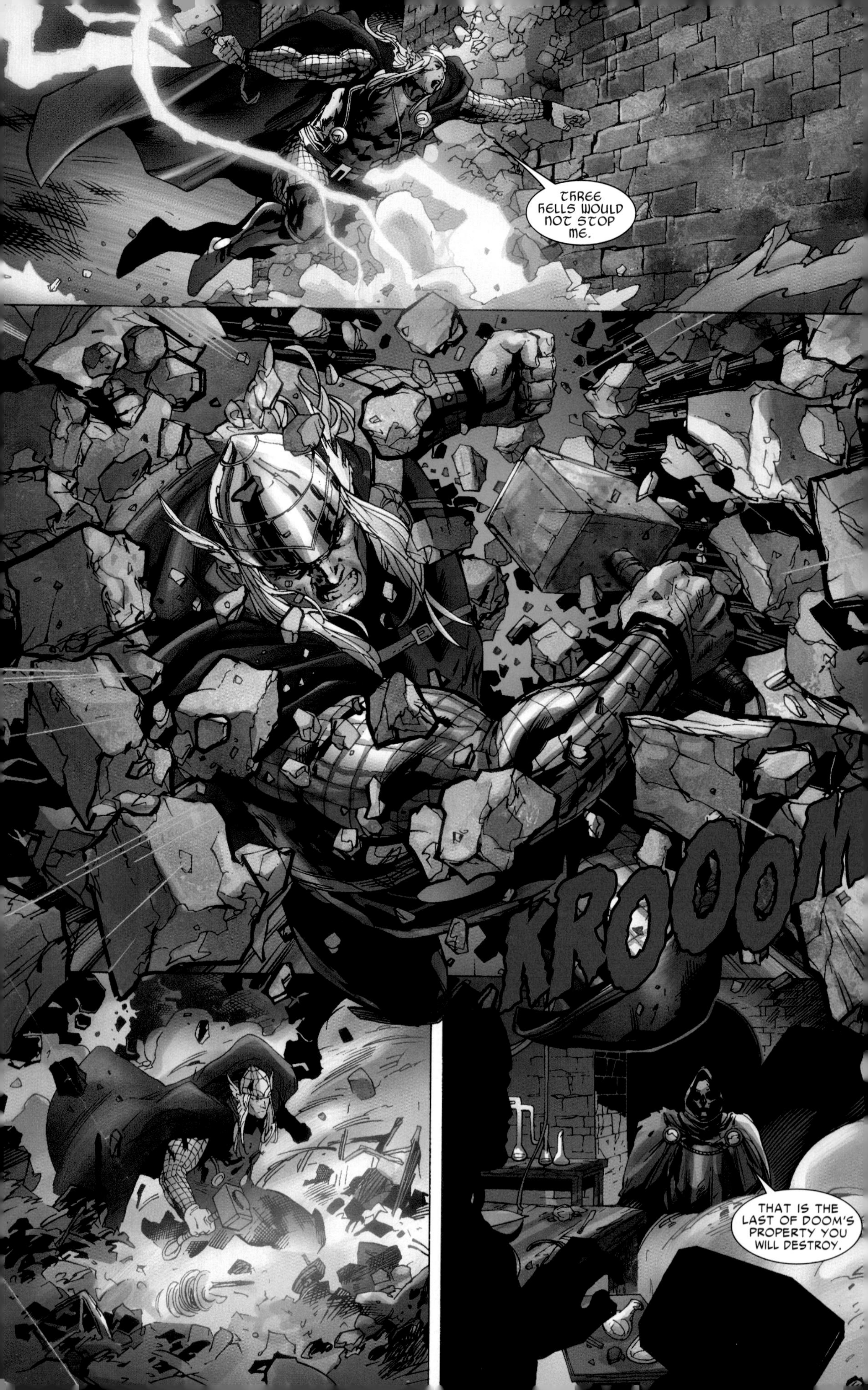
THREE HELLS WOULD NOT STOP ME.
KROOOM
THAT IS THE LAST OF DOOM'S PROPERTY YOU WILL DESTROY.

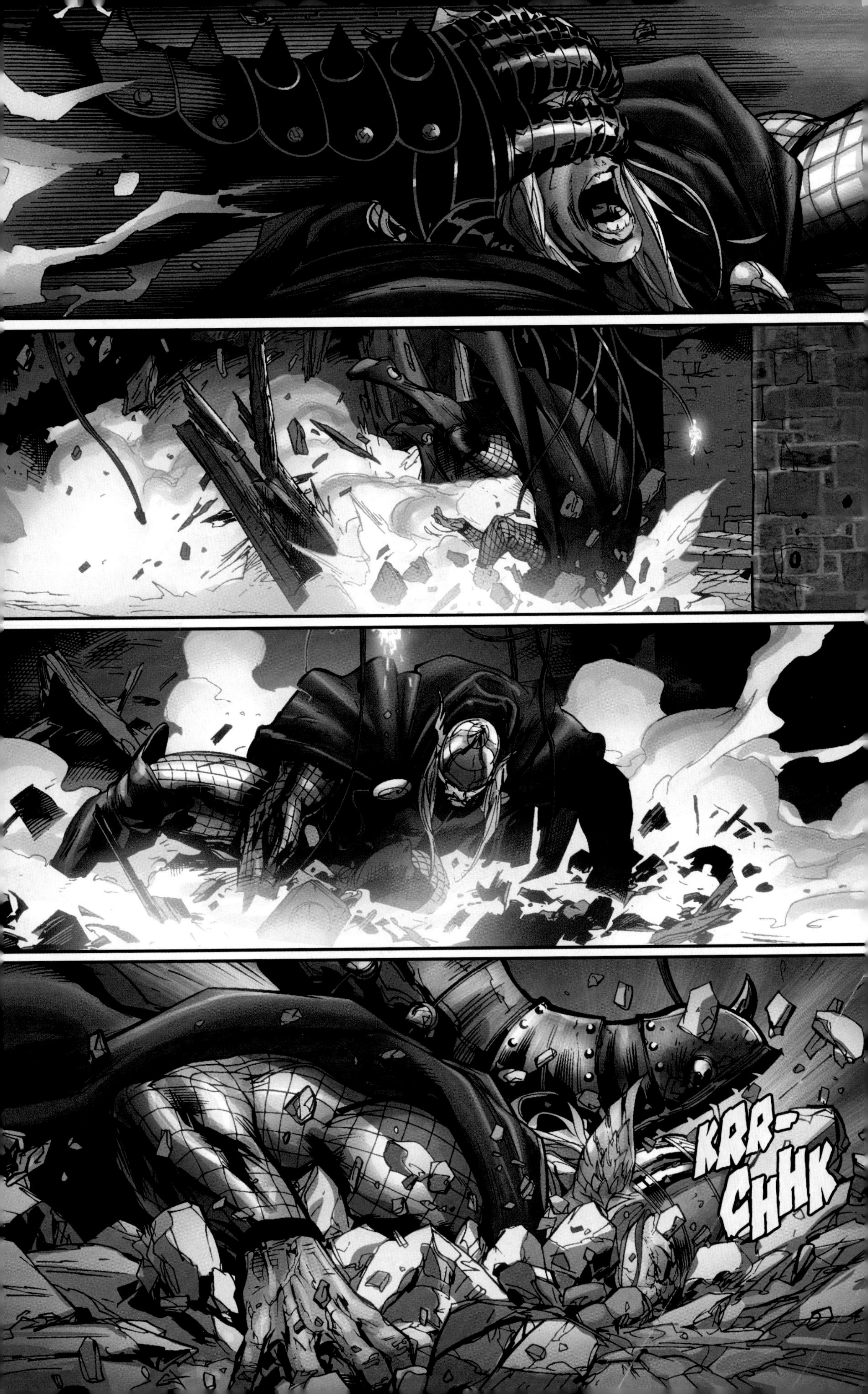
KRR-
CHHK

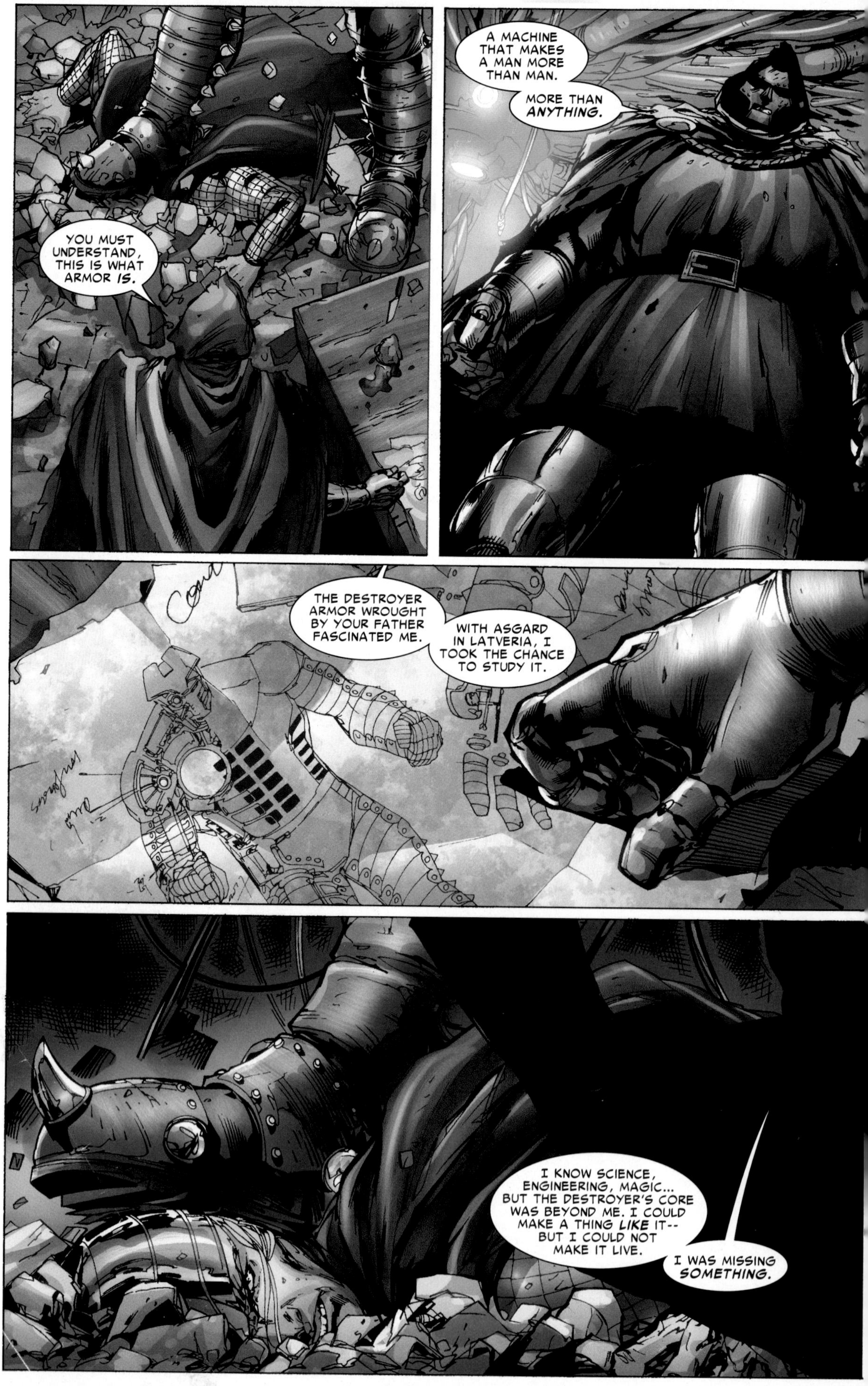
YOU MUST UNDERSTAND, THIS IS WHAT ARMOR *IS.*
A MACHINE THAT MAKES A MAN MORE THAN MAN.
MORE THAN *ANYTHING.*
THE DESTROYER ARMOR WROUGHT BY YOUR FATHER FASCINATED ME.
WITH ASGARD IN LATVERIA, I TOOK THE CHANCE TO STUDY IT.
I KNOW SCIENCE, ENGINEERING, MAGIC... BUT THE DESTROYER'S CORE WAS BEYOND ME. I COULD MAKE A THING *LIKE* IT-- BUT I COULD NOT MAKE IT LIVE.
I WAS MISSING *SOMETHING.*

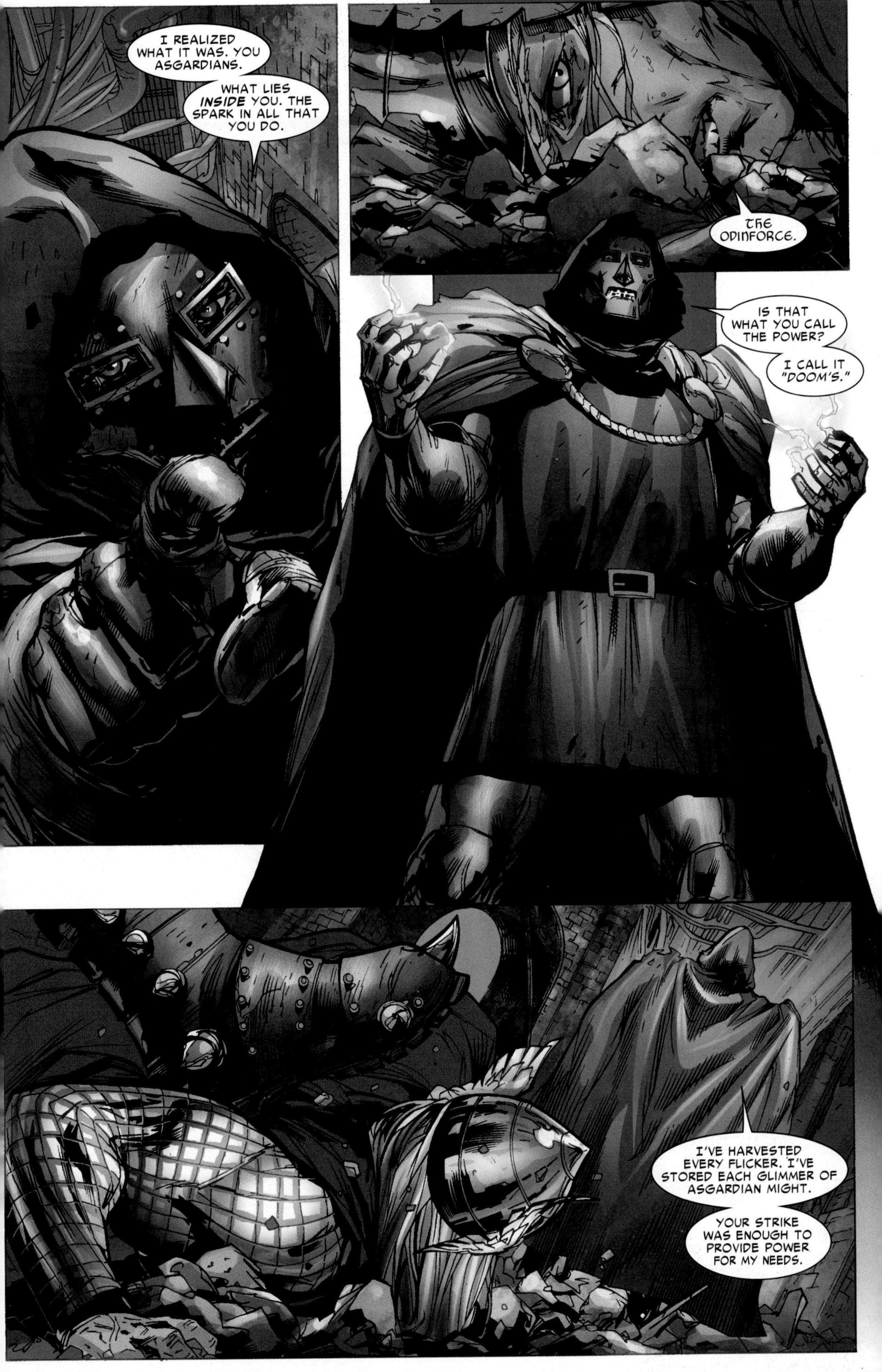
I REALIZED WHAT IT WAS. YOU ASGARDIANS.
WHAT LIES *INSIDE* YOU. THE SPARK IN ALL THAT YOU DO.
THE ODINFORCE.
IS THAT WHAT YOU CALL THE POWER?
I CALL IT "DOOM'S."
I'VE HARVESTED EVERY FLICKER. I'VE STORED EACH GLIMMER OF ASGARDIAN MIGHT.
YOUR STRIKE WAS ENOUGH TO PROVIDE POWER FOR MY NEEDS.

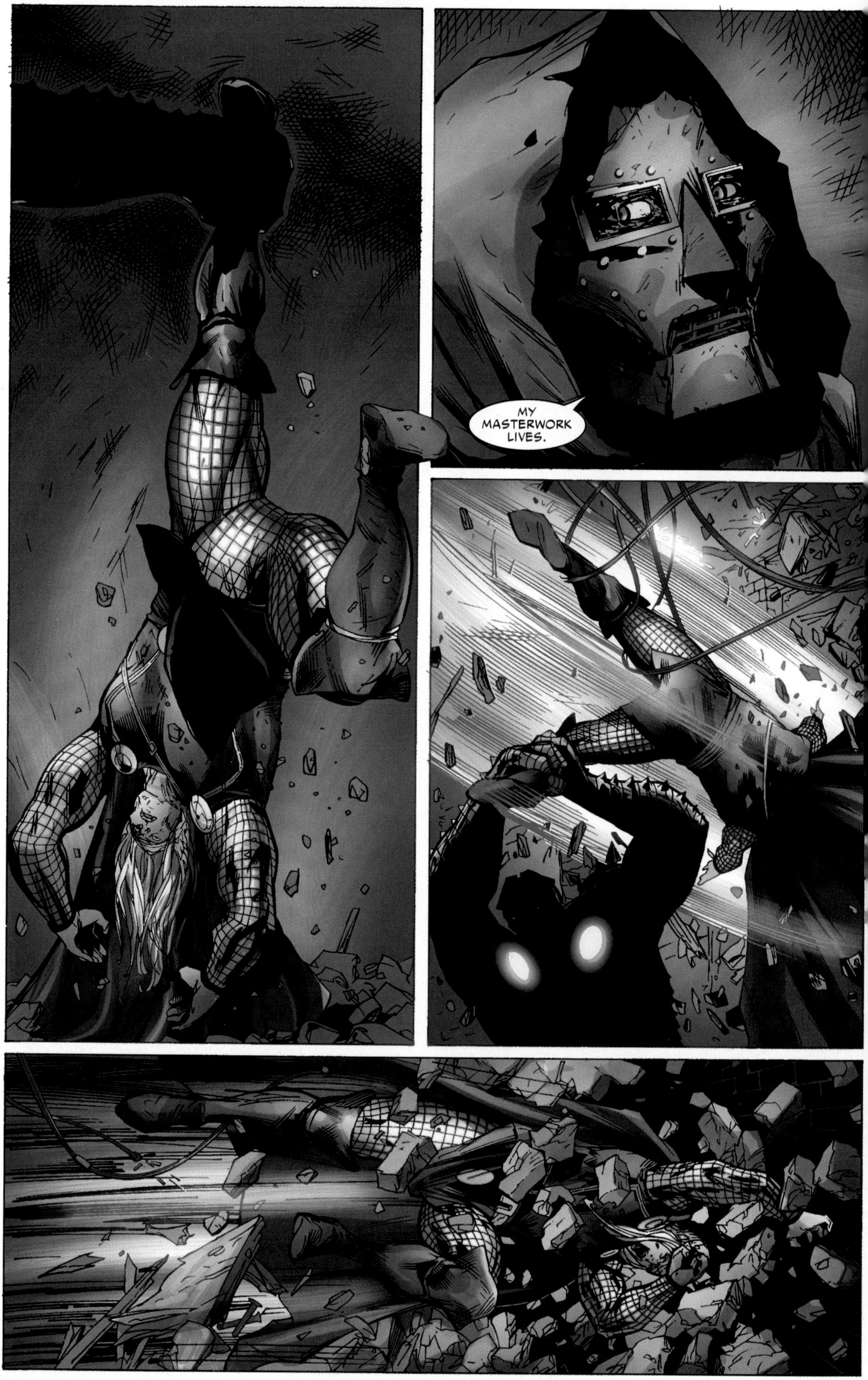

MY MASTERWORK LIVES.

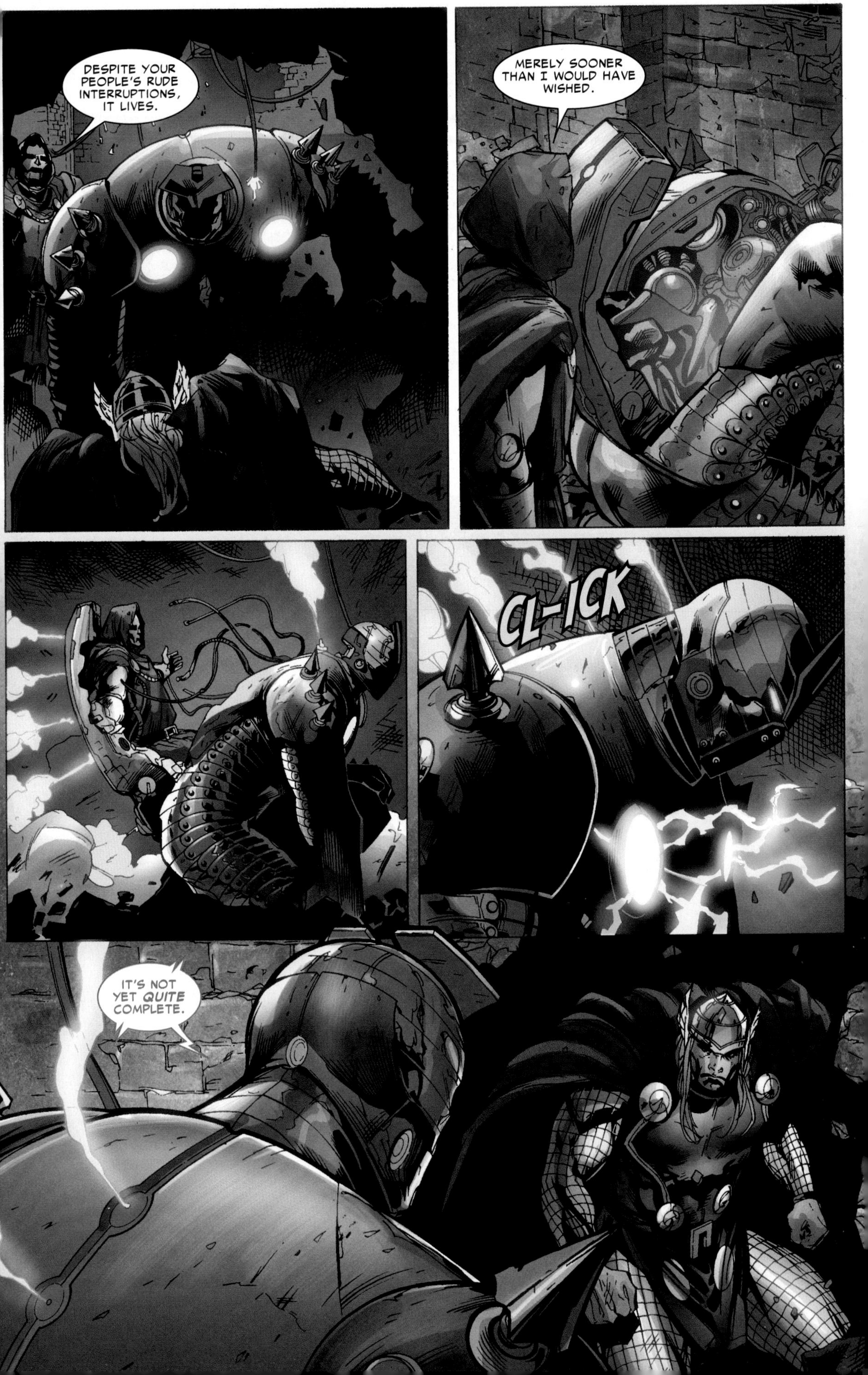
DESPITE YOUR PEOPLE'S RUDE INTERRUPTIONS, IT LIVES.
MERELY SOONER THAN I WOULD HAVE WISHED.
CL-ICK
IT'S NOT YET *QUITE* COMPLETE.

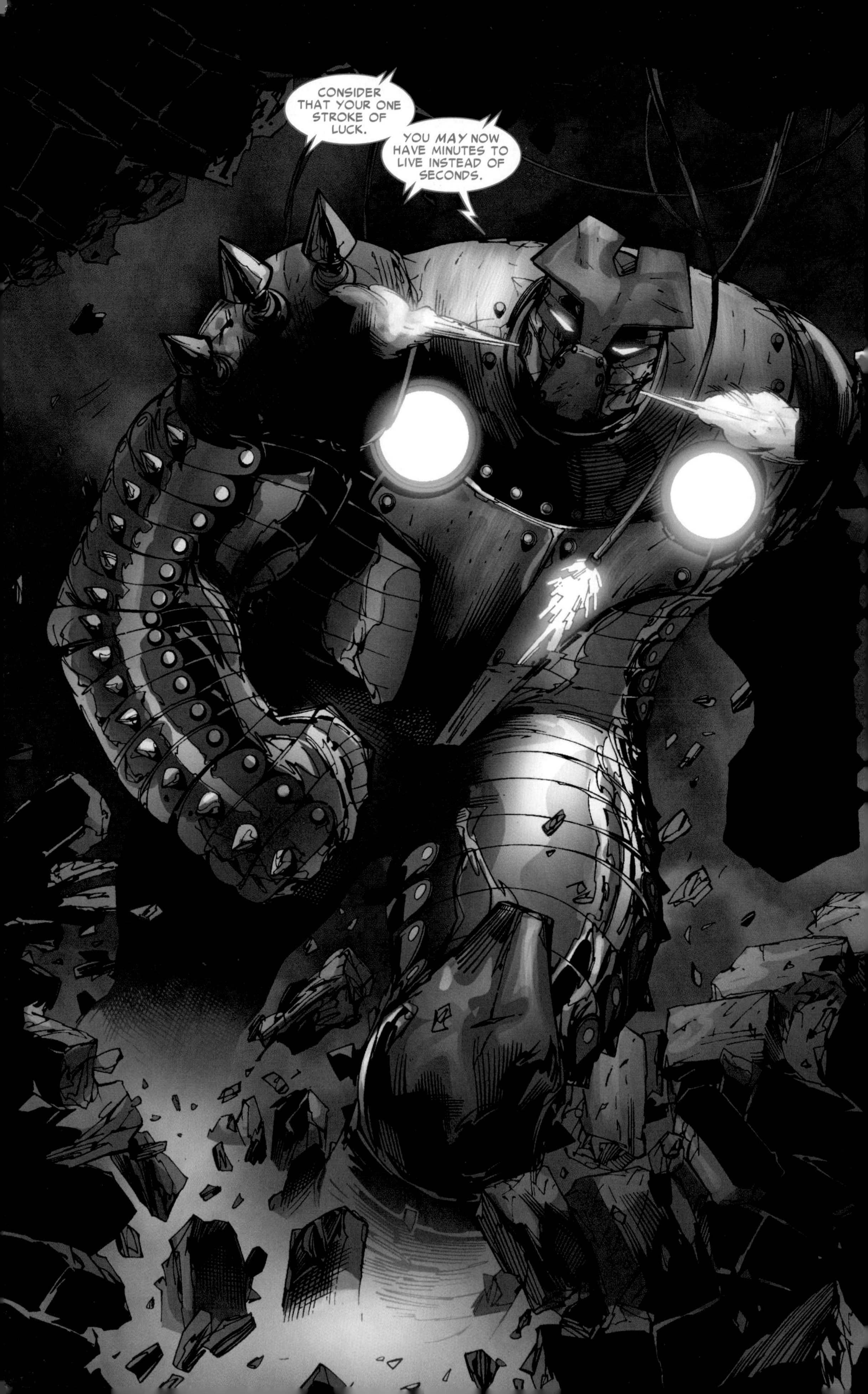
CONSIDER THAT YOUR ONE STROKE OF LUCK.
YOU MAY NOW HAVE MINUTES TO LIVE INSTEAD OF SECONDS.

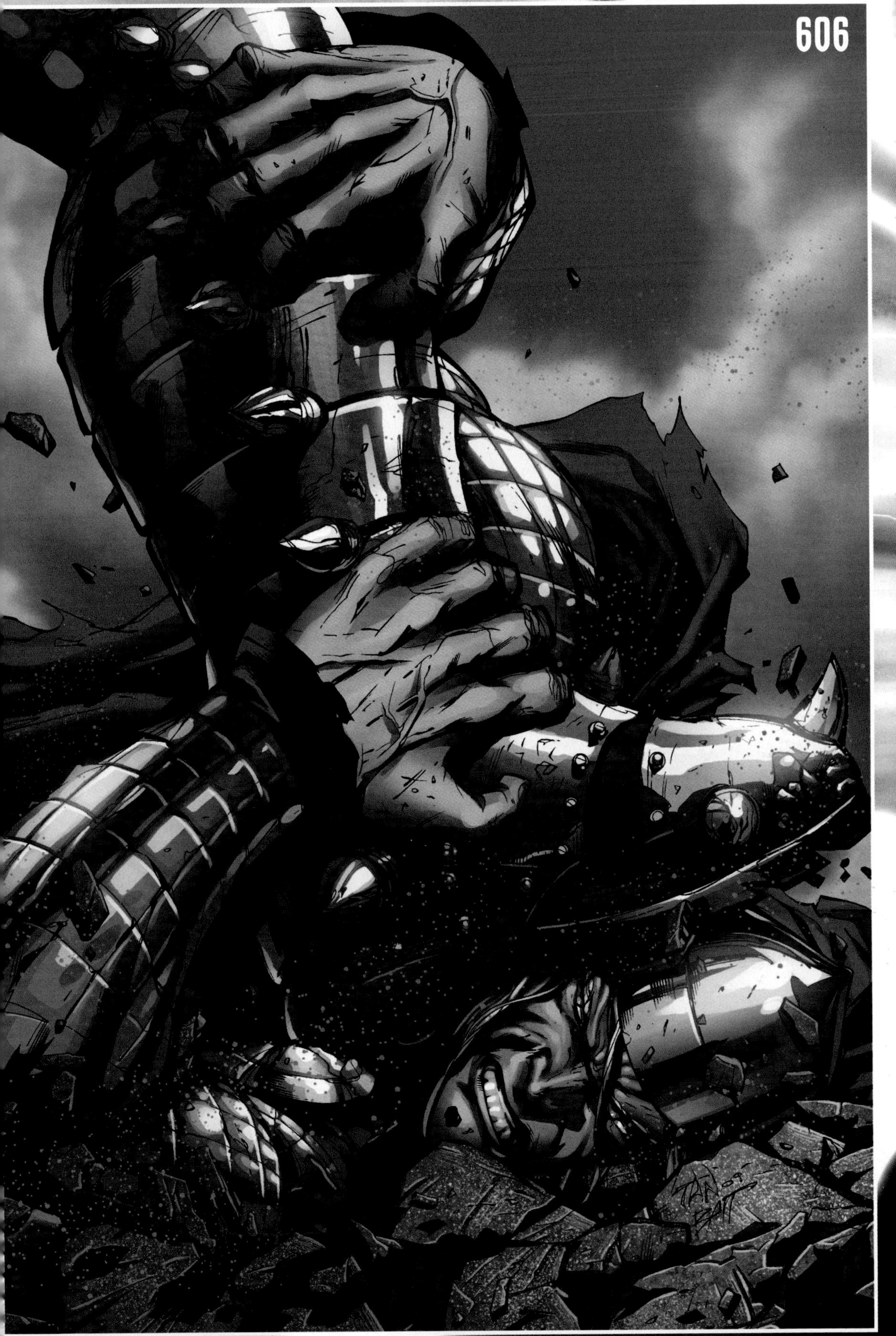
606

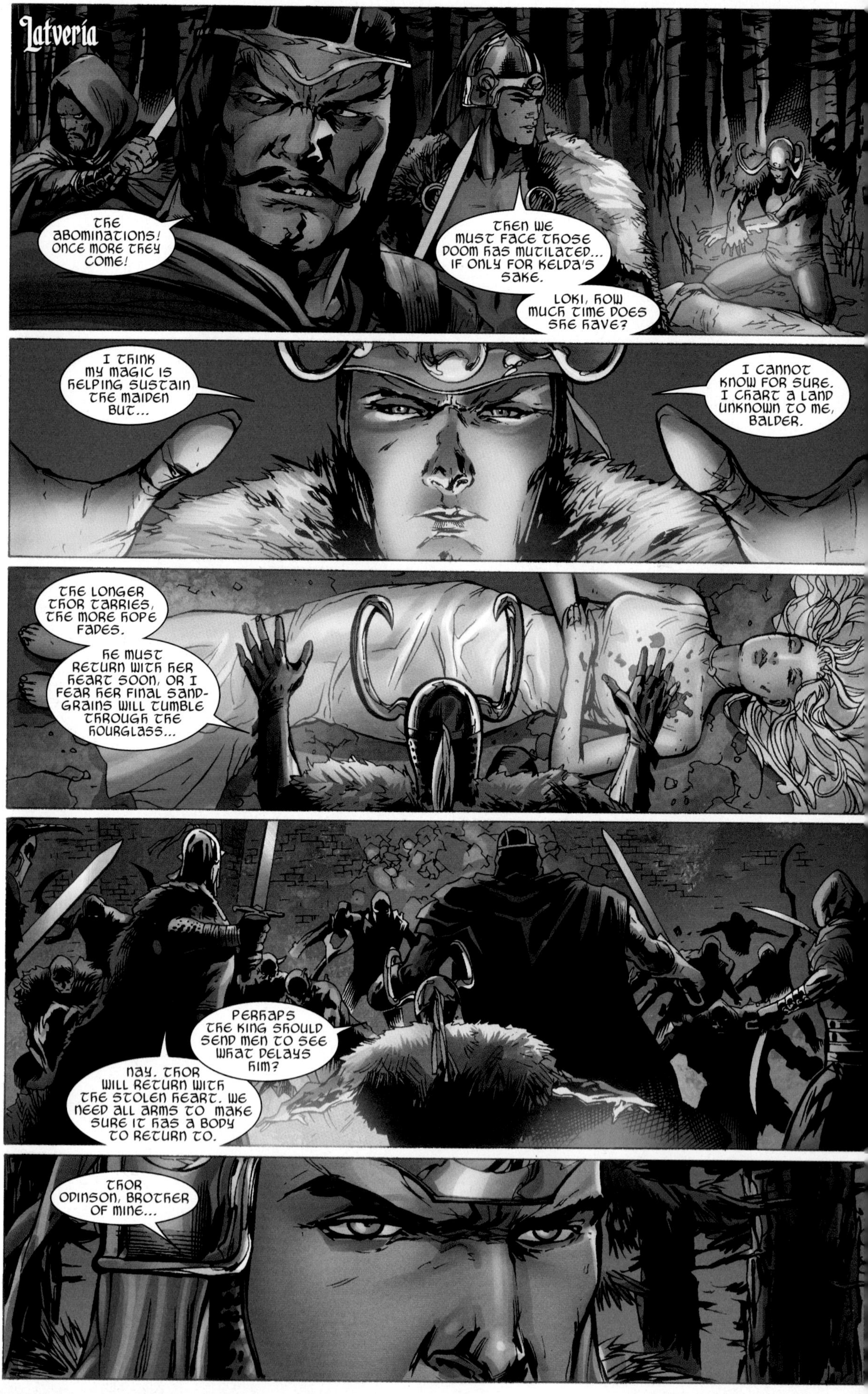
Latveria
THE ABOMINATIONS! ONCE MORE THEY COME!
THEN WE MUST FACE THOSE DOOM HAS MUTILATED... IF ONLY FOR KELDA'S SAKE.
LOKI, HOW MUCH TIME DOES SHE HAVE?
I THINK MY MAGIC IS HELPING SUSTAIN THE MAIDEN BUT...
I CANNOT KNOW FOR SURE. I CHART A LAND UNKNOWN TO ME, BALDER.
THE LONGER THOR TARRIES, THE MORE HOPE FADES.
HE MUST RETURN WITH HER HEART SOON, OR I FEAR HER FINAL SAND-GRAINS WILL TUMBLE THROUGH THE HOURGLASS...
PERHAPS THE KING SHOULD SEND MEN TO SEE WHAT DELAYS HIM?
NAY. THOR WILL RETURN WITH THE STOLEN HEART. WE NEED ALL ARMS TO MAKE SURE IT HAS A BODY TO RETURN TO.
THOR ODINSON, BROTHER OF MINE...

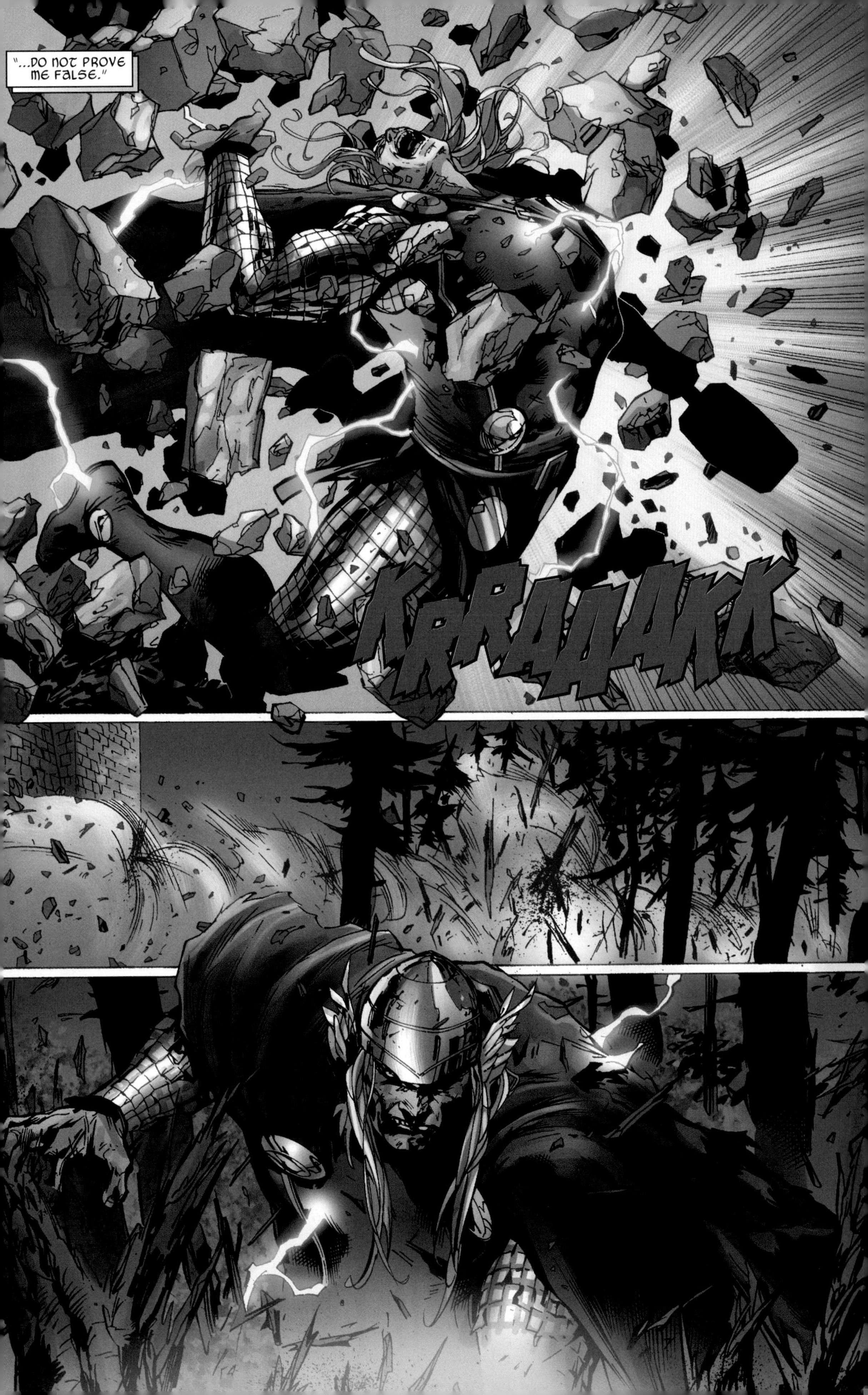
"...DO NOT PROVE ME FALSE."
KRRAAAKK

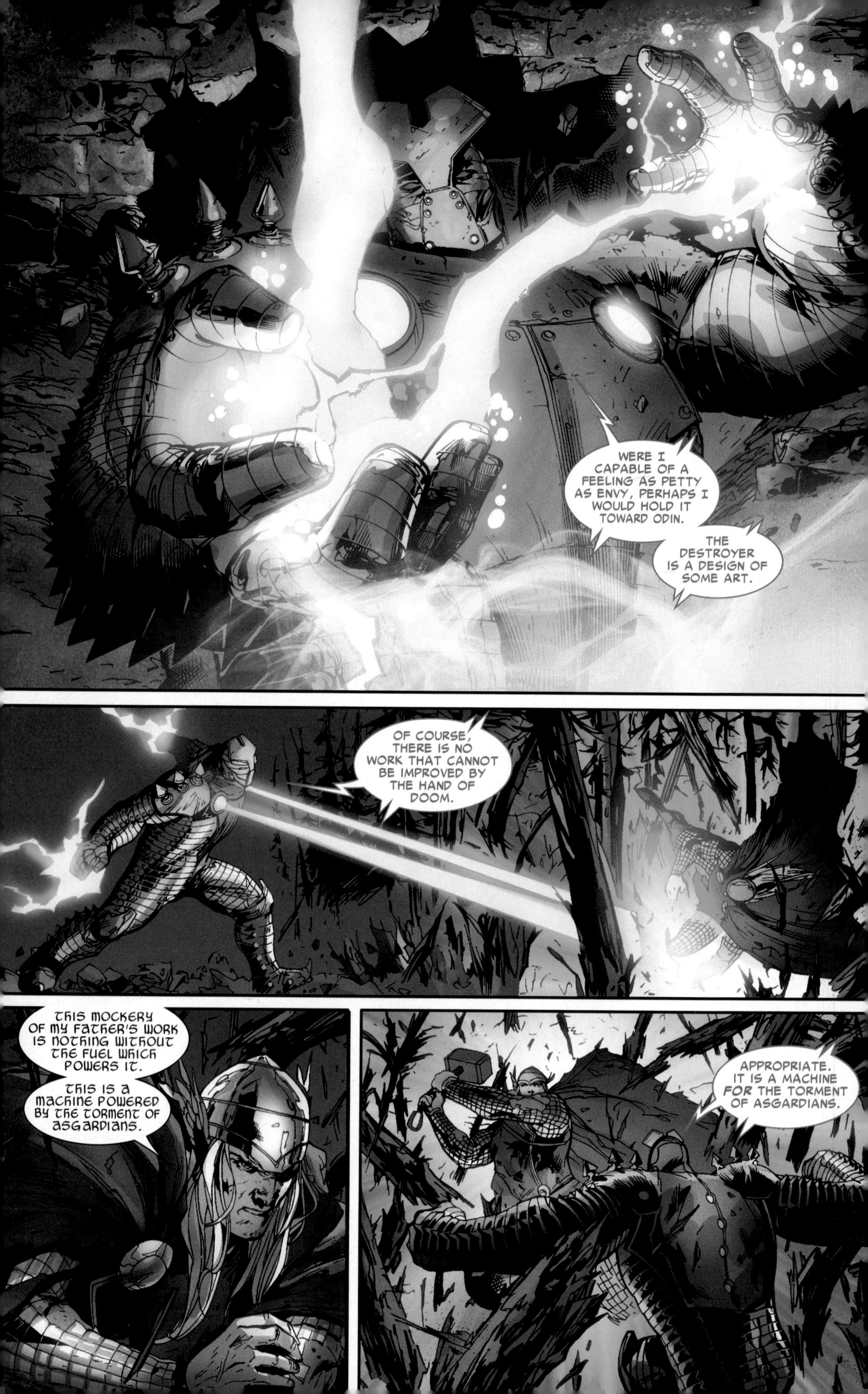
WERE I CAPABLE OF A FEELING AS PETTY AS ENVY, PERHAPS I WOULD HOLD IT TOWARD ODIN.
THE DESTROYER IS A DESIGN OF SOME ART.
OF COURSE, THERE IS NO WORK THAT CANNOT BE IMPROVED BY THE HAND OF DOOM.
THIS MOCKERY OF MY FATHER'S WORK IS NOTHING WITHOUT THE FUEL WHICH POWERS IT.
THIS IS A MACHINE POWERED BY THE TORMENT OF ASGARDIANS.
APPROPRIATE. IT IS A MACHINE FOR THE TORMENT OF ASGARDIANS.

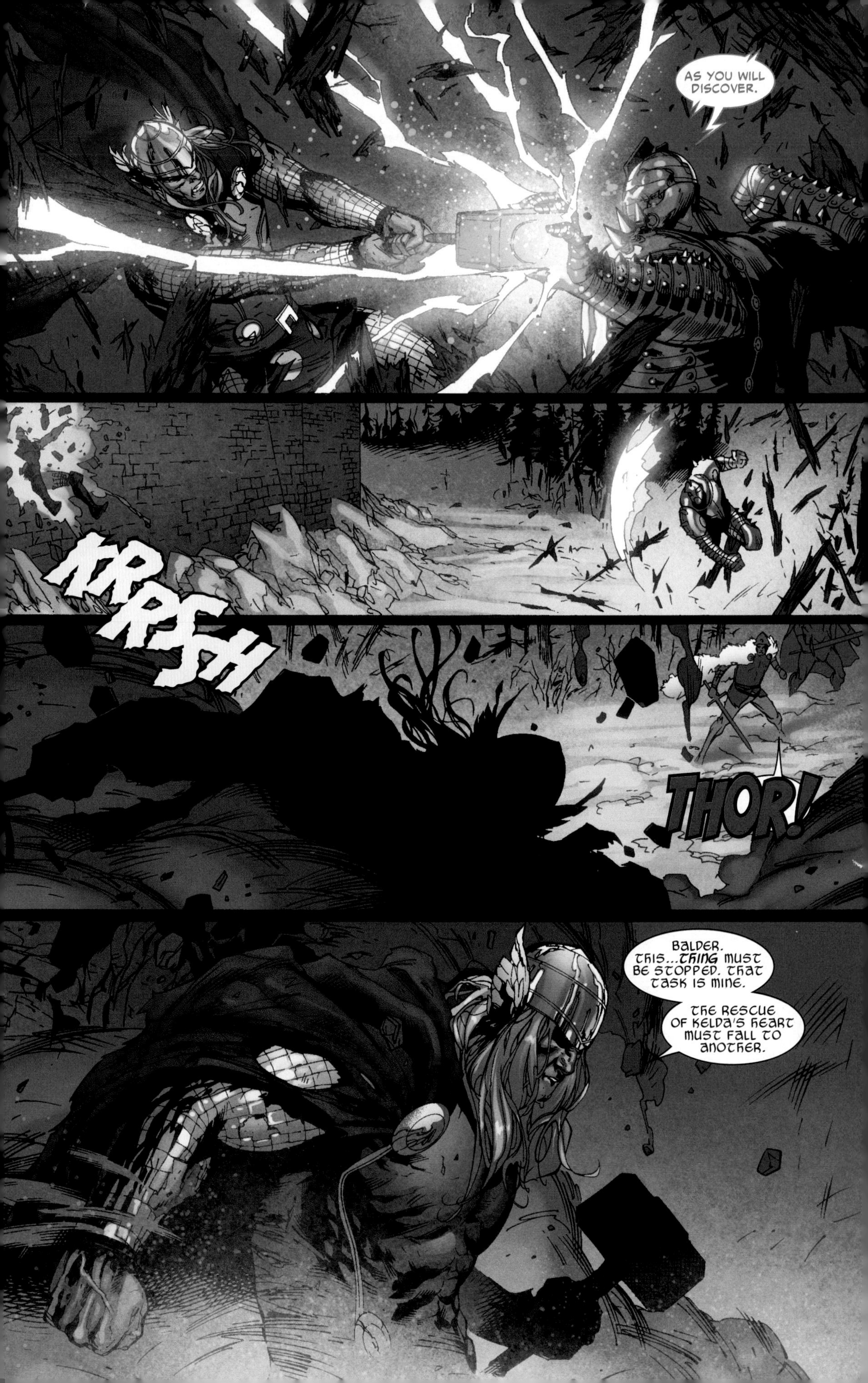
AS YOU WILL DISCOVER.
KRRSH
THOR!
BALDER. THIS...THING MUST BE STOPPED. THAT TASK IS MINE.
THE RESCUE OF KELDA'S HEART MUST FALL TO ANOTHER.

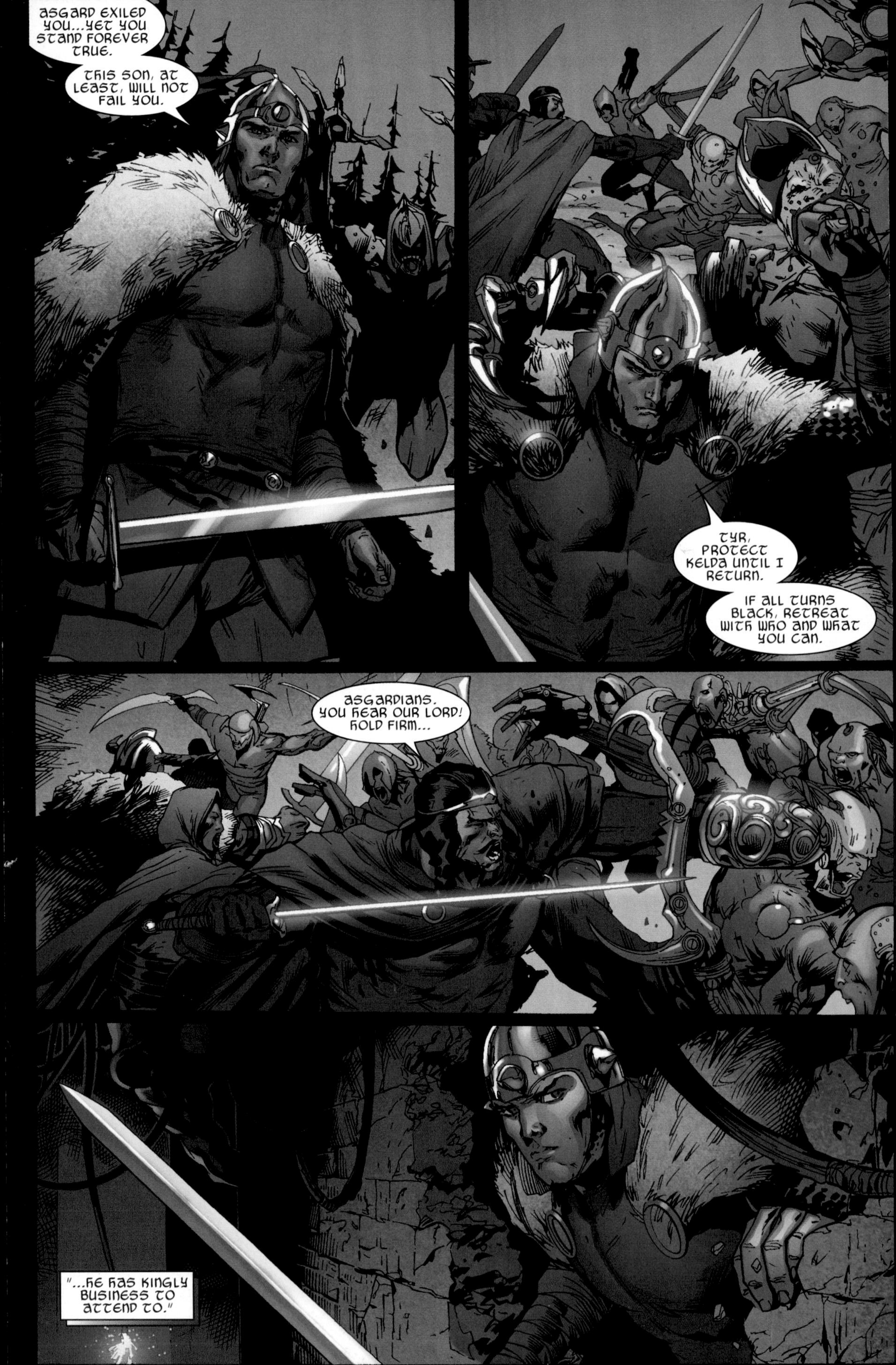
ASGARD EXILED YOU...YET YOU STAND FOREVER TRUE.
THIS SON, AT LEAST, WILL NOT FAIL YOU.
TYR, PROTECT KELDA UNTIL I RETURN.
IF ALL TURNS BLACK, RETREAT WITH WHO AND WHAT YOU CAN.
ASGARDIANS. YOU HEAR OUR LORD! HOLD FIRM...
"...HE HAS KINGLY BUSINESS TO ATTEND TO."

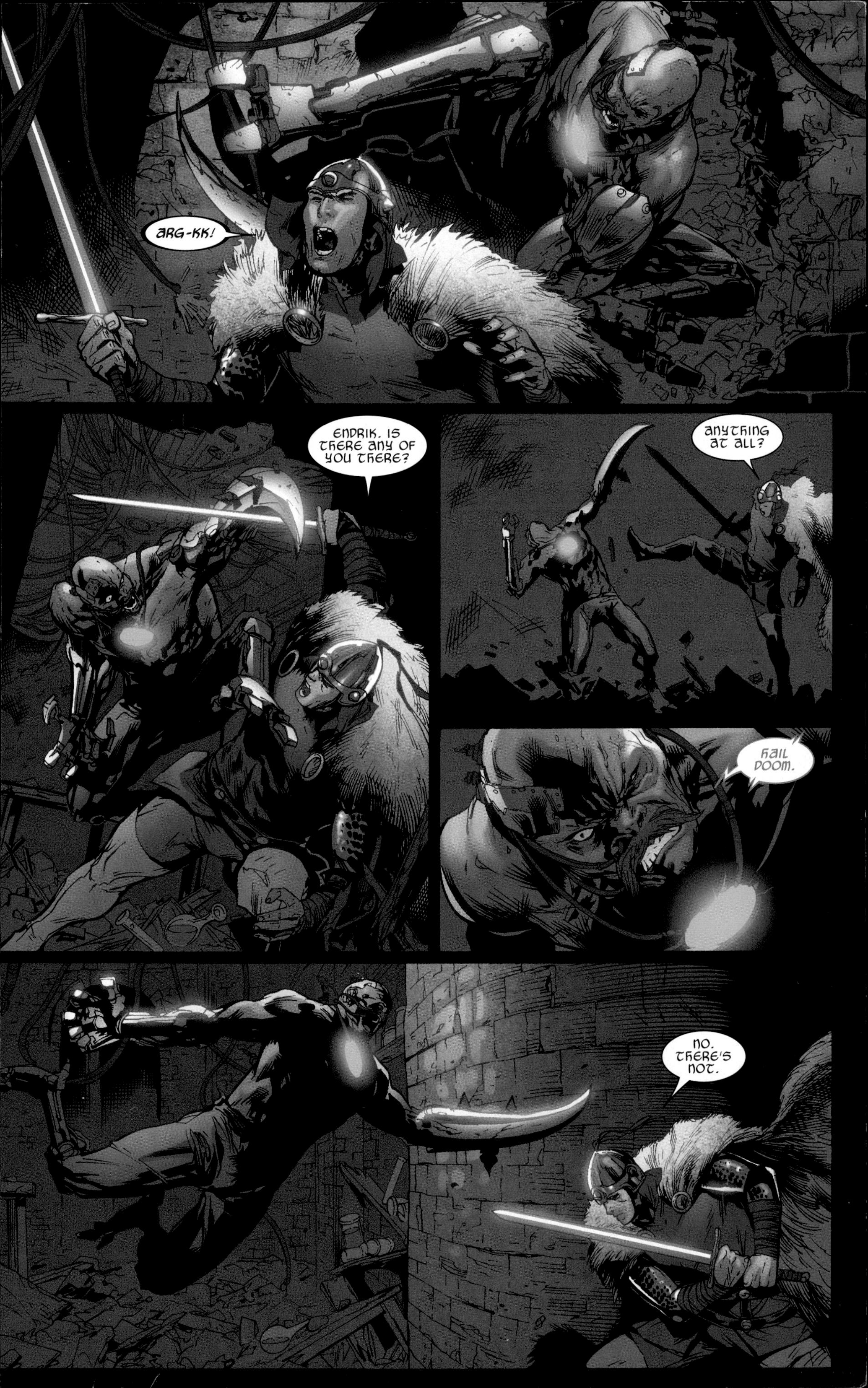
ARG-KK!
ENDRIK. IS THERE ANY OF YOU THERE?
ANYTHING AT ALL?
HAIL DOOM.
NO. THERE'S NOT.

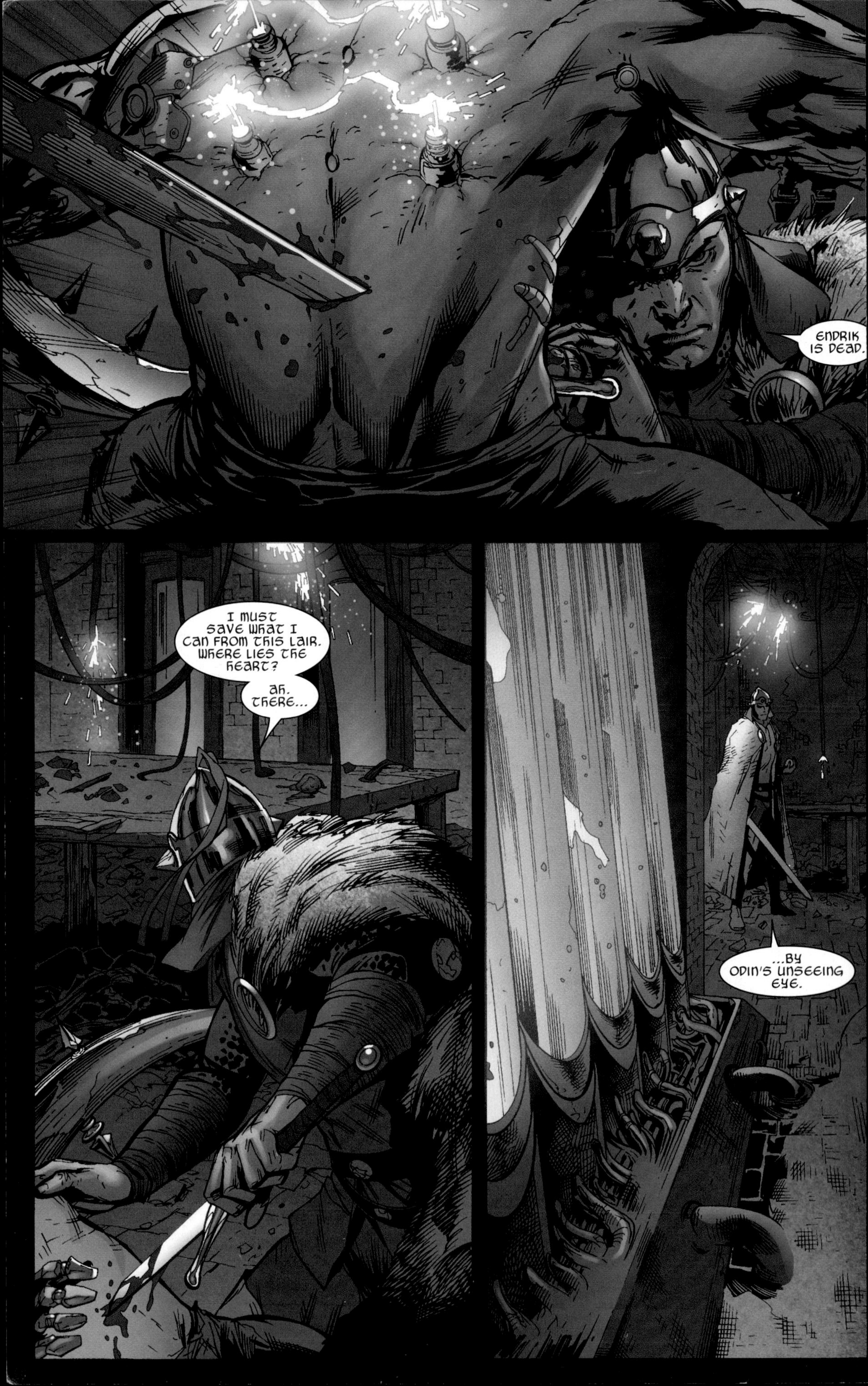
ENDRIK IS DEAD.
I MUST SAVE WHAT I CAN FROM THIS LAIR. WHERE LIES THE HEART?
AH. THERE...
...BY ODIN'S UNSEEING EYE.

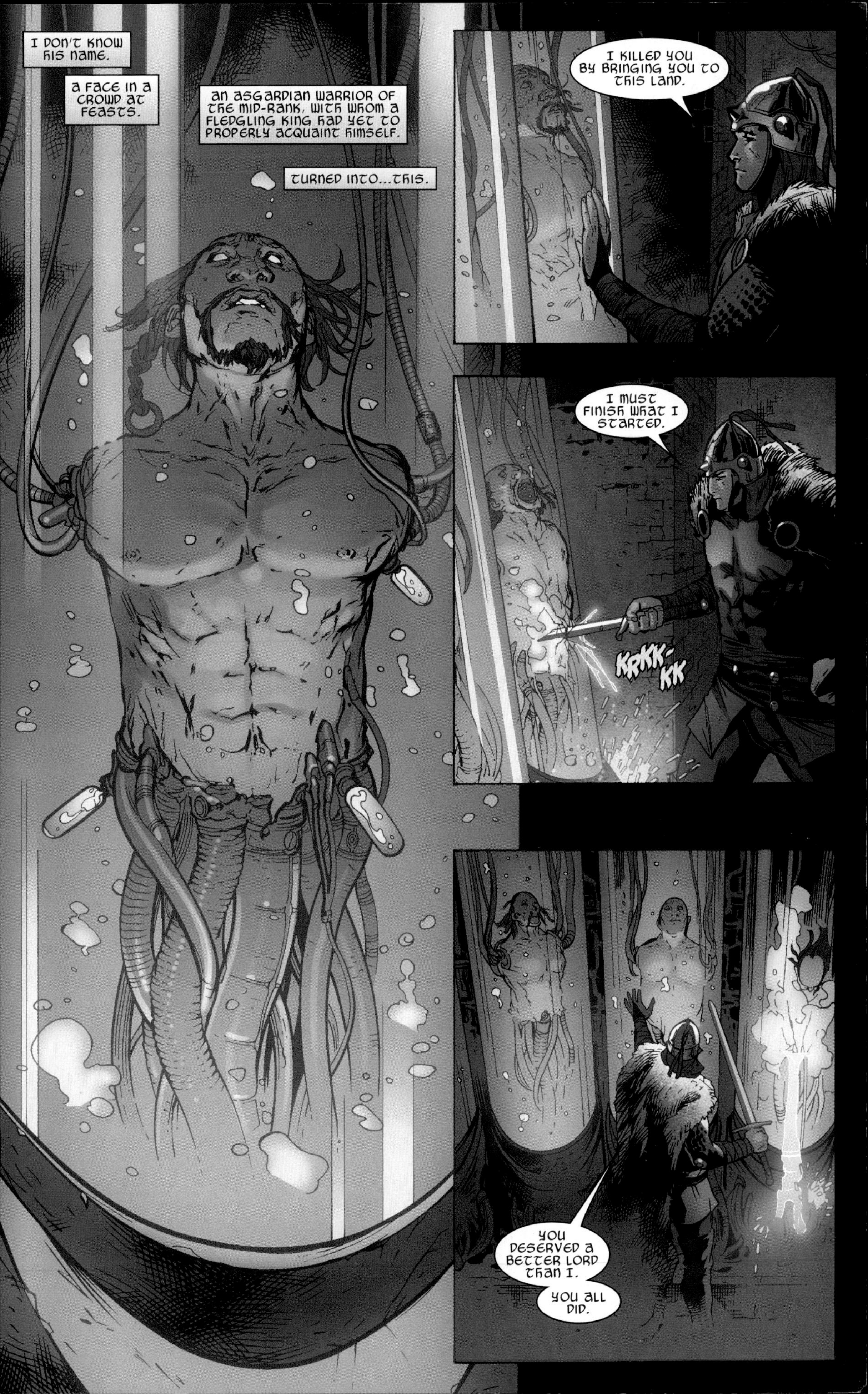
I DON'T KNOW HIS NAME.
A FACE IN A CROWD AT FEASTS.
AN ASGARDIAN WARRIOR OF THE MID-RANK, WITH WHOM A FLEDGLING KING HAD YET TO PROPERLY ACQUAINT HIMSELF.
TURNED INTO...THIS.
I KILLED YOU BY BRINGING YOU TO THIS LAND.
I MUST FINISH WHAT I STARTED.
KRKK-KK
YOU DESERVED A BETTER LORD THAN I.
YOU ALL DID.

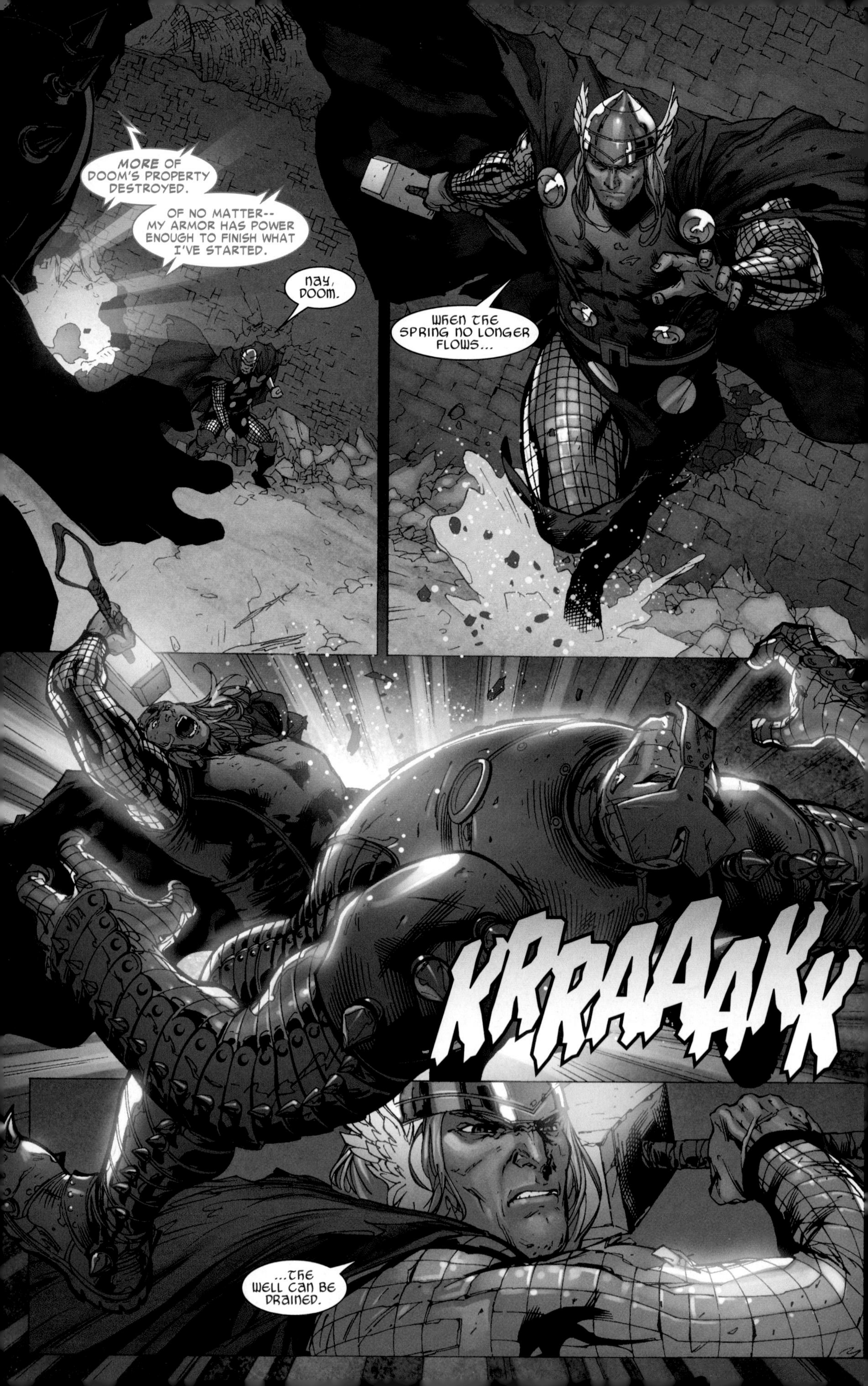
MORE OF DOOM'S PROPERTY DESTROYED.
OF NO MATTER-- MY ARMOR HAS POWER ENOUGH TO FINISH WHAT I'VE STARTED.
NAY, DOOM.
WHEN THE SPRING NO LONGER FLOWS...
KRRAAAKK
...THE WELL CAN BE DRAINED.

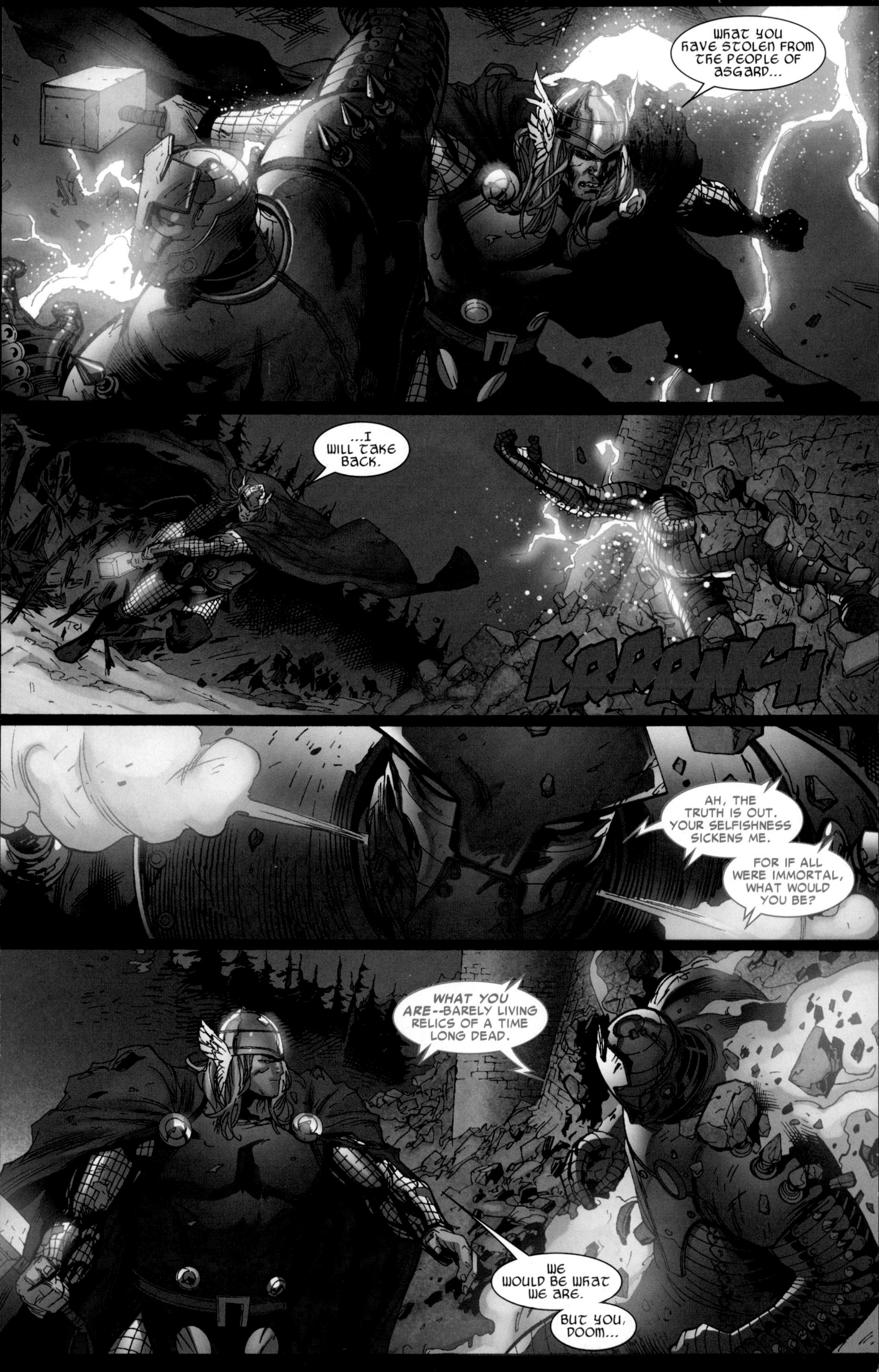
WHAT YOU HAVE STOLEN FROM THE PEOPLE OF ASGARD...
...I WILL TAKE BACK.
KRRRNCH
AH, THE TRUTH IS OUT. YOUR SELFISHNESS SICKENS ME.
FOR IF ALL WERE IMMORTAL, WHAT WOULD YOU BE?
WHAT YOU ARE--BARELY LIVING RELICS OF A TIME LONG DEAD.
WE WOULD BE WHAT WE ARE.
BUT YOU, DOOM...

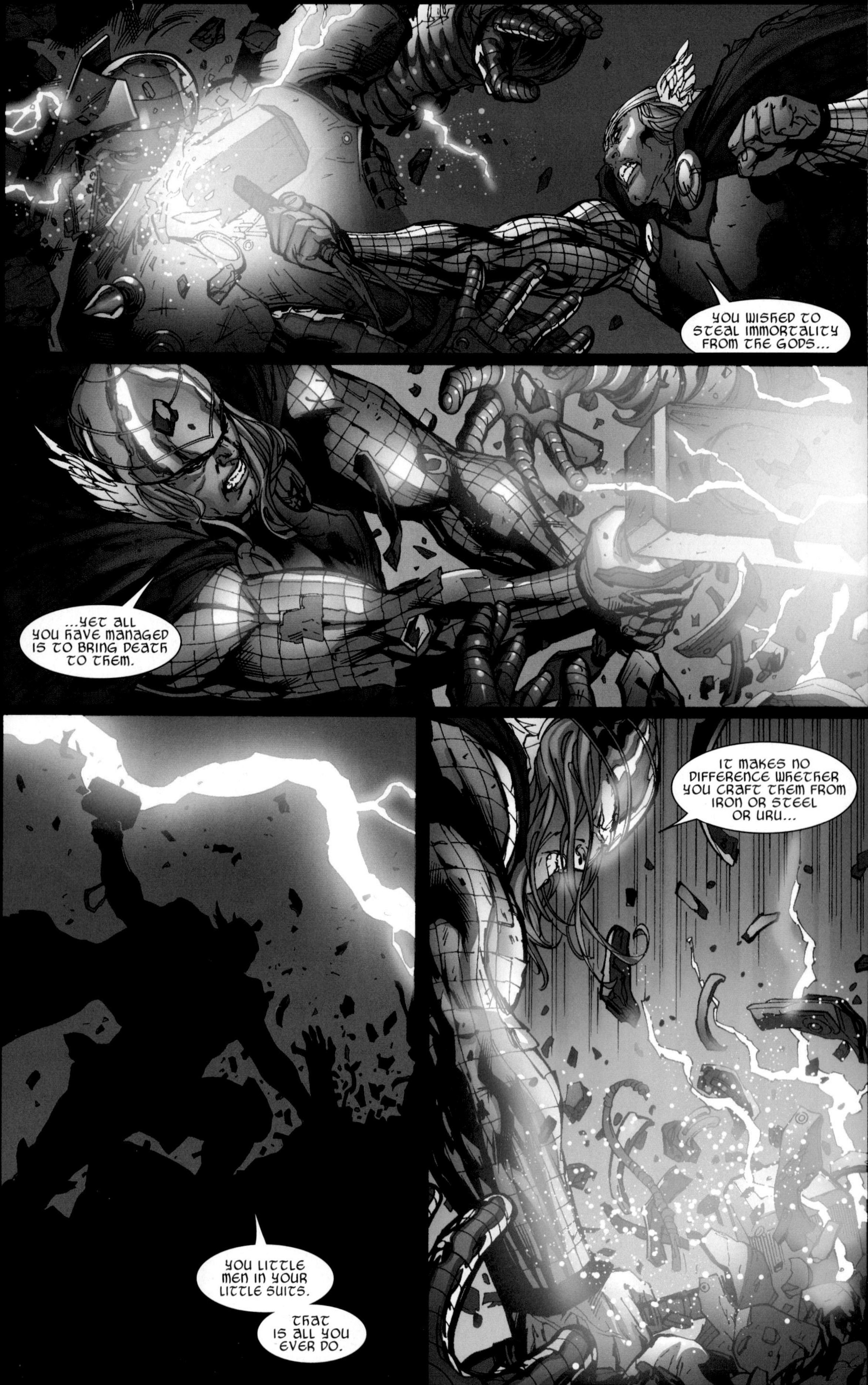
YOU WISHED TO STEAL IMMORTALITY FROM THE GODS...
...YET ALL YOU HAVE MANAGED IS TO BRING DEATH TO THEM.
IT MAKES NO DIFFERENCE WHETHER YOU CRAFT THEM FROM IRON OR STEEL OR URU...
YOU LITTLE MEN IN YOUR LITTLE SUITS.
THAT IS ALL YOU EVER DO.

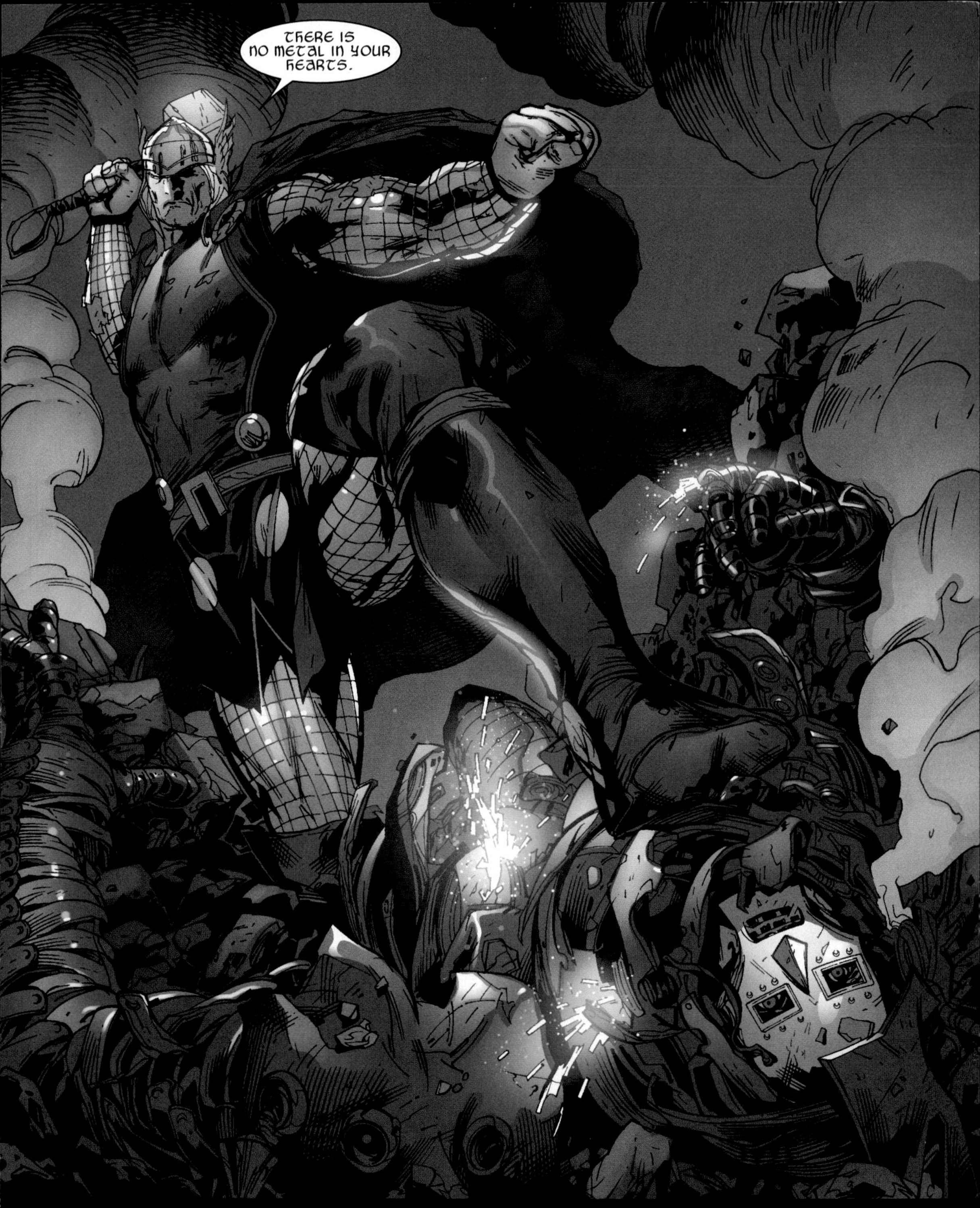
THERE IS NO METAL IN YOUR HEARTS.
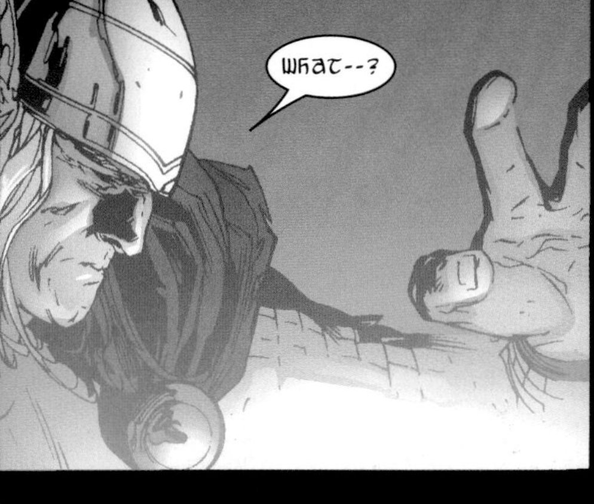
WHAT--?
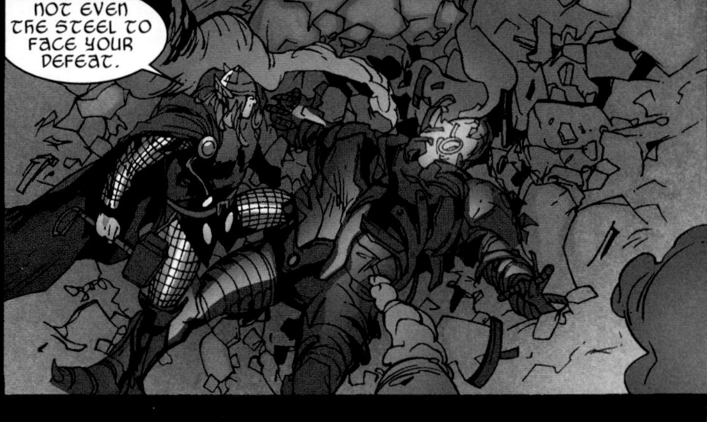
NOT EVEN THE STEEL TO FACE YOUR DEFEAT.

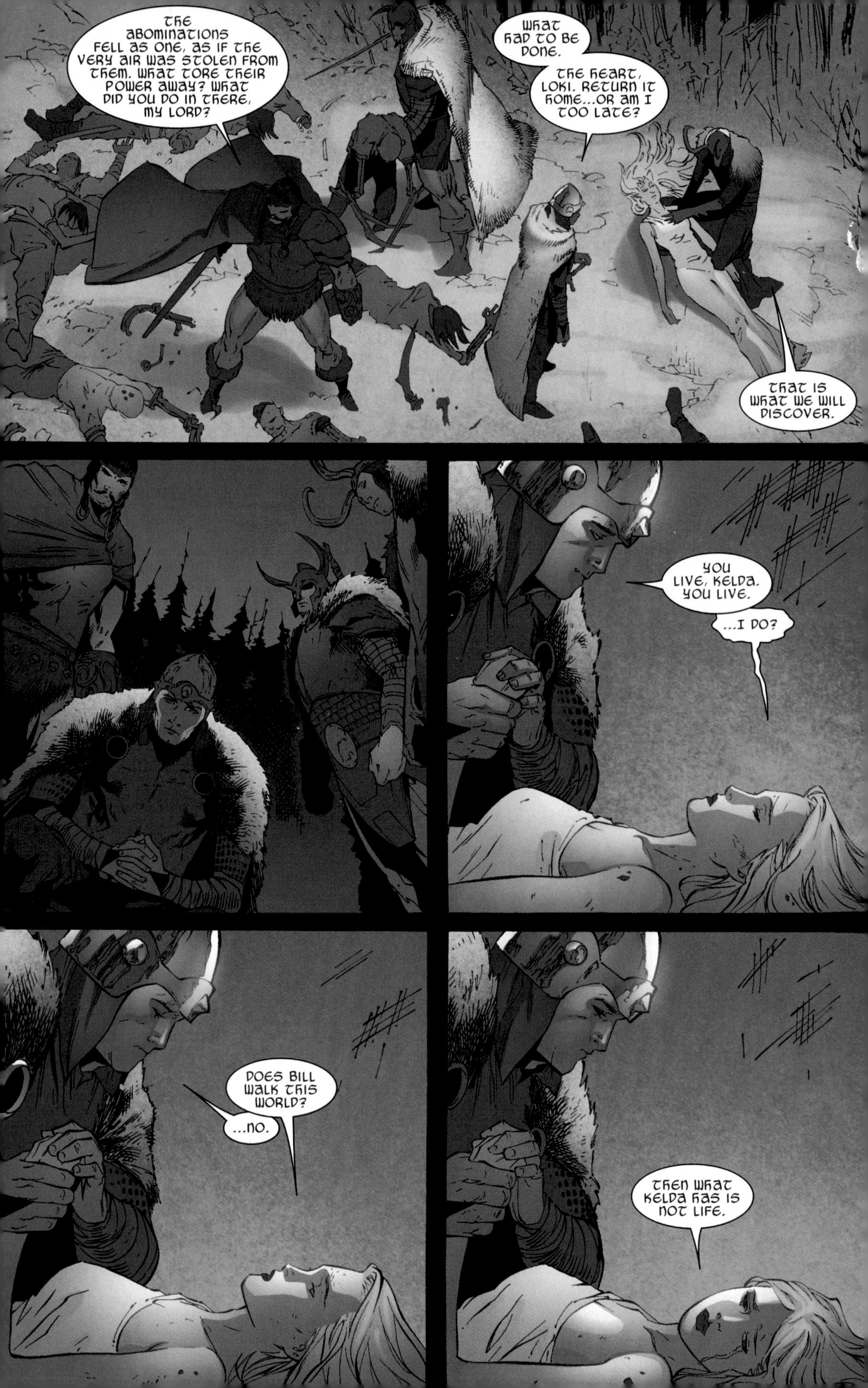
THE ABOMINATIONS FELL AS ONE, AS IF THE VERY AIR WAS STOLEN FROM THEM. WHAT TORE THEIR POWER AWAY? WHAT DID YOU DO IN THERE, MY LORD?
WHAT HAD TO BE DONE.
THE HEART, LOKI. RETURN IT HOME...OR AM I TOO LATE?
THAT IS WHAT WE WILL DISCOVER.
YOU LIVE, KELDA. YOU LIVE.
...I DO?
DOES BILL WALK THIS WORLD?
...NO.
THEN WHAT KELDA HAS IS NOT LIFE.

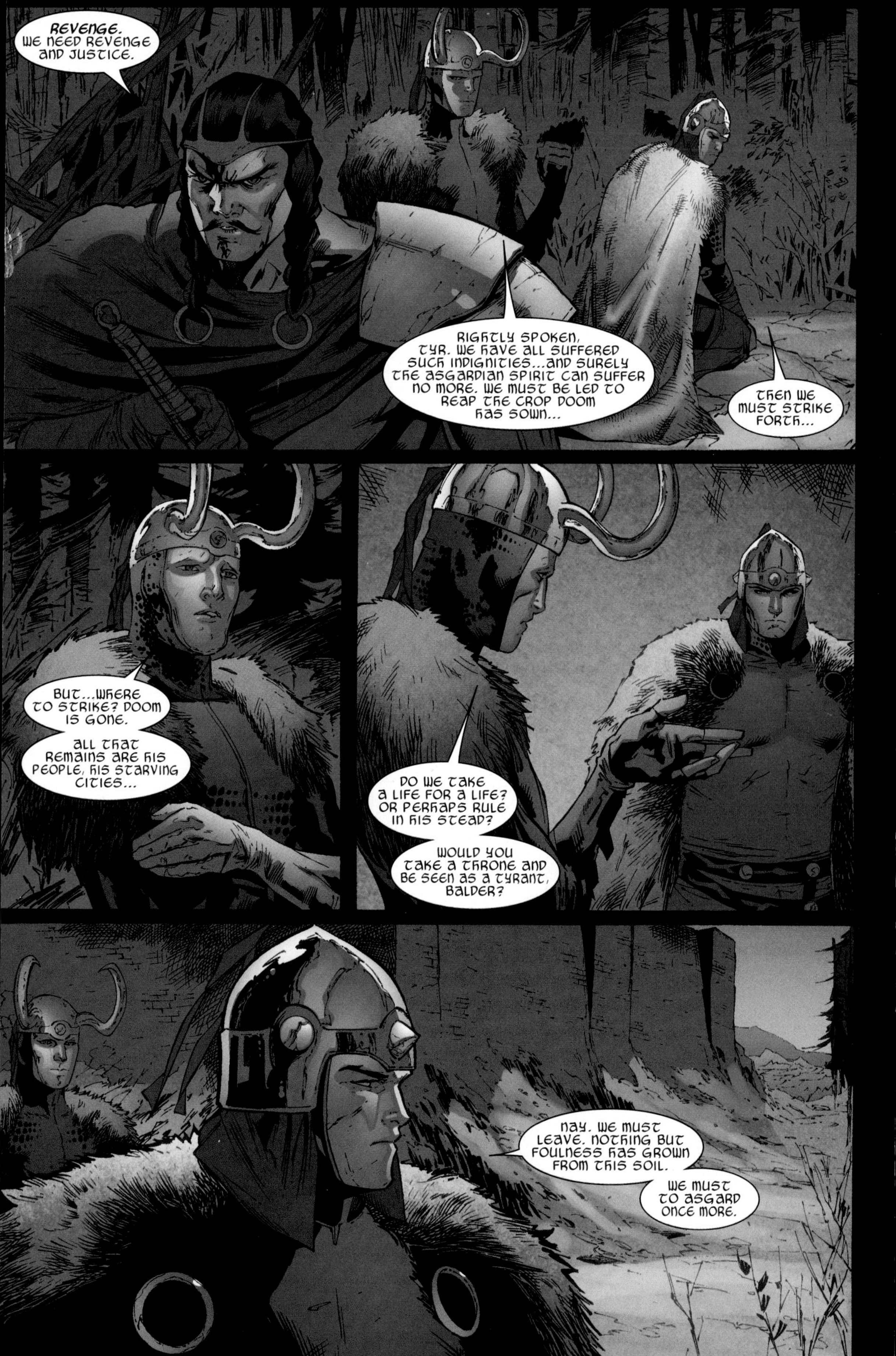
REVENGE. WE NEED REVENGE AND JUSTICE.
RIGHTLY SPOKEN, TYR. WE HAVE ALL SUFFERED SUCH INDIGNITIES...AND SURELY THE ASGARDIAN SPIRIT CAN SUFFER NO MORE. WE MUST BE LED TO REAP THE CROP DOOM HAS SOWN...
THEN WE MUST STRIKE FORTH...
BUT...WHERE TO STRIKE? DOOM IS GONE.
ALL THAT REMAINS ARE HIS PEOPLE, HIS STARVING CITIES...
DO WE TAKE A LIFE FOR A LIFE? OR PERHAPS RULE IN HIS STEAD?
WOULD YOU TAKE A THRONE AND BE SEEN AS A TYRANT, BALDER?
NAY. WE MUST LEAVE. NOTHING BUT FOULNESS HAS GROWN FROM THIS SOIL.
WE MUST TO ASGARD ONCE MORE.

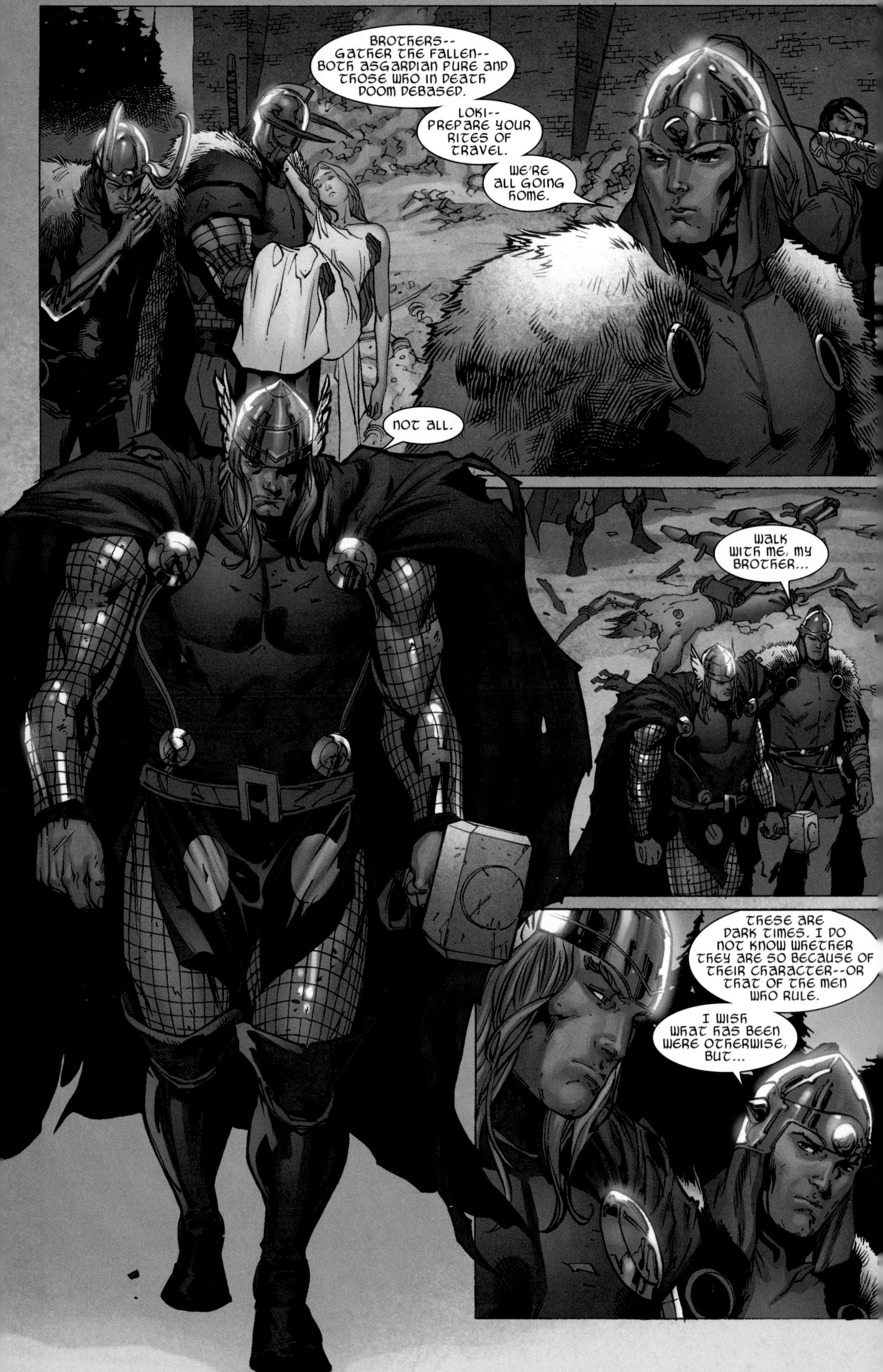
BROTHERS-- GATHER THE FALLEN-- BOTH ASGARDIAN PURE AND THOSE WHO IN DEATH DOOM DEBASED.
LOKI-- PREPARE YOUR RITES OF TRAVEL.
WE'RE ALL GOING HOME.
NOT ALL.
WALK WITH ME, MY BROTHER...
THESE ARE DARK TIMES. I DO NOT KNOW WHETHER THEY ARE SO BECAUSE OF THEIR CHARACTER--OR THAT OF THE MEN WHO RULE.
I WISH WHAT HAS BEEN WERE OTHERWISE, BUT...

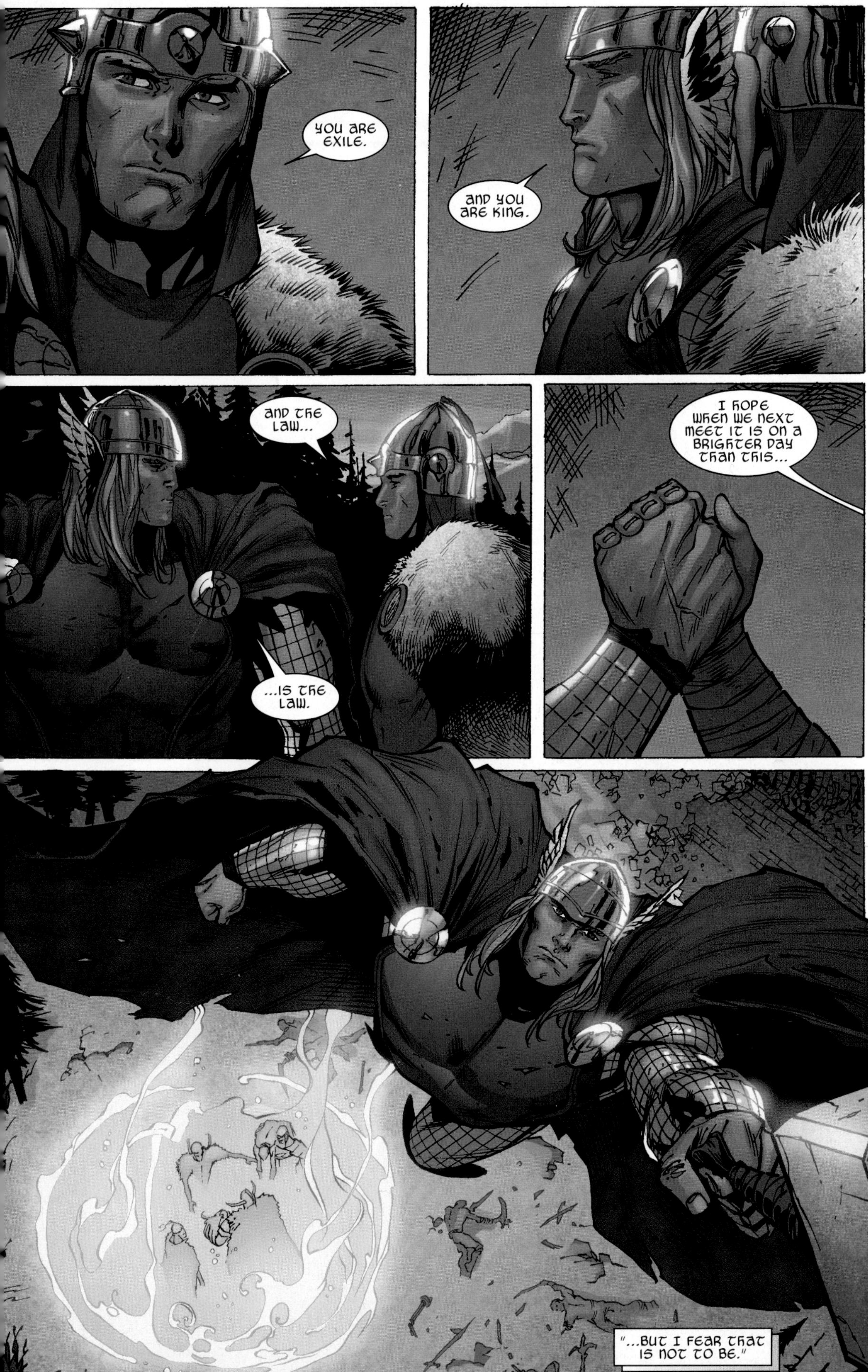
YOU ARE EXILE.
AND YOU ARE KING.
AND THE LAW...
...IS THE LAW.
I HOPE WHEN WE NEXT MEET IT IS ON A BRIGHTER DAY THAN THIS...
"...BUT I FEAR THAT IS NOT TO BE."

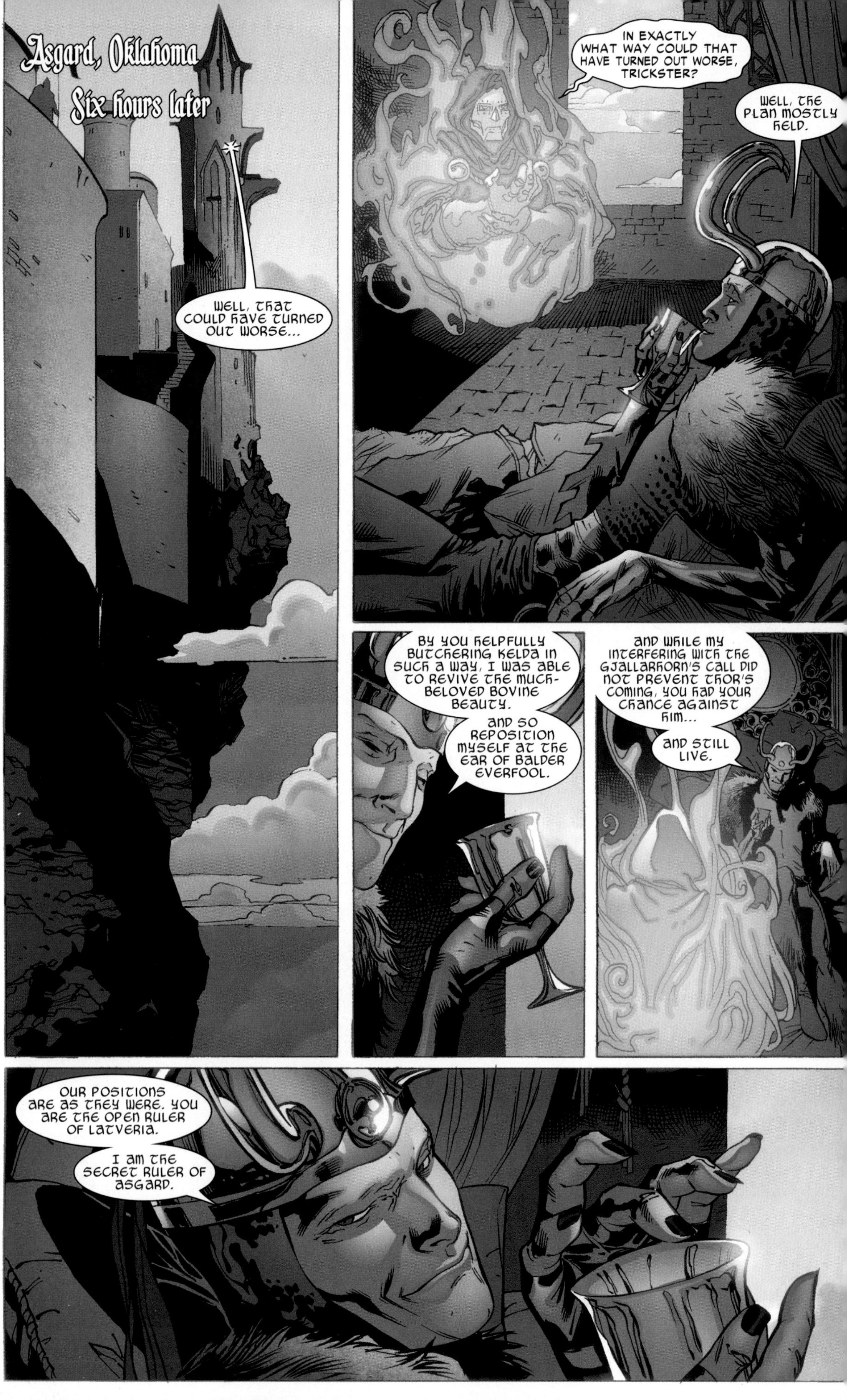
Asgard, Oklahoma
Six hours later
WELL, THAT COULD HAVE TURNED OUT WORSE...
IN EXACTLY WHAT WAY COULD THAT HAVE TURNED OUT WORSE, TRICKSTER?
WELL, THE PLAN MOSTLY HELD.
BY YOU HELPFULLY BUTCHERING KELDA IN SUCH A WAY, I WAS ABLE TO REVIVE THE MUCH-BELOVED BOVINE BEAUTY.
AND SO REPOSITION MYSELF AT THE EAR OF BALDER EVERFOOL.
AND WHILE MY INTERFERING WITH THE GJALLARHORN'S CALL DID NOT PREVENT THOR'S COMING, YOU HAD YOUR CHANCE AGAINST HIM...
AND STILL LIVE.
OUR POSITIONS ARE AS THEY WERE. YOU ARE THE OPEN RULER OF LATVERIA.
I AM THE SECRET RULER OF ASGARD.

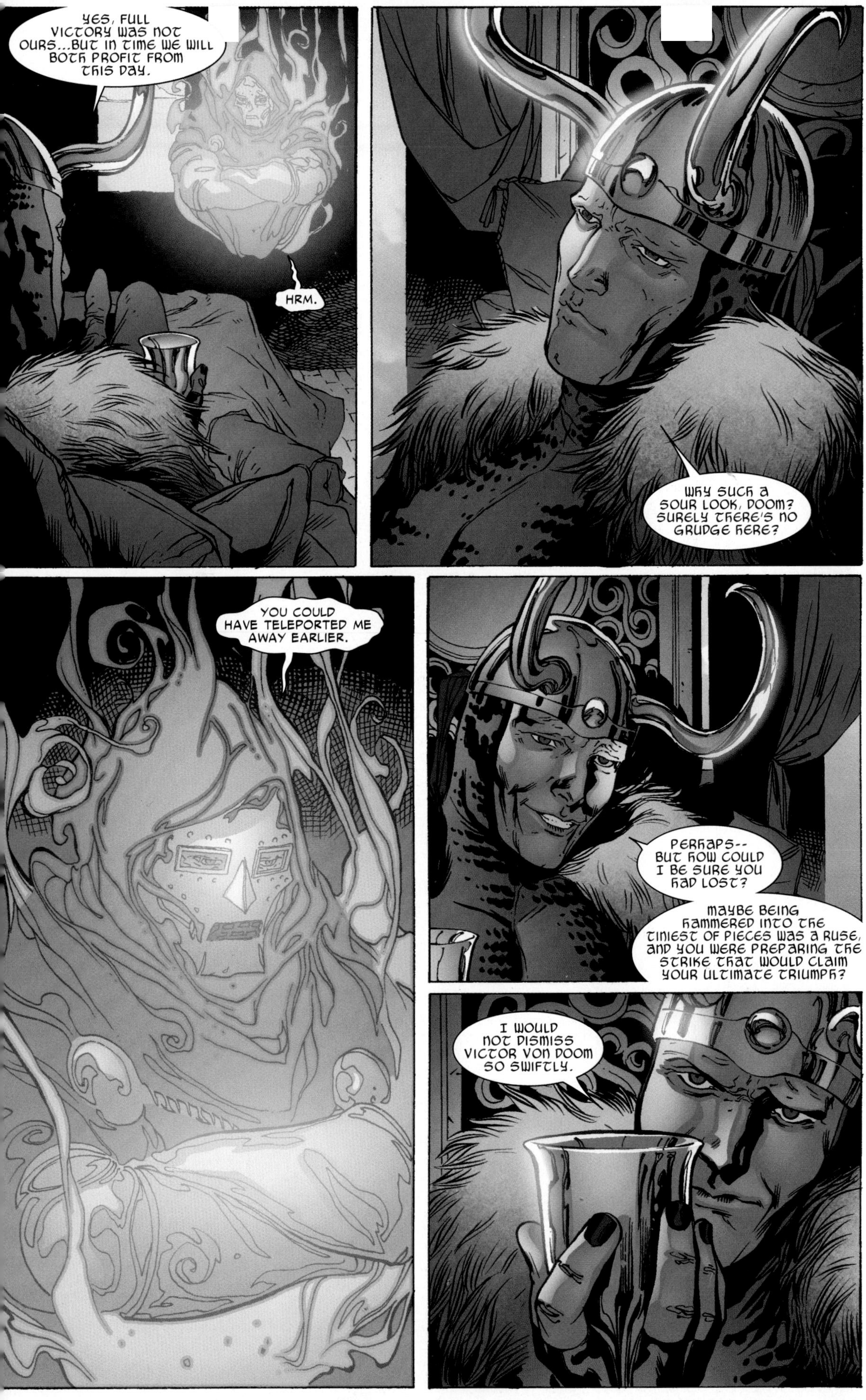

YES, FULL VICTORY WAS NOT OURS...BUT IN TIME WE WILL BOTH PROFIT FROM THIS DAY.
HRM.
WHY SUCH A SOUR LOOK, DOOM? SURELY THERE'S NO GRUDGE HERE?
YOU COULD HAVE TELEPORTED ME AWAY EARLIER.
PERHAPS-- BUT HOW COULD I BE SURE YOU HAD LOST?
MAYBE BEING HAMMERED INTO THE TINIEST OF PIECES WAS A RUSE, AND YOU WERE PREPARING THE STRIKE THAT WOULD CLAIM YOUR ULTIMATE TRIUMPH?
I WOULD NOT DISMISS VICTOR VON DOOM SO SWIFTLY.

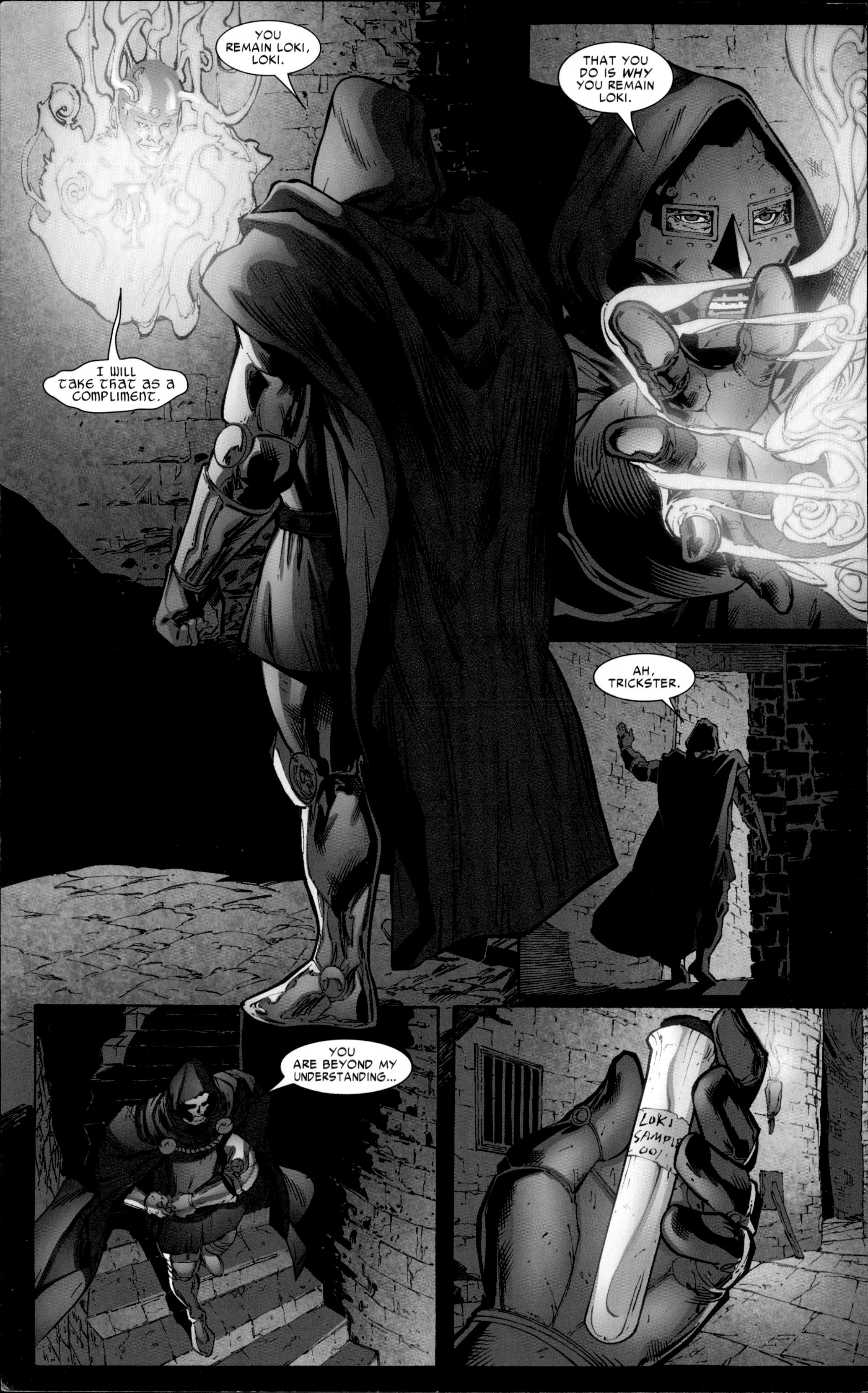
YOU REMAIN LOKI, LOKI.
I WILL TAKE THAT AS A COMPLIMENT.
THAT YOU DO IS WHY YOU REMAIN LOKI.
AH, TRICKSTER.
YOU ARE BEYOND MY UNDERSTANDING...
LOKI SAMPLE 001

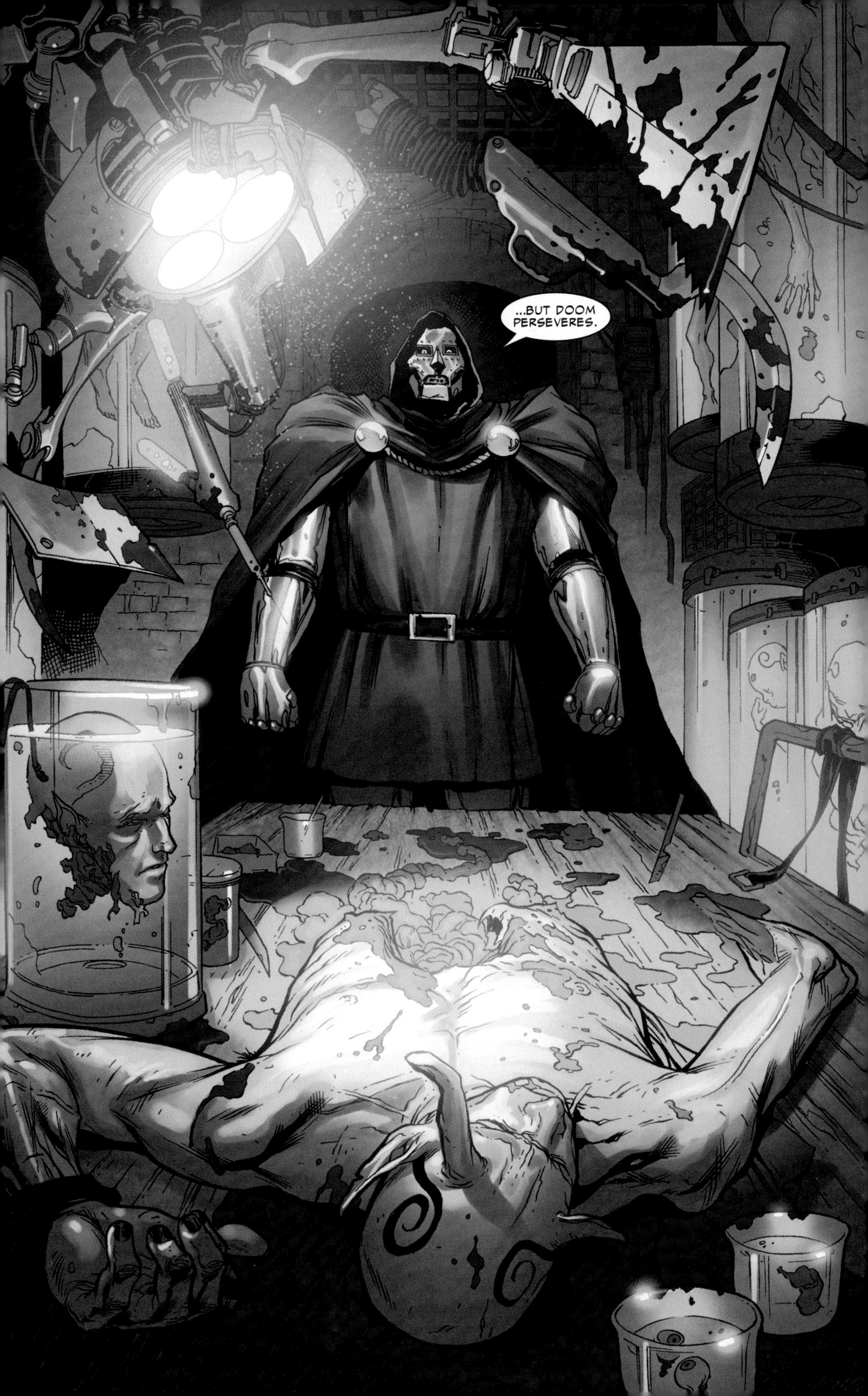
...BUT DOOM PERSEVERES.

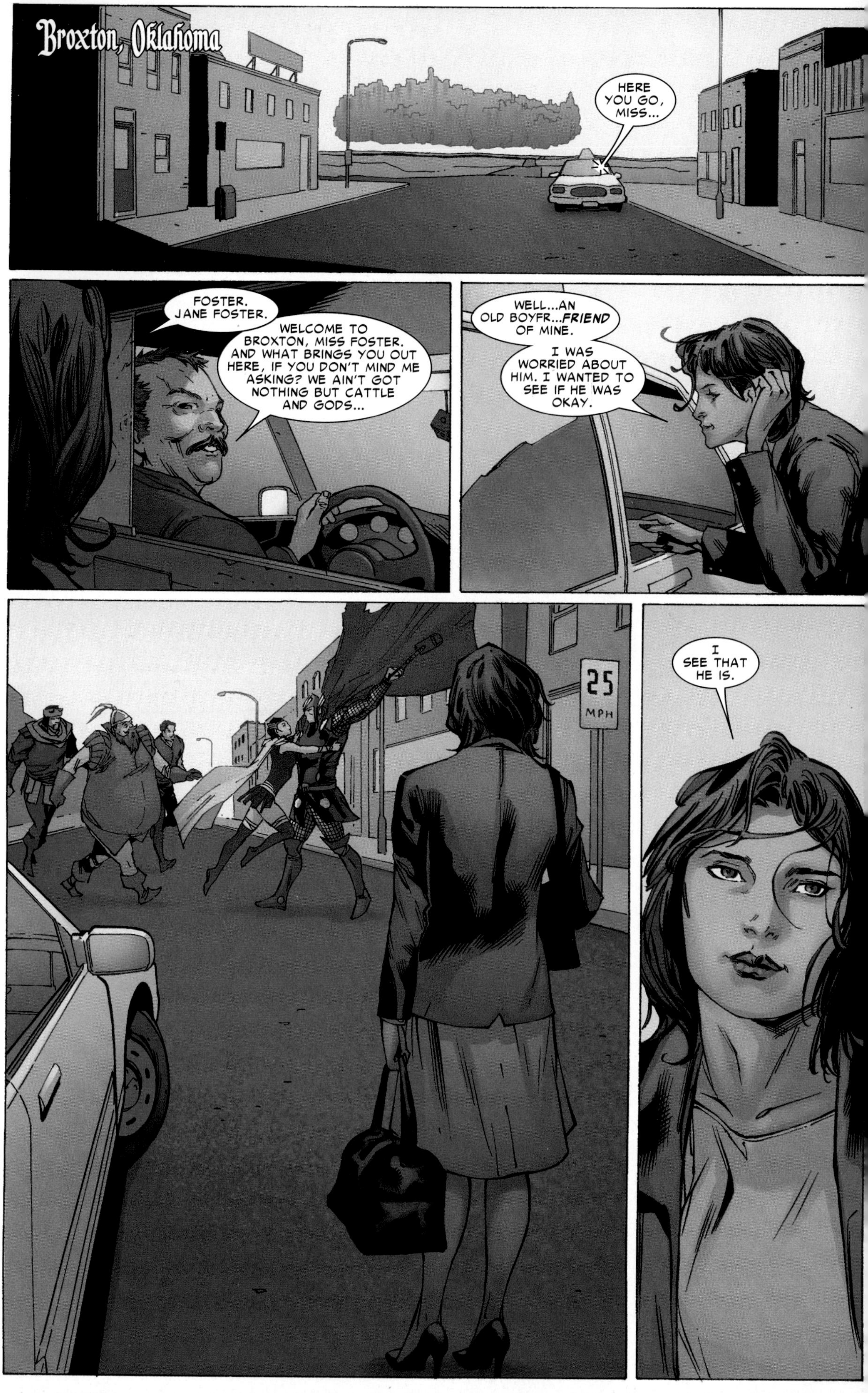
Broxton, Oklahoma
HERE YOU GO, MISS...
FOSTER. JANE FOSTER.
WELCOME TO BROXTON, MISS FOSTER. AND WHAT BRINGS YOU OUT HERE, IF YOU DON'T MIND ME ASKING? WE AIN'T GOT NOTHING BUT CATTLE AND GODS...
WELL...AN OLD BOYFR...*FRIEND* OF MINE.
I WAS WORRIED ABOUT HIM. I WANTED TO SEE IF HE WAS OKAY.
25 MPH
I SEE THAT HE IS.

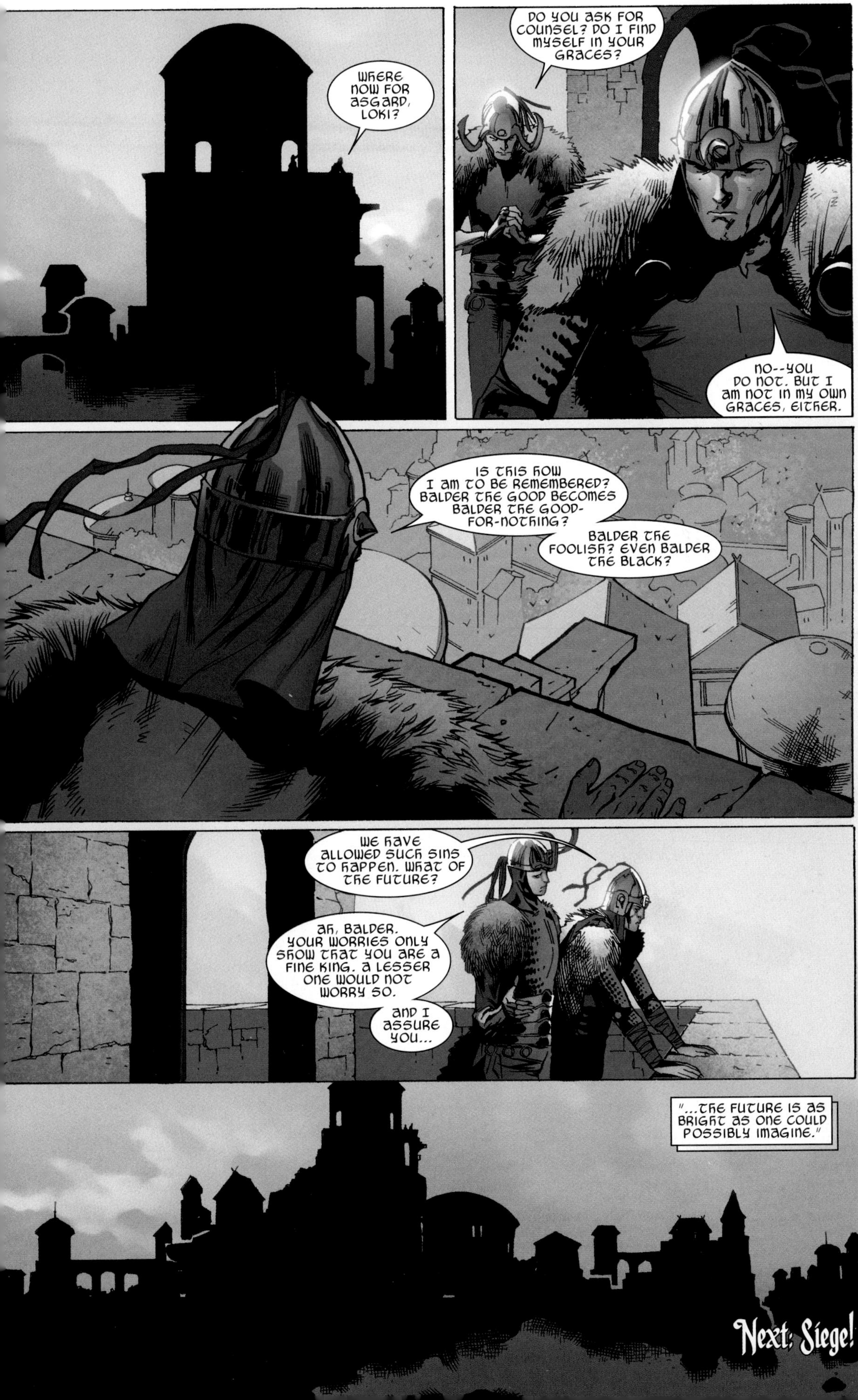
WHERE NOW FOR ASGARD, LOKI?
DO YOU ASK FOR COUNSEL? DO I FIND MYSELF IN YOUR GRACES?
NO--YOU DO NOT. BUT I AM NOT IN MY OWN GRACES, EITHER.
IS THIS HOW I AM TO BE REMEMBERED? BALDER THE GOOD BECOMES BALDER THE GOOD-FOR-NOTHING?
BALDER THE FOOLISH? EVEN BALDER THE BLACK?
WE HAVE ALLOWED SUCH SINS TO HAPPEN. WHAT OF THE FUTURE?
AH, BALDER. YOUR WORRIES ONLY SHOW THAT YOU ARE A FINE KING. A LESSER ONE WOULD NOT WORRY SO.
AND I ASSURE YOU...
"...THE FUTURE IS AS BRIGHT AS ONE COULD POSSIBLY IMAGINE."
Next: Siege!

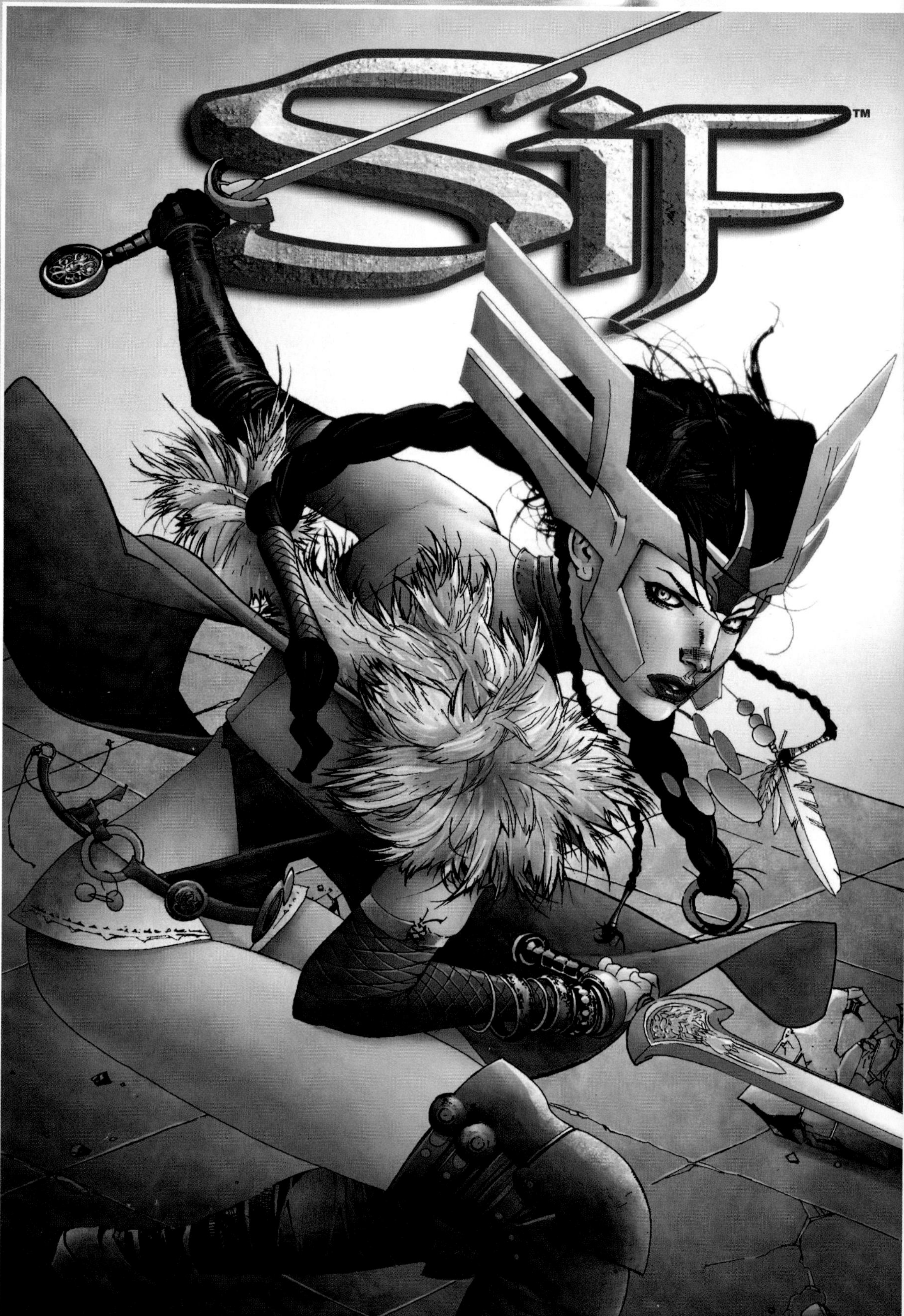
SIF™

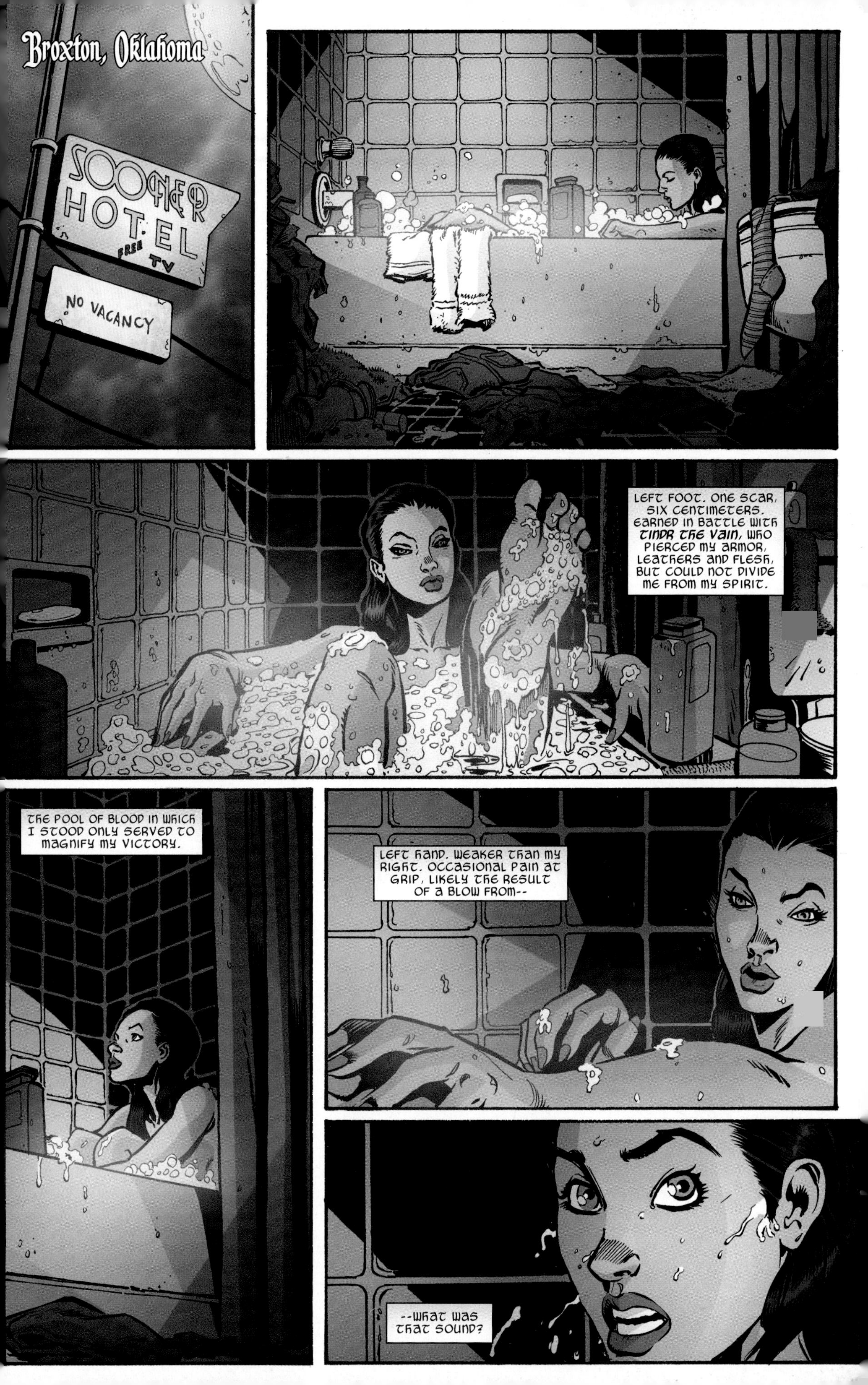
Broxton, Oklahoma
SOONER HOTEL
FREE TV
NO VACANCY
LEFT FOOT. ONE SCAR, SIX CENTIMETERS. EARNED IN BATTLE WITH TINDR THE VAIN, WHO PIERCED MY ARMOR, LEATHERS AND FLESH, BUT COULD NOT DIVIDE ME FROM MY SPIRIT.
THE POOL OF BLOOD IN WHICH I STOOD ONLY SERVED TO MAGNIFY MY VICTORY.
LEFT HAND. WEAKER THAN MY RIGHT. OCCASIONAL PAIN AT GRIP, LIKELY THE RESULT OF A BLOW FROM--
--WHAT WAS THAT SOUND?

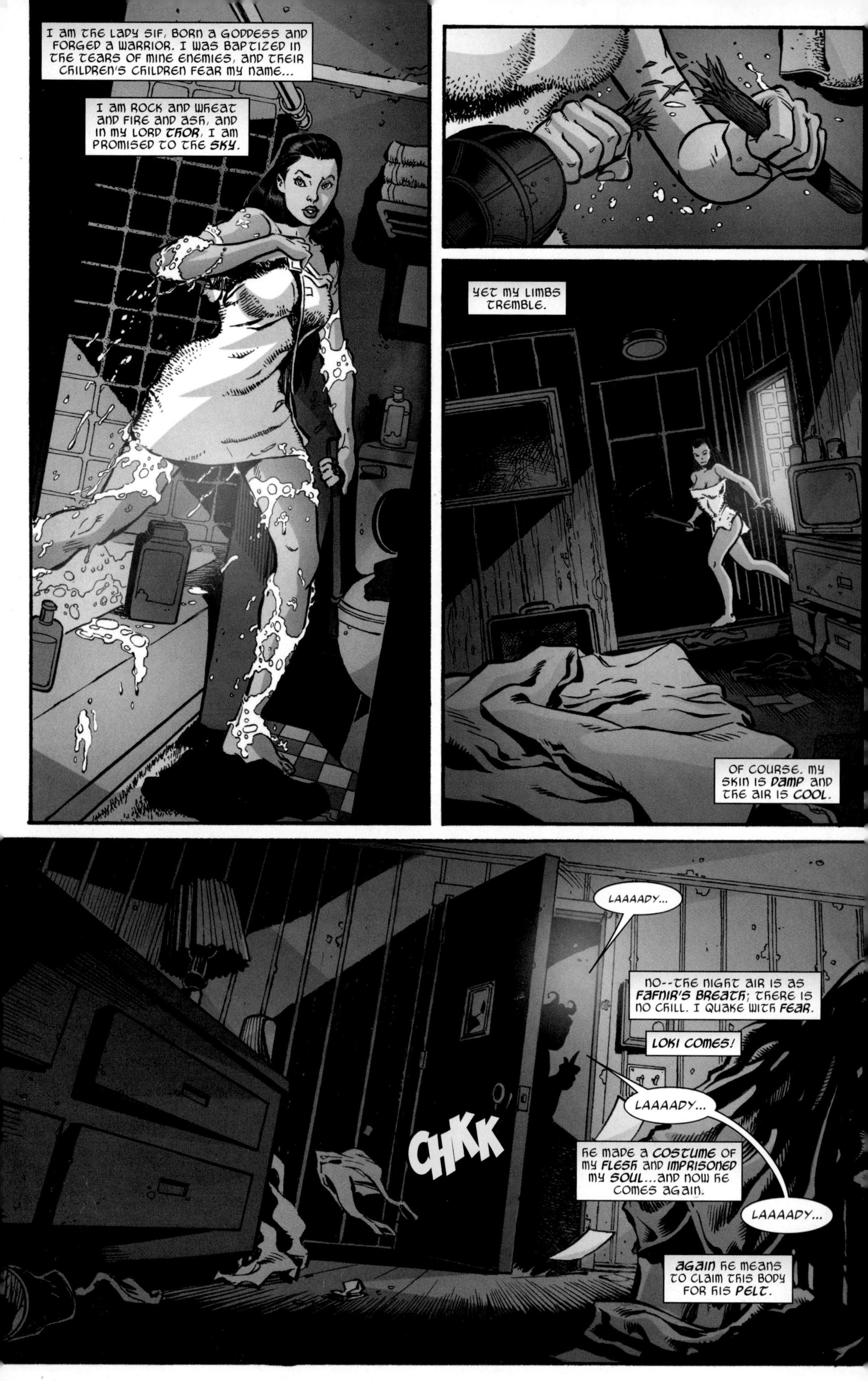
I AM THE LADY SIF, BORN A GODDESS AND FORGED A WARRIOR. I WAS BAPTIZED IN THE TEARS OF MINE ENEMIES, AND THEIR CHILDREN'S CHILDREN FEAR MY NAME...
I AM ROCK AND WHEAT AND FIRE AND ASH, AND IN MY LORD THOR, I AM PROMISED TO THE SKY.
YET MY LIMBS TREMBLE.
OF COURSE. MY SKIN IS DAMP AND THE AIR IS COOL.
LAAAADY...
NO--THE NIGHT AIR IS AS FAFNIR'S BREATH; THERE IS NO CHILL. I QUAKE WITH FEAR.
LOKI COMES!
LAAAADY...
CHKK
HE MADE A COSTUME OF MY FLESH AND IMPRISONED MY SOUL...AND NOW HE COMES AGAIN.
LAAAADY...
AGAIN HE MEANS TO CLAIM THIS BODY FOR HIS PELT.

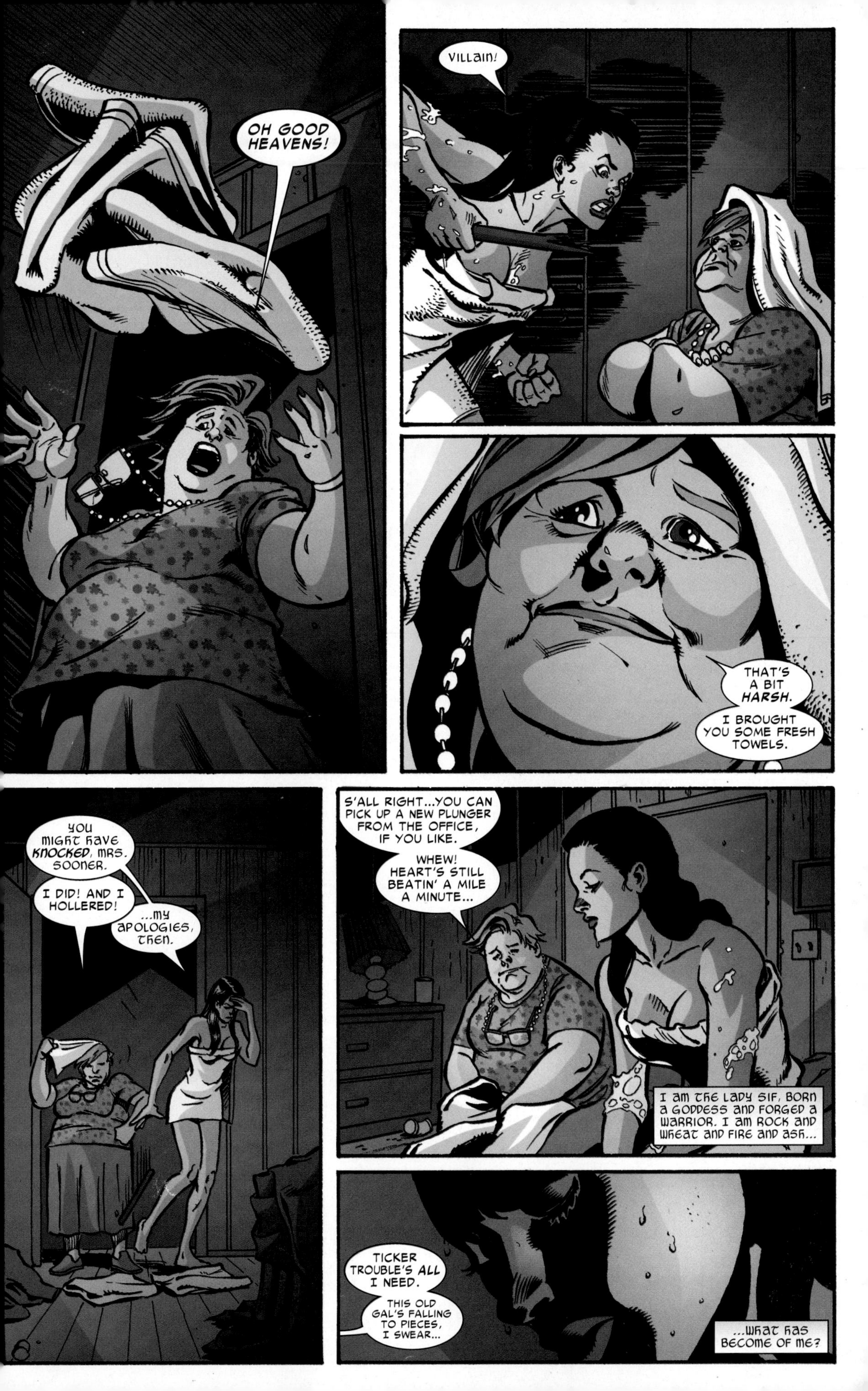
OH GOOD HEAVENS!
VILLAIN!
THAT'S A BIT HARSH.
I BROUGHT YOU SOME FRESH TOWELS.
YOU MIGHT HAVE KNOCKED, MRS. SOONER.
I DID! AND I HOLLERED!
...MY APOLOGIES, THEN.
S'ALL RIGHT...YOU CAN PICK UP A NEW PLUNGER FROM THE OFFICE, IF YOU LIKE.
WHEW! HEART'S STILL BEATIN' A MILE A MINUTE...
I AM THE LADY SIF, BORN A GODDESS AND FORGED A WARRIOR. I AM ROCK AND WHEAT AND FIRE AND ASH...
TICKER TROUBLE'S ALL I NEED.
THIS OLD GAL'S FALLING TO PIECES, I SWEAR...
...WHAT HAS BECOME OF ME?

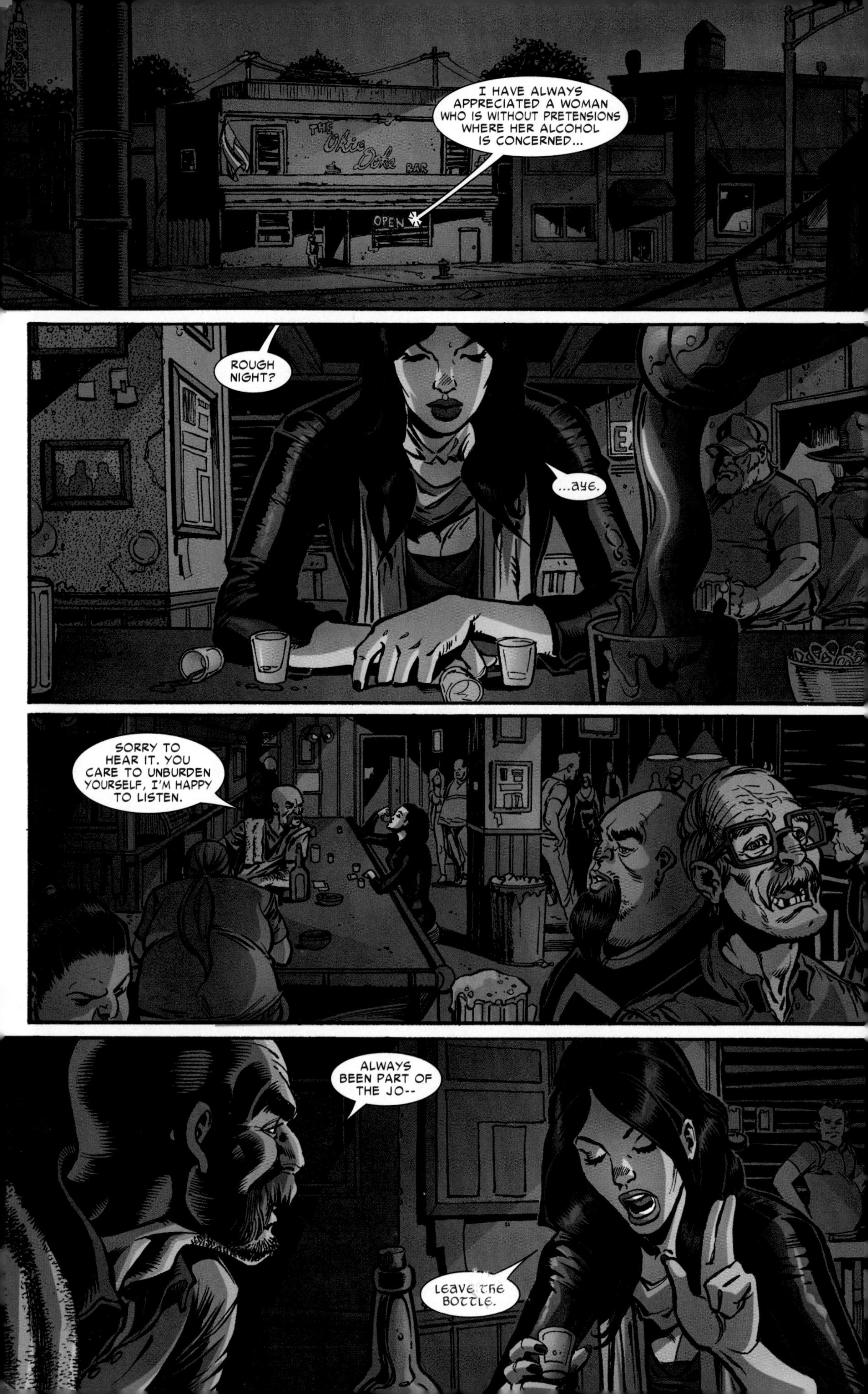
THE Okie Doke BAR
OPEN
I HAVE ALWAYS APPRECIATED A WOMAN WHO IS WITHOUT PRETENSIONS WHERE HER ALCOHOL IS CONCERNED...
ROUGH NIGHT?
...aye.
SORRY TO HEAR IT. YOU CARE TO UNBURDEN YOURSELF, I'M HAPPY TO LISTEN.
ALWAYS BEEN PART OF THE JO--
LEAVE THE BOTTLE.

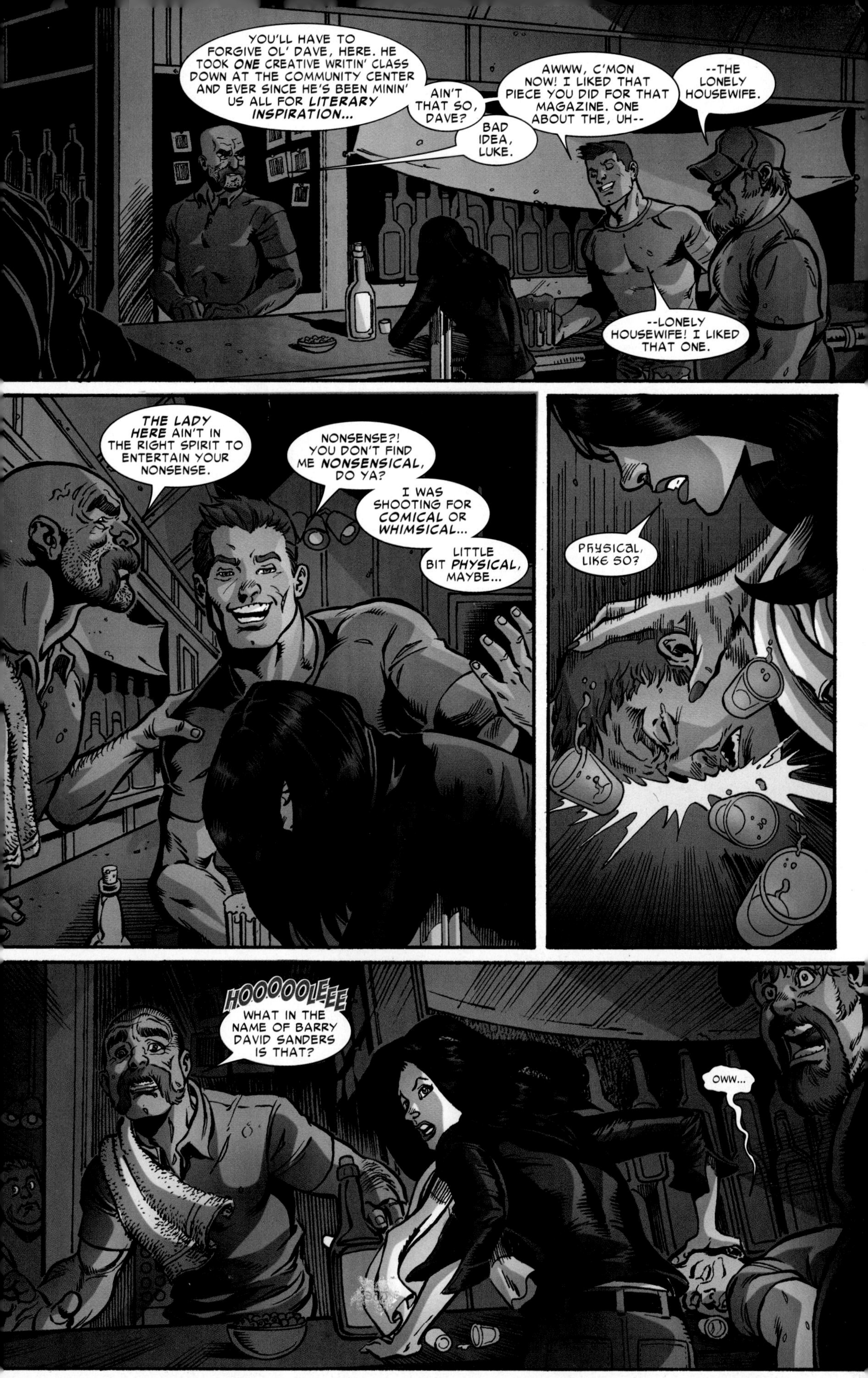
YOU'LL HAVE TO FORGIVE OL' DAVE, HERE. HE TOOK ONE CREATIVE WRITIN' CLASS DOWN AT THE COMMUNITY CENTER AND EVER SINCE HE'S BEEN MININ' US ALL FOR LITERARY INSPIRATION...
AIN'T THAT SO, DAVE?
BAD IDEA, LUKE.
AWWW, C'MON NOW! I LIKED THAT PIECE YOU DID FOR THAT MAGAZINE. ONE ABOUT THE, UH--
--THE LONELY HOUSEWIFE.
--LONELY HOUSEWIFE! I LIKED THAT ONE.
THE LADY HERE AIN'T IN THE RIGHT SPIRIT TO ENTERTAIN YOUR NONSENSE.
NONSENSE?! YOU DON'T FIND ME NONSENSICAL, DO YA?
I WAS SHOOTING FOR COMICAL OR WHIMSICAL...
LITTLE BIT PHYSICAL, MAYBE...
PHYSICAL, LIKE SO?
HOOOOOLEEE
WHAT IN THE NAME OF BARRY DAVID SANDERS IS THAT?
OWW...

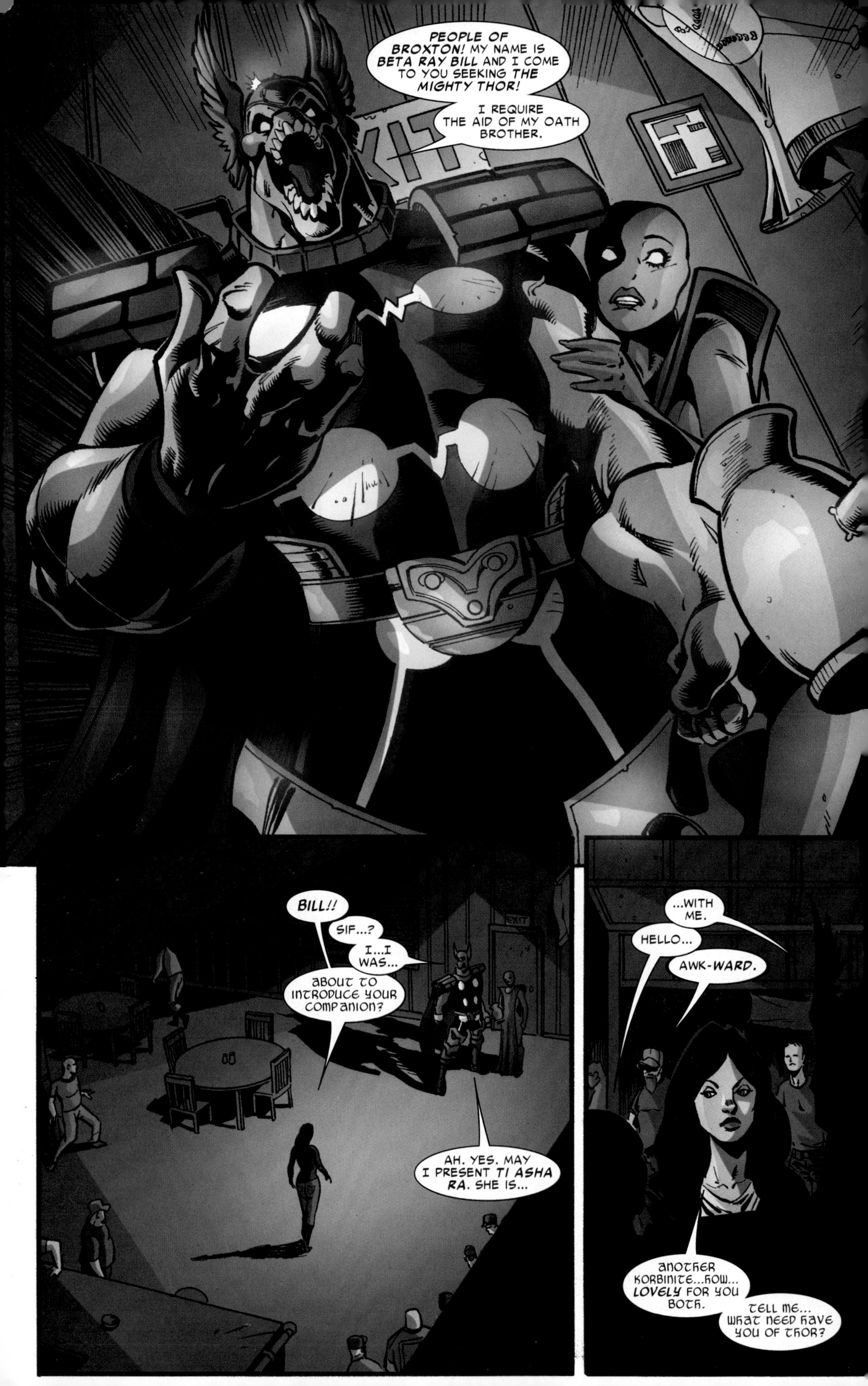
PEOPLE OF BROXTON! MY NAME IS BETA RAY BILL AND I COME TO YOU SEEKING THE MIGHTY THOR!
I REQUIRE THE AID OF MY OATH BROTHER.
BILL!!
SIF...?
I...I WAS...
ABOUT TO INTRODUCE YOUR COMPANION?
AH. YES. MAY I PRESENT TI ASHA RA. SHE IS...
...WITH ME.
HELLO...
AWK-WARD.
ANOTHER KORBINITE...HOW... LOVELY FOR YOU BOTH.
TELL ME... WHAT NEED HAVE YOU OF THOR?

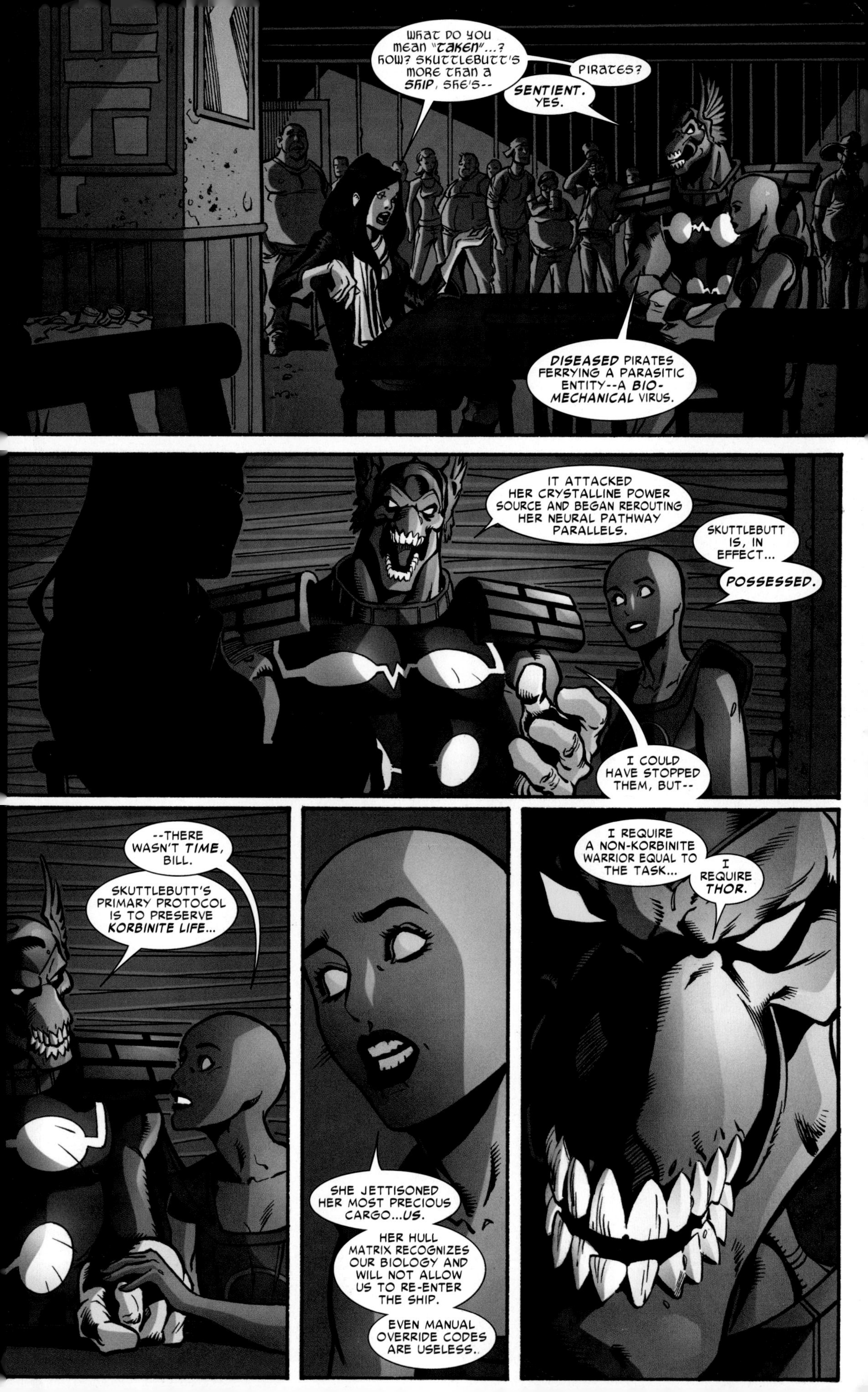

WHAT DO YOU MEAN "TAKEN"...? HOW? SKUTTLEBUTT'S MORE THAN A SHIP, SHE'S--
PIRATES?
SENTIENT. YES.
DISEASED PIRATES FERRYING A PARASITIC ENTITY--A BIO-MECHANICAL VIRUS.
IT ATTACKED HER CRYSTALLINE POWER SOURCE AND BEGAN REROUTING HER NEURAL PATHWAY PARALLELS.
SKUTTLEBUTT IS, IN EFFECT...
POSSESSED.
I COULD HAVE STOPPED THEM, BUT--
--THERE WASN'T TIME, BILL.
SKUTTLEBUTT'S PRIMARY PROTOCOL IS TO PRESERVE KORBINITE LIFE...
SHE JETTISONED HER MOST PRECIOUS CARGO...US.
HER HULL MATRIX RECOGNIZES OUR BIOLOGY AND WILL NOT ALLOW US TO RE-ENTER THE SHIP.
EVEN MANUAL OVERRIDE CODES ARE USELESS.
I REQUIRE A NON-KORBINITE WARRIOR EQUAL TO THE TASK...
I REQUIRE THOR.

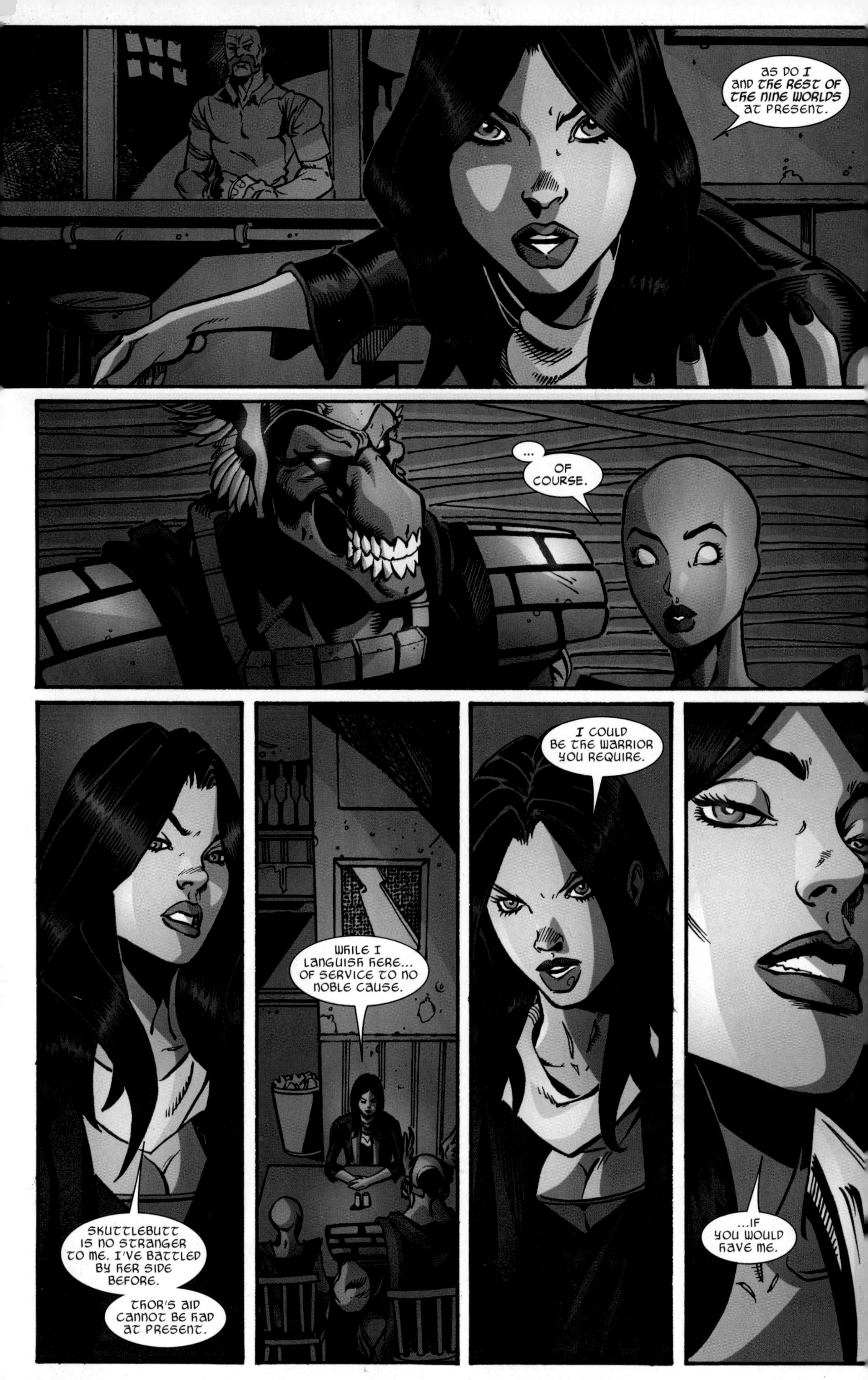
AS DO I AND THE REST OF THE NINE WORLDS AT PRESENT.
... OF COURSE.
SKUTTLEBUTT IS NO STRANGER TO ME. I'VE BATTLED BY HER SIDE BEFORE.
THOR'S AID CANNOT BE HAD AT PRESENT.
WHILE I LANGUISH HERE... OF SERVICE TO NO NOBLE CAUSE.
I COULD BE THE WARRIOR YOU REQUIRE.
...IF YOU WOULD HAVE ME.

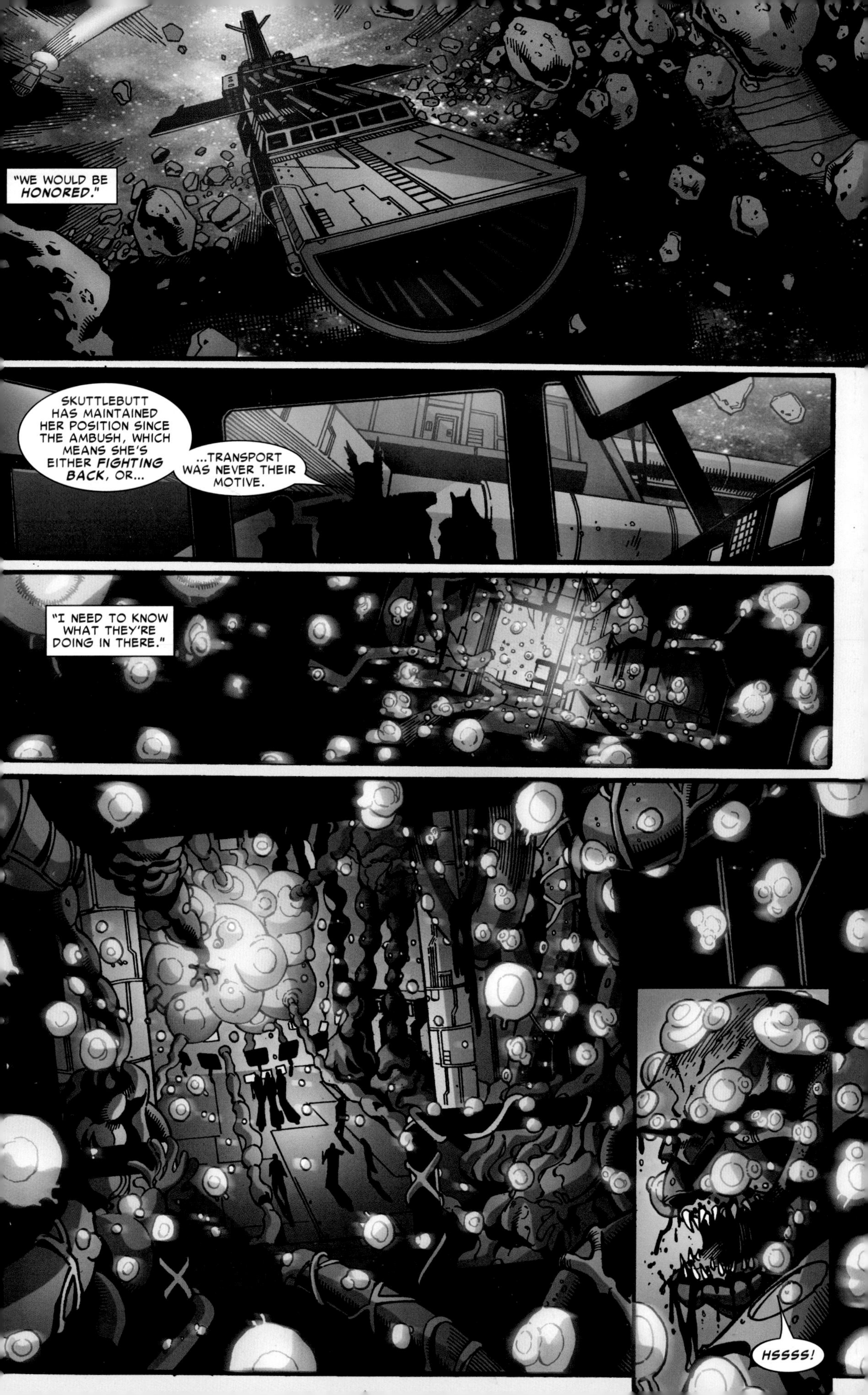
"WE WOULD BE HONORED."
SKUTTLEBUTT HAS MAINTAINED HER POSITION SINCE THE AMBUSH, WHICH MEANS SHE'S EITHER FIGHTING BACK, OR...
...TRANSPORT WAS NEVER THEIR MOTIVE.
"I NEED TO KNOW WHAT THEY'RE DOING IN THERE."
HSSSS!

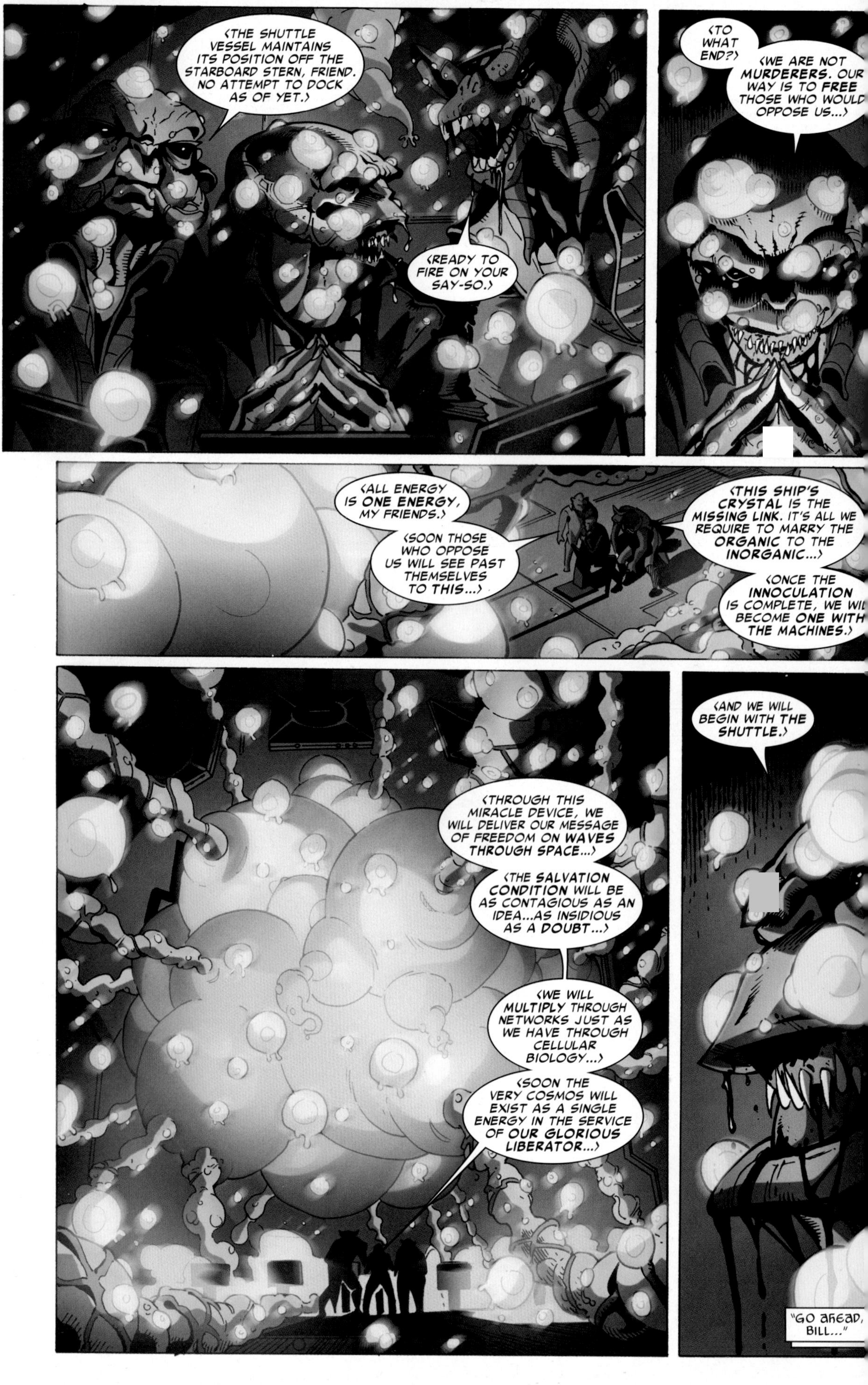
‹THE SHUTTLE VESSEL MAINTAINS ITS POSITION OFF THE STARBOARD STERN, FRIEND. NO ATTEMPT TO DOCK AS OF YET.›
‹READY TO FIRE ON YOUR SAY-SO.›
‹TO WHAT END?›
‹WE ARE NOT MURDERERS. OUR WAY IS TO FREE THOSE WHO WOULD OPPOSE US...›
‹ALL ENERGY IS ONE ENERGY, MY FRIENDS.›
‹SOON THOSE WHO OPPOSE US WILL SEE PAST THEMSELVES TO THIS...›
‹THIS SHIP'S CRYSTAL IS THE MISSING LINK. IT'S ALL WE REQUIRE TO MARRY THE ORGANIC TO THE INORGANIC...›
‹ONCE THE INNOCULATION IS COMPLETE, WE WIL BECOME ONE WITH THE MACHINES.›
‹THROUGH THIS MIRACLE DEVICE, WE WILL DELIVER OUR MESSAGE OF FREEDOM ON WAVES THROUGH SPACE...›
‹THE SALVATION CONDITION WILL BE AS CONTAGIOUS AS AN IDEA...AS INSIDIOUS AS A DOUBT...›
‹WE WILL MULTIPLY THROUGH NETWORKS JUST AS WE HAVE THROUGH CELLULAR BIOLOGY...›
‹SOON THE VERY COSMOS WILL EXIST AS A SINGLE ENERGY IN THE SERVICE OF OUR GLORIOUS LIBERATOR...›
‹AND WE WILL BEGIN WITH THE SHUTTLE.›
"GO AHEAD, BILL..."

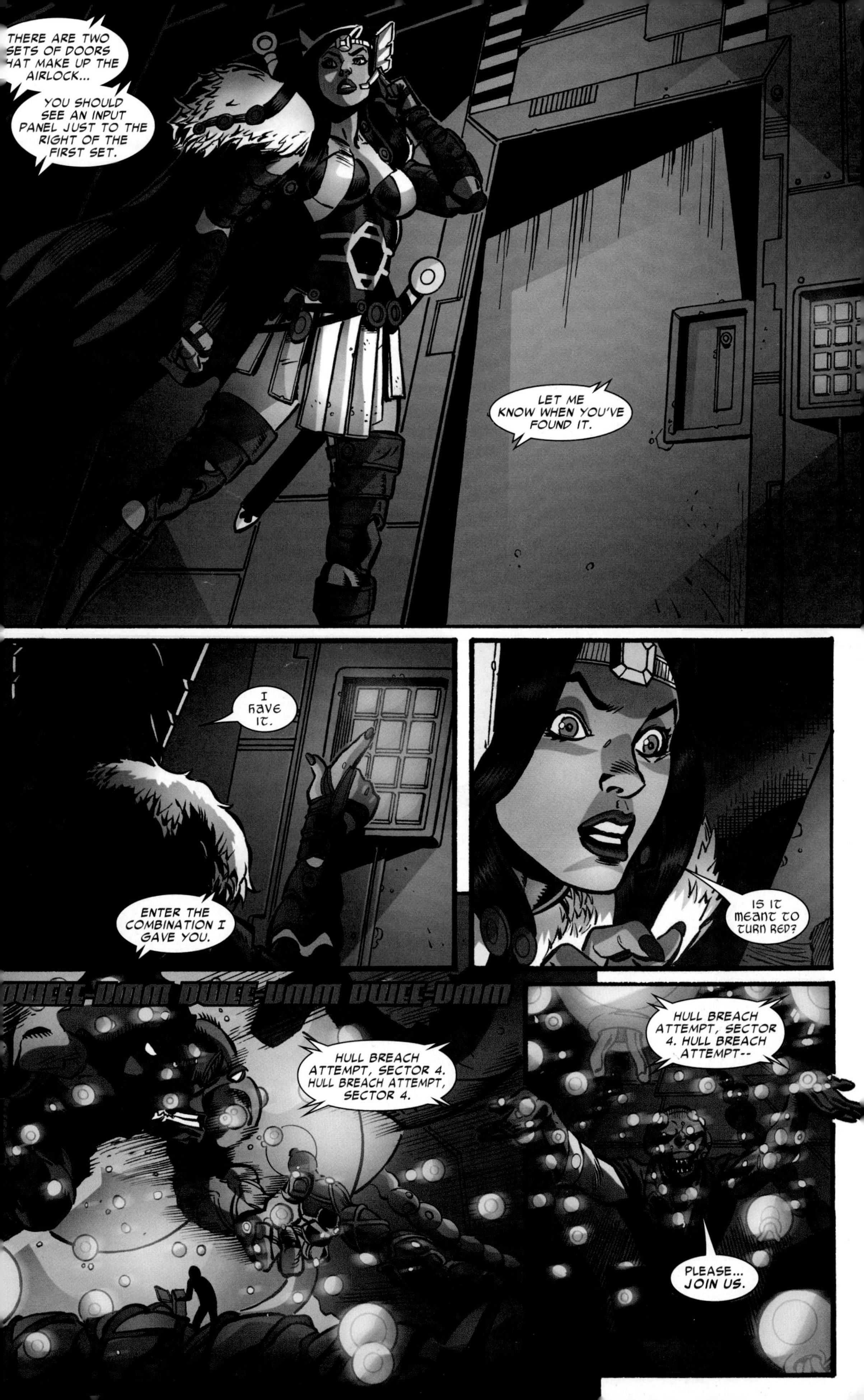
THERE ARE TWO SETS OF DOORS HAT MAKE UP THE AIRLOCK...
YOU SHOULD SEE AN INPUT PANEL JUST TO THE RIGHT OF THE FIRST SET.
LET ME KNOW WHEN YOU'VE FOUND IT.
I HAVE IT.
ENTER THE COMBINATION I GAVE YOU.
IS IT MEANT TO TURN RED?
DWEE-VMM DWEE-VMM DWEE-VMM
HULL BREACH ATTEMPT, SECTOR 4. HULL BREACH ATTEMPT, SECTOR 4.
HULL BREACH ATTEMPT, SECTOR 4. HULL BREACH ATTEMPT--
PLEASE... JOIN US.

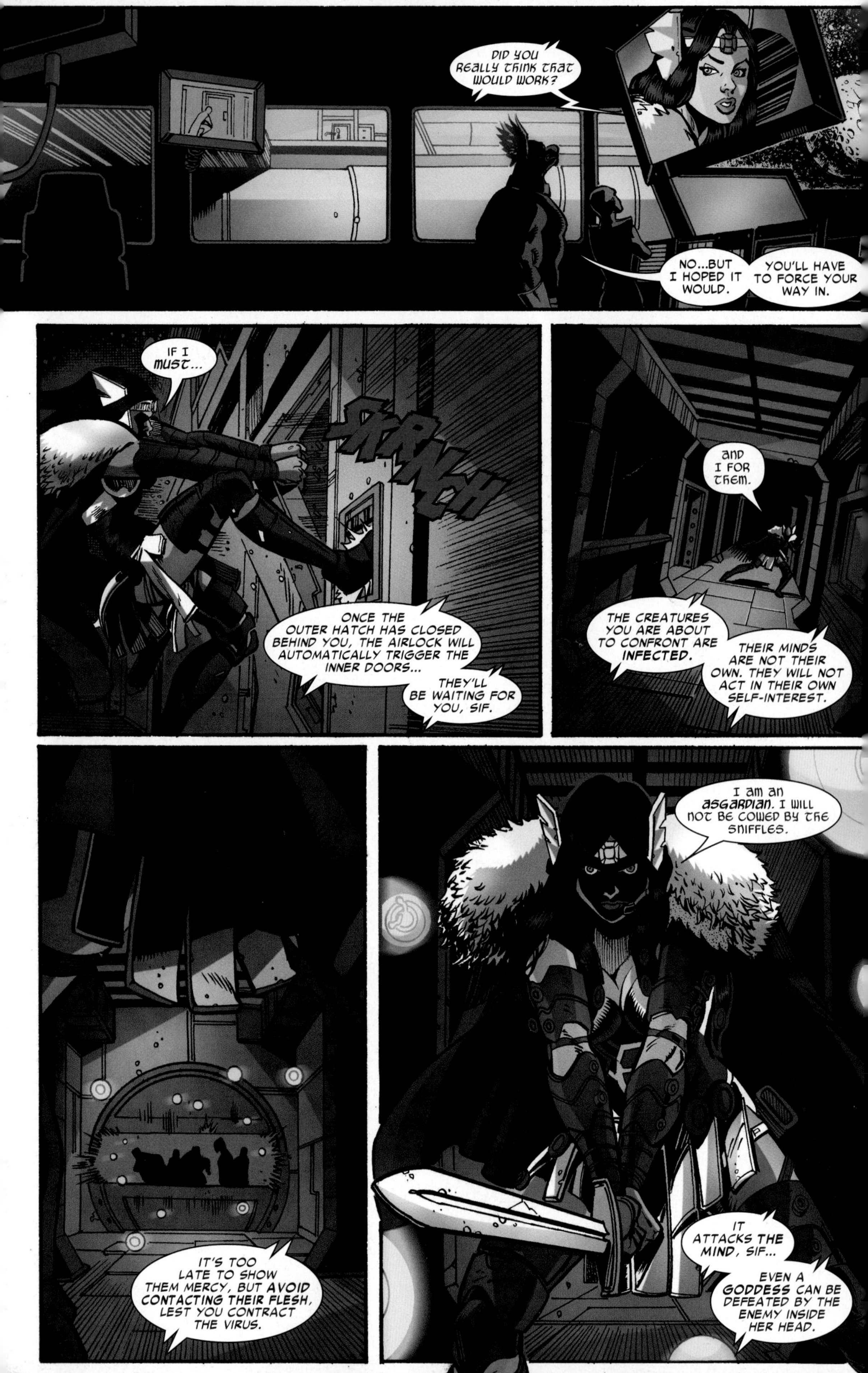

DID YOU REALLY THINK THAT WOULD WORK?
NO...BUT I HOPED IT WOULD.
YOU'LL HAVE TO FORCE YOUR WAY IN.
IF I MUST...
SKRNCH
ONCE THE OUTER HATCH HAS CLOSED BEHIND YOU, THE AIRLOCK WILL AUTOMATICALLY TRIGGER THE INNER DOORS...
THEY'LL BE WAITING FOR YOU, SIF.
AND I FOR THEM.
THE CREATURES YOU ARE ABOUT TO CONFRONT ARE INFECTED.
THEIR MINDS ARE NOT THEIR OWN. THEY WILL NOT ACT IN THEIR OWN SELF-INTEREST.
IT'S TOO LATE TO SHOW THEM MERCY, BUT AVOID CONTACTING THEIR FLESH, LEST YOU CONTRACT THE VIRUS.
I AM AN ASGARDIAN. I WILL NOT BE COWED BY THE SNIFFLES.
IT ATTACKS THE MIND, SIF...
EVEN A GODDESS CAN BE DEFEATED BY THE ENEMY INSIDE HER HEAD.

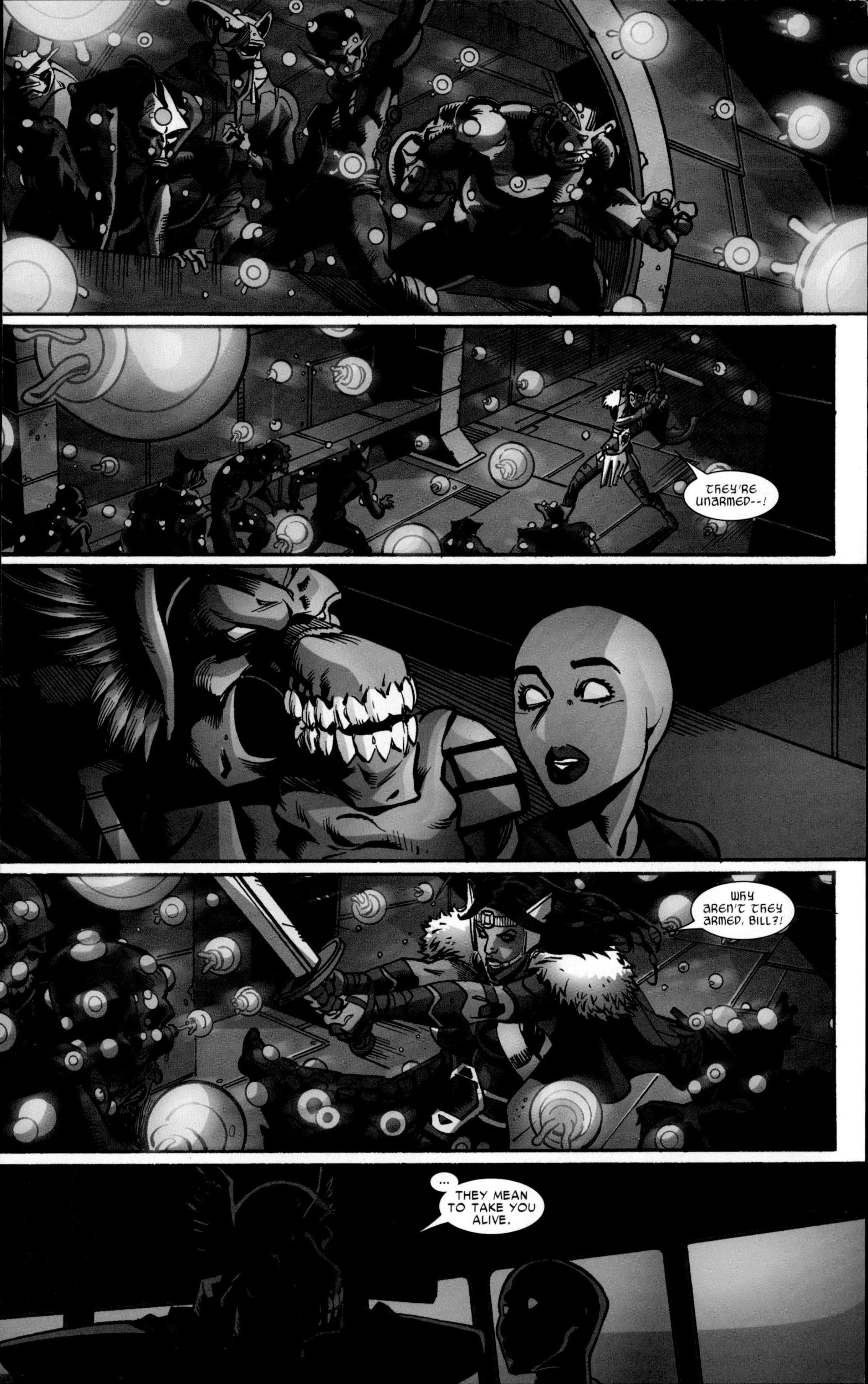
THEY'RE UNARMED--!
WHY AREN'T THEY ARMED, BILL?!
...THEY MEAN TO TAKE YOU ALIVE.

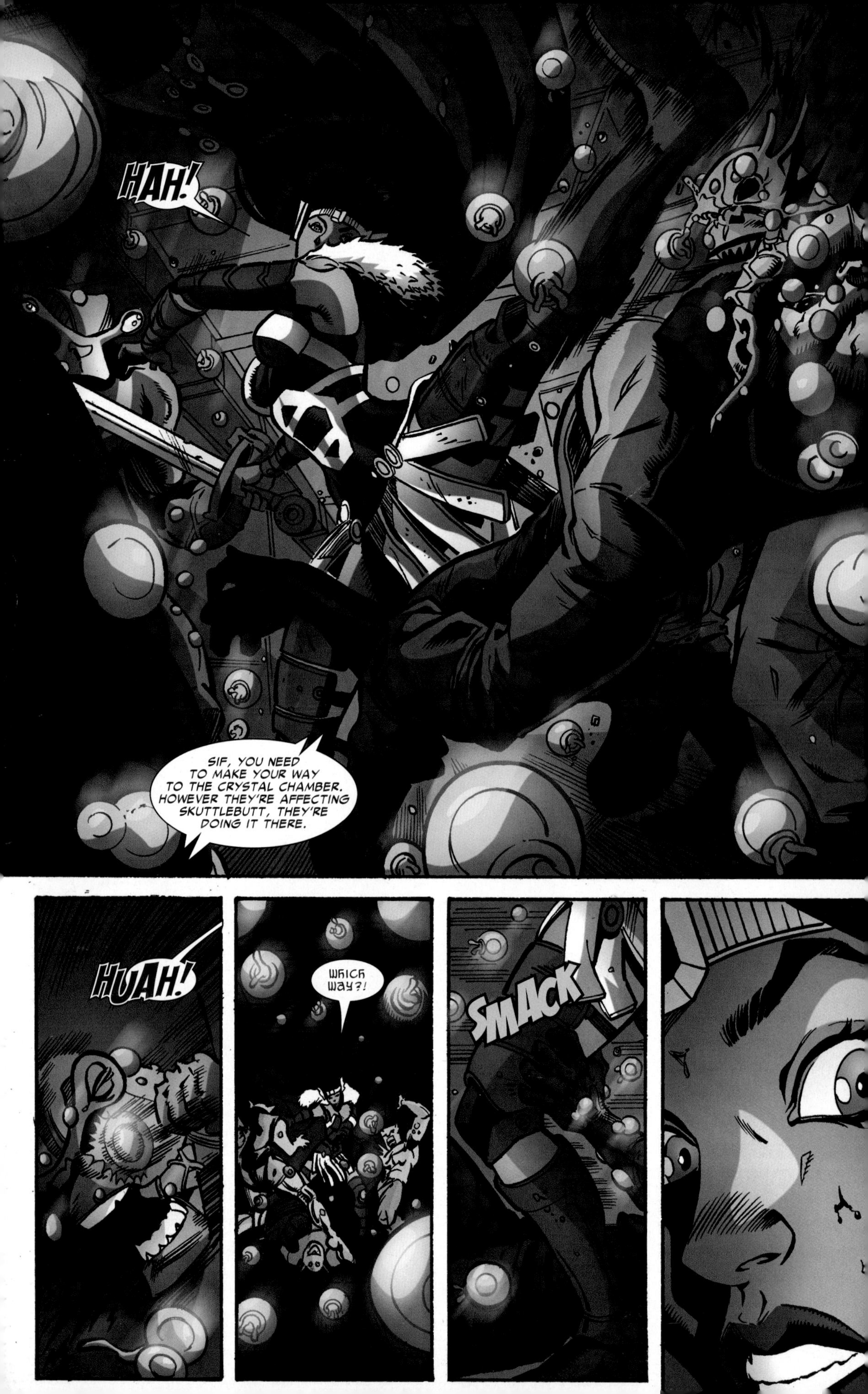
HAH!
SIF, YOU NEED TO MAKE YOUR WAY TO THE CRYSTAL CHAMBER. HOWEVER THEY'RE AFFECTING SKUTTLEBUTT, THEY'RE DOING IT THERE.
HUAH!
WHICH WAY?!
SMACK

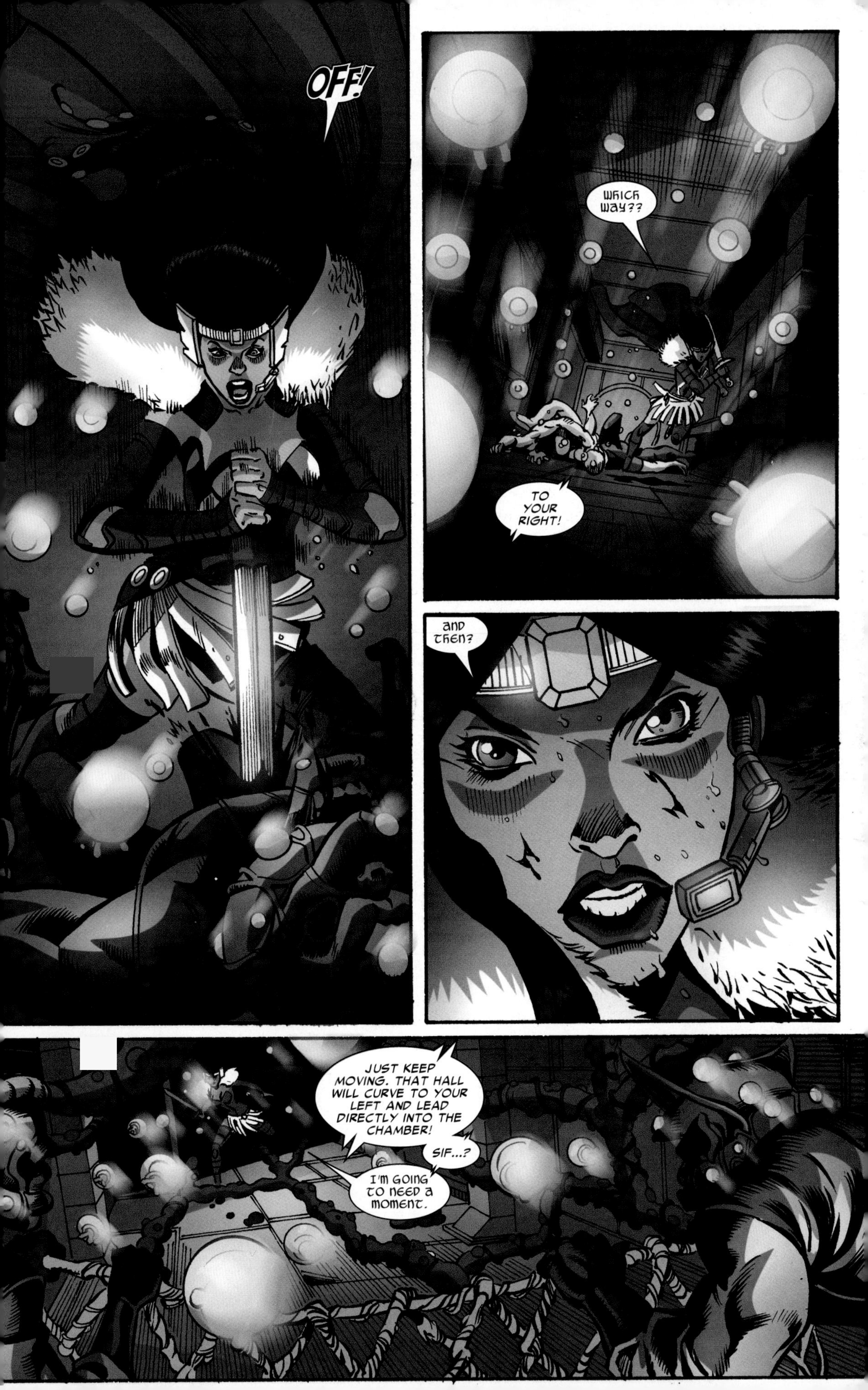
OFF!
WHICH WAY??
TO YOUR RIGHT!
AND THEN?
JUST KEEP MOVING. THAT HALL WILL CURVE TO YOUR LEFT AND LEAD DIRECTLY INTO THE CHAMBER!
SIF...?
I'M GOING TO NEED A MOMENT.

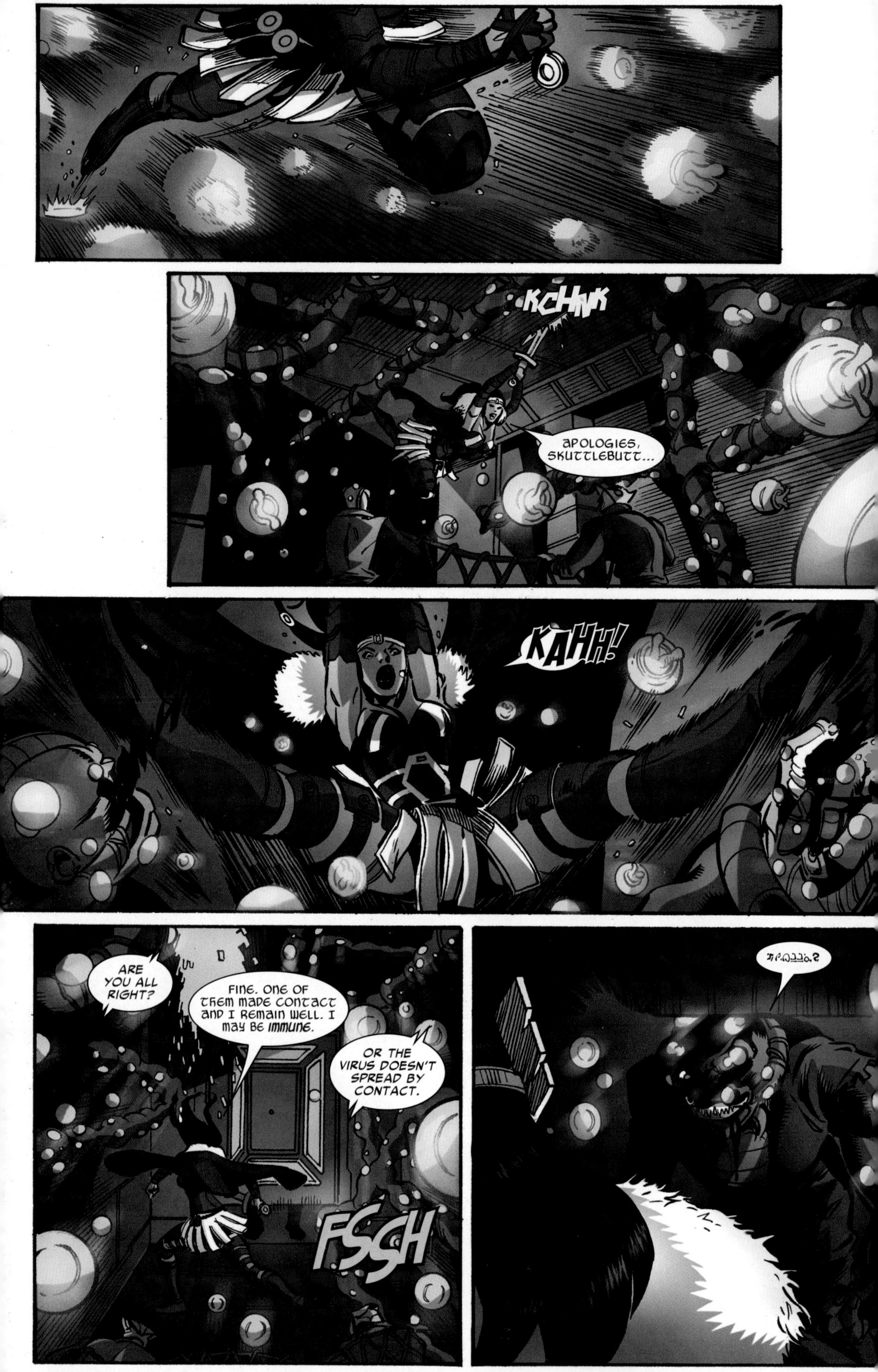
KCHNK
APOLOGIES, SKUTTLEBUTT...
KAHH!
ARE YOU ALL RIGHT?
FINE. ONE OF THEM MADE CONTACT AND I REMAIN WELL. I MAY BE IMMUNE.
OR THE VIRUS DOESN'T SPREAD BY CONTACT.
FSSH

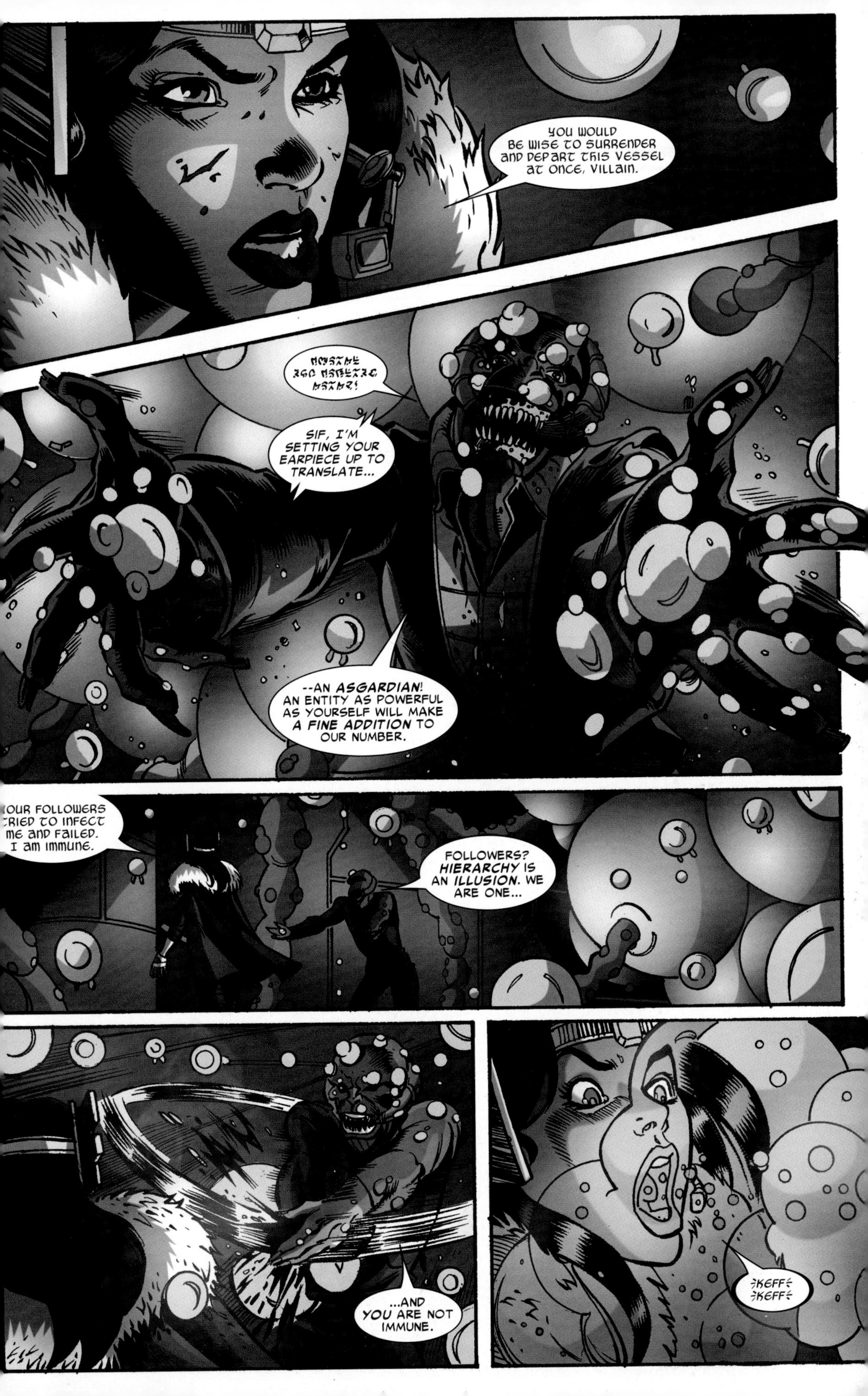
YOU WOULD BE WISE TO SURRENDER AND DEPART THIS VESSEL AT ONCE, VILLAIN.
SIF, I'M SETTING YOUR EARPIECE UP TO TRANSLATE...
--AN ASGARDIAN! AN ENTITY AS POWERFUL AS YOURSELF WILL MAKE A FINE ADDITION TO OUR NUMBER.
OUR FOLLOWERS TRIED TO INFECT ME AND FAILED. I AM IMMUNE.
FOLLOWERS? HIERARCHY IS AN ILLUSION. WE ARE ONE...
...AND YOU ARE NOT IMMUNE.
KEFF
KEFF

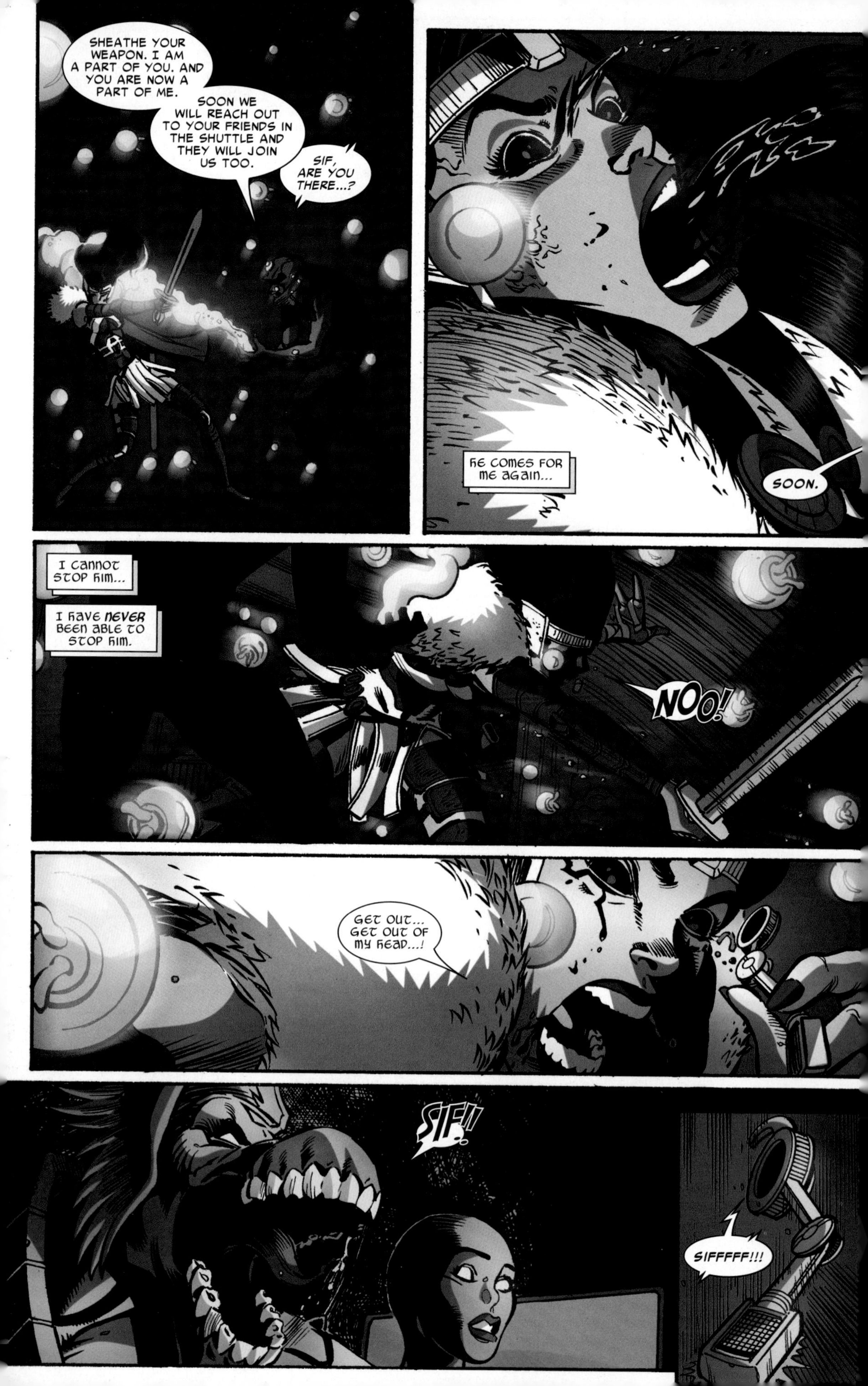
SHEATHE YOUR WEAPON. I AM A PART OF YOU. AND YOU ARE NOW A PART OF ME.
SOON WE WILL REACH OUT TO YOUR FRIENDS IN THE SHUTTLE AND THEY WILL JOIN US TOO.
SIF, ARE YOU THERE...?
HE COMES FOR ME AGAIN...
SOON.
I CANNOT STOP HIM...
I HAVE NEVER BEEN ABLE TO STOP HIM.
NOO!
GET OUT... GET OUT OF MY HEAD...!
SIF!!
SIFFFFF!!!

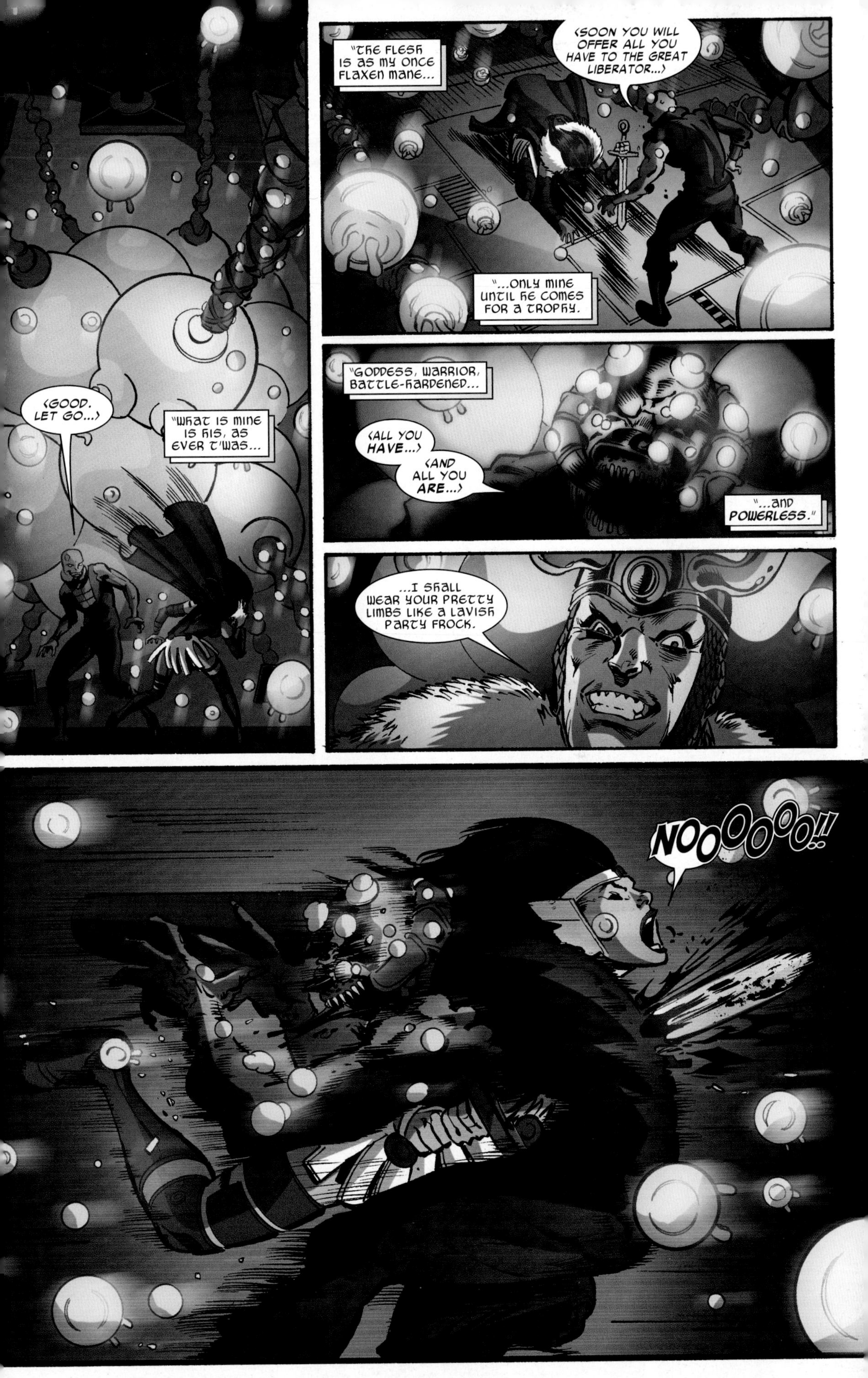
<GOOD. LET GO...>
"WHAT IS MINE IS HIS, AS EVER T'WAS...
"THE FLESH IS AS MY ONCE FLAXEN MANE...
<SOON YOU WILL OFFER ALL YOU HAVE TO THE GREAT LIBERATOR...>
"...ONLY MINE UNTIL HE COMES FOR A TROPHY.
"GODDESS, WARRIOR, BATTLE-HARDENED...
<ALL YOU HAVE...>
<AND ALL YOU ARE...>
"...AND POWERLESS."
...I SHALL WEAR YOUR PRETTY LIMBS LIKE A LAVISH PARTY FROCK.
NOOOOOO!!

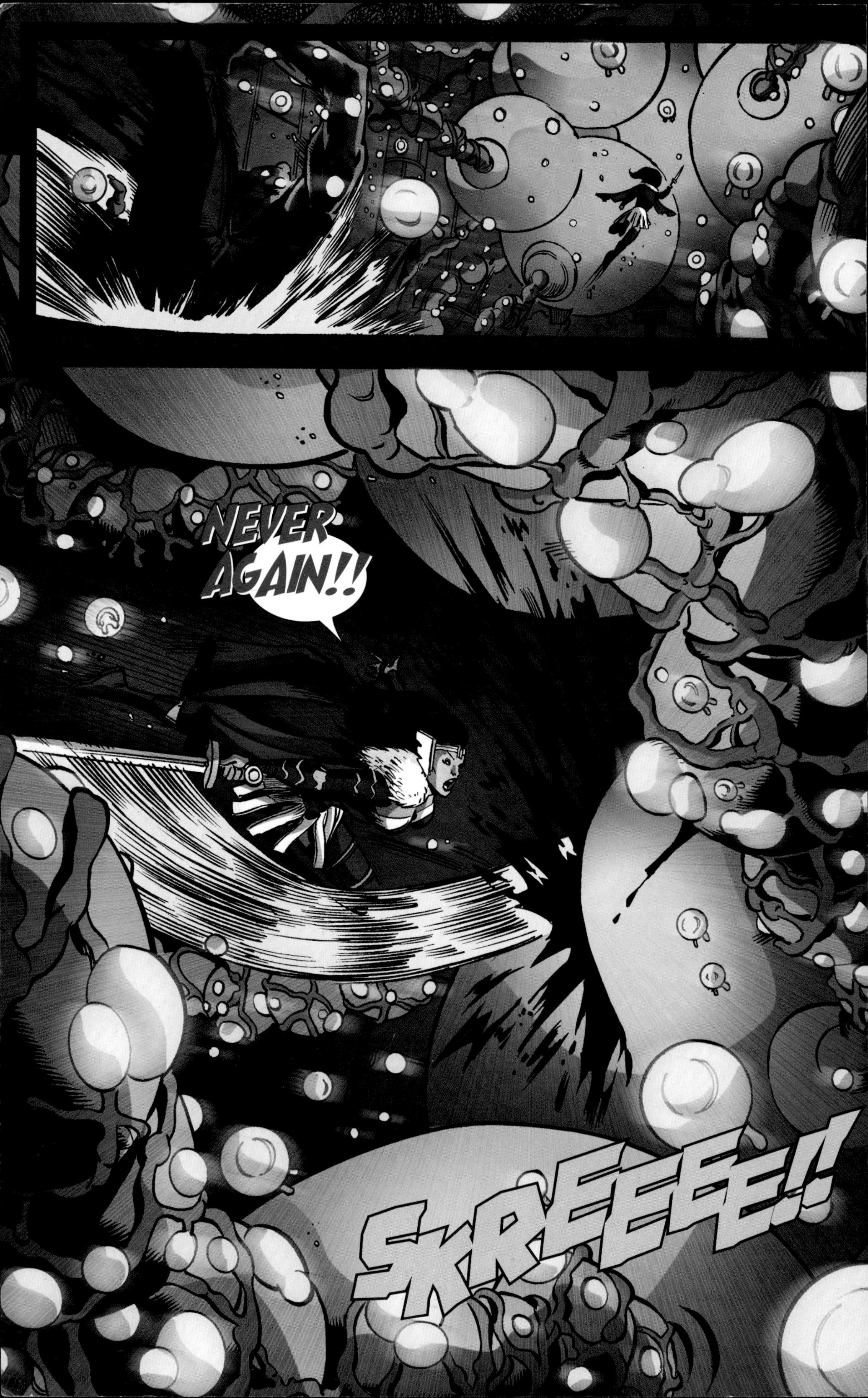
NEVER AGAIN!!
SKREEEE!!

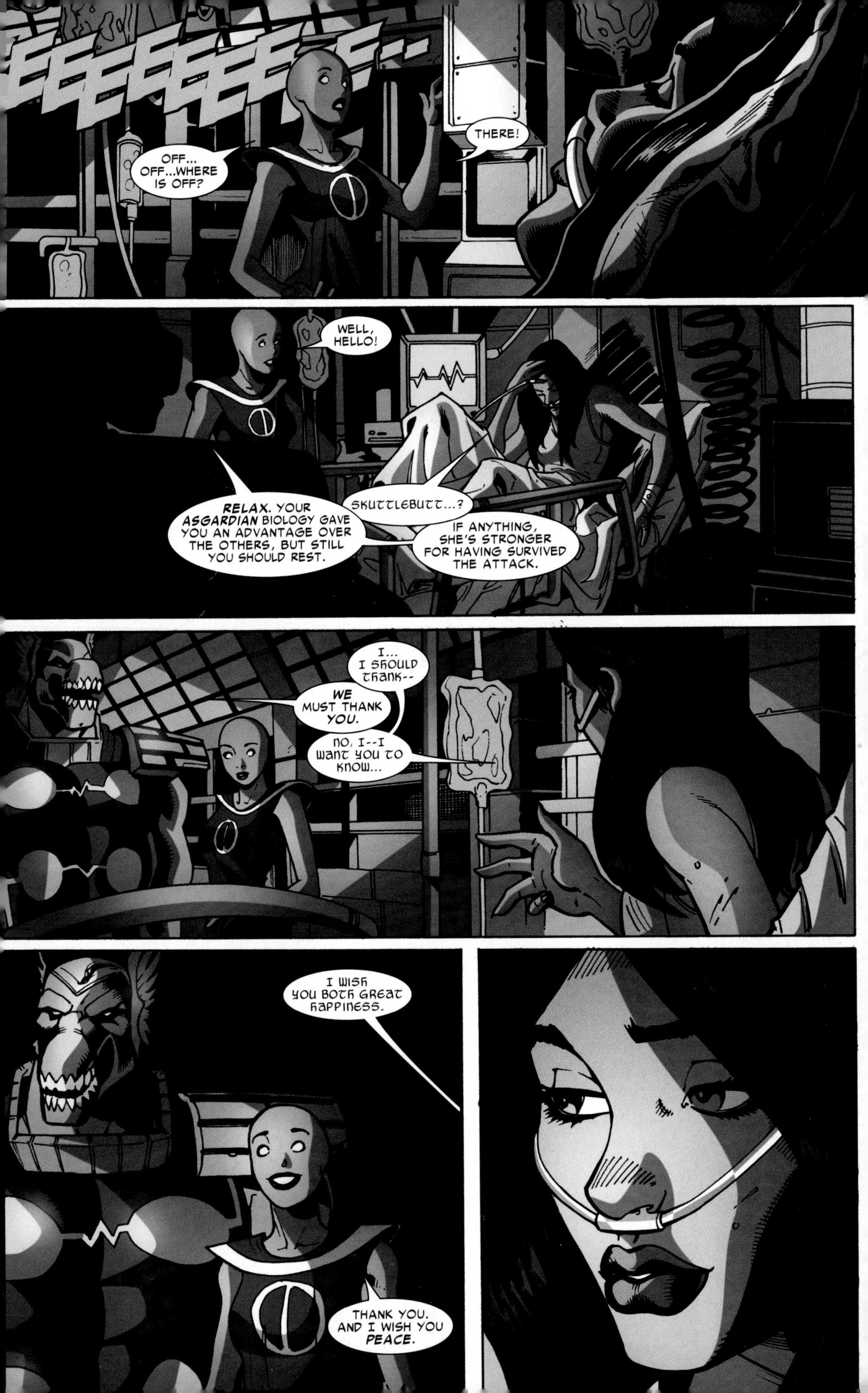
EEEEEEEEE--
OFF... OFF...WHERE IS OFF?
THERE!
WELL, HELLO!
SKUTTLEBUTT...?
RELAX. YOUR ASGARDIAN BIOLOGY GAVE YOU AN ADVANTAGE OVER THE OTHERS, BUT STILL YOU SHOULD REST.
IF ANYTHING, SHE'S STRONGER FOR HAVING SURVIVED THE ATTACK.
I... I SHOULD THANK--
WE MUST THANK YOU.
NO, I--I WANT YOU TO KNOW...
I WISH YOU BOTH GREAT HAPPINESS.
THANK YOU. AND I WISH YOU PEACE.

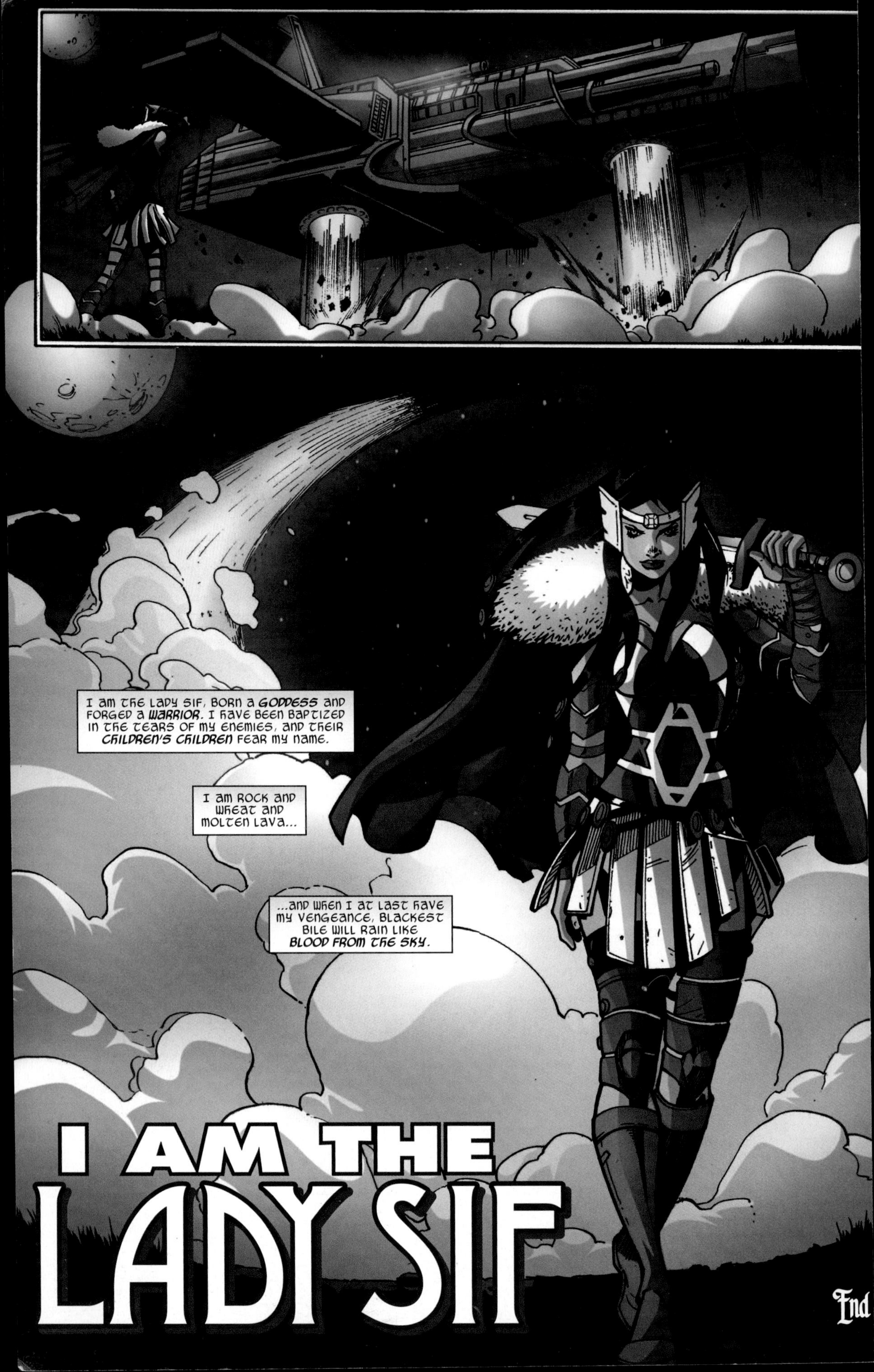
I AM THE LADY SIF, BORN A GODDESS AND FORGED A WARRIOR. I HAVE BEEN BAPTIZED IN THE TEARS OF MY ENEMIES, AND THEIR CHILDREN'S CHILDREN FEAR MY NAME.
I AM ROCK AND WHEAT AND MOLTEN LAVA...
...AND WHEN I AT LAST HAVE MY VENGEANCE, BLACKEST BILE WILL RAIN LIKE BLOOD FROM THE SKY.
I AM THE LADY SIF
End

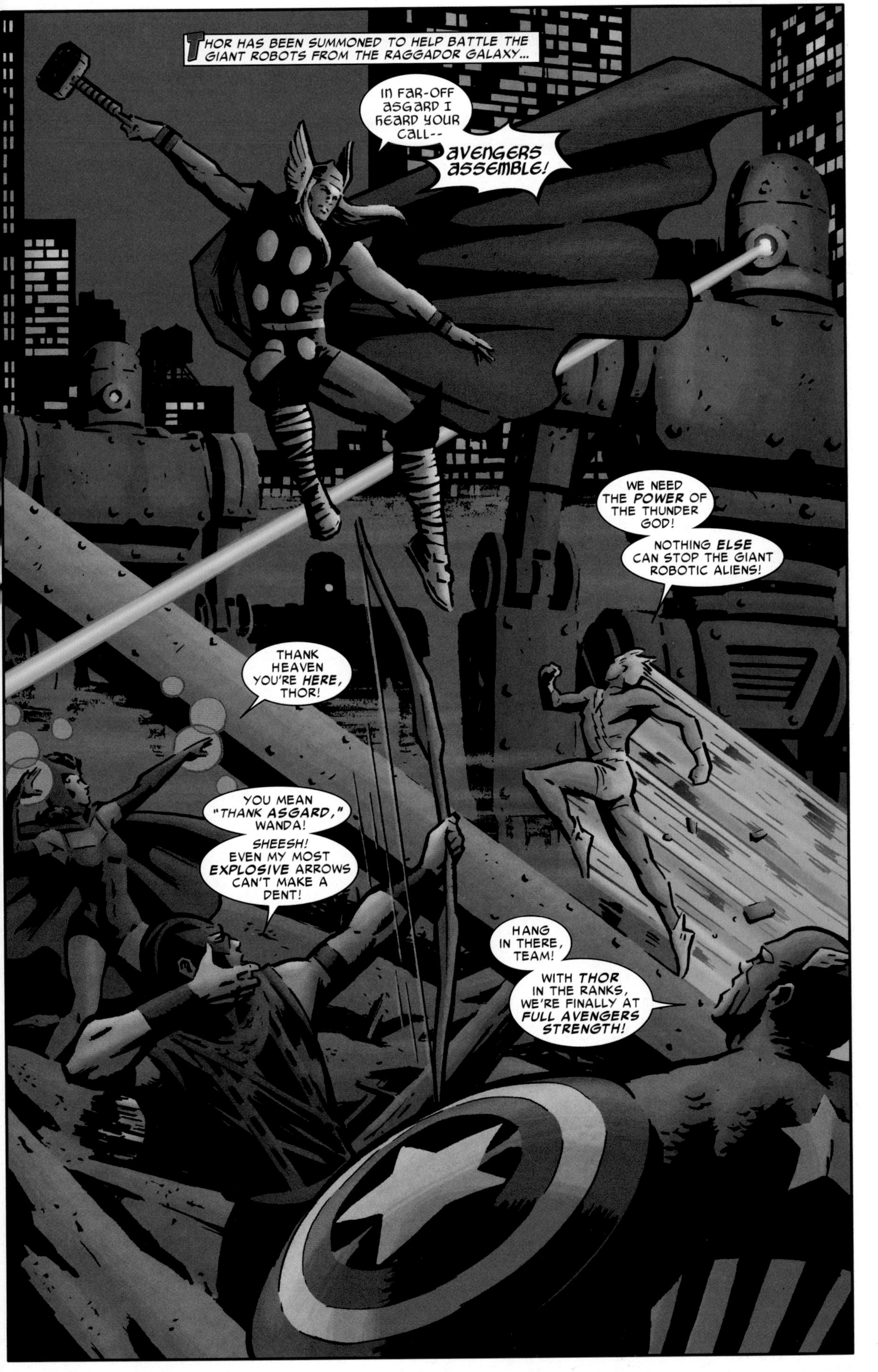
THOR HAS BEEN SUMMONED TO HELP BATTLE THE GIANT ROBOTS FROM THE RAGGADOR GALAXY...
IN FAR-OFF ASGARD I HEARD YOUR CALL--
AVENGERS ASSEMBLE!
WE NEED THE POWER OF THE THUNDER GOD!
NOTHING ELSE CAN STOP THE GIANT ROBOTIC ALIENS!
THANK HEAVEN YOU'RE HERE, THOR!
YOU MEAN "THANK ASGARD," WANDA!
SHEESH! EVEN MY MOST EXPLOSIVE ARROWS CAN'T MAKE A DENT!
HANG IN THERE, TEAM!
WITH THOR IN THE RANKS, WE'RE FINALLY AT FULL AVENGERS STRENGTH!

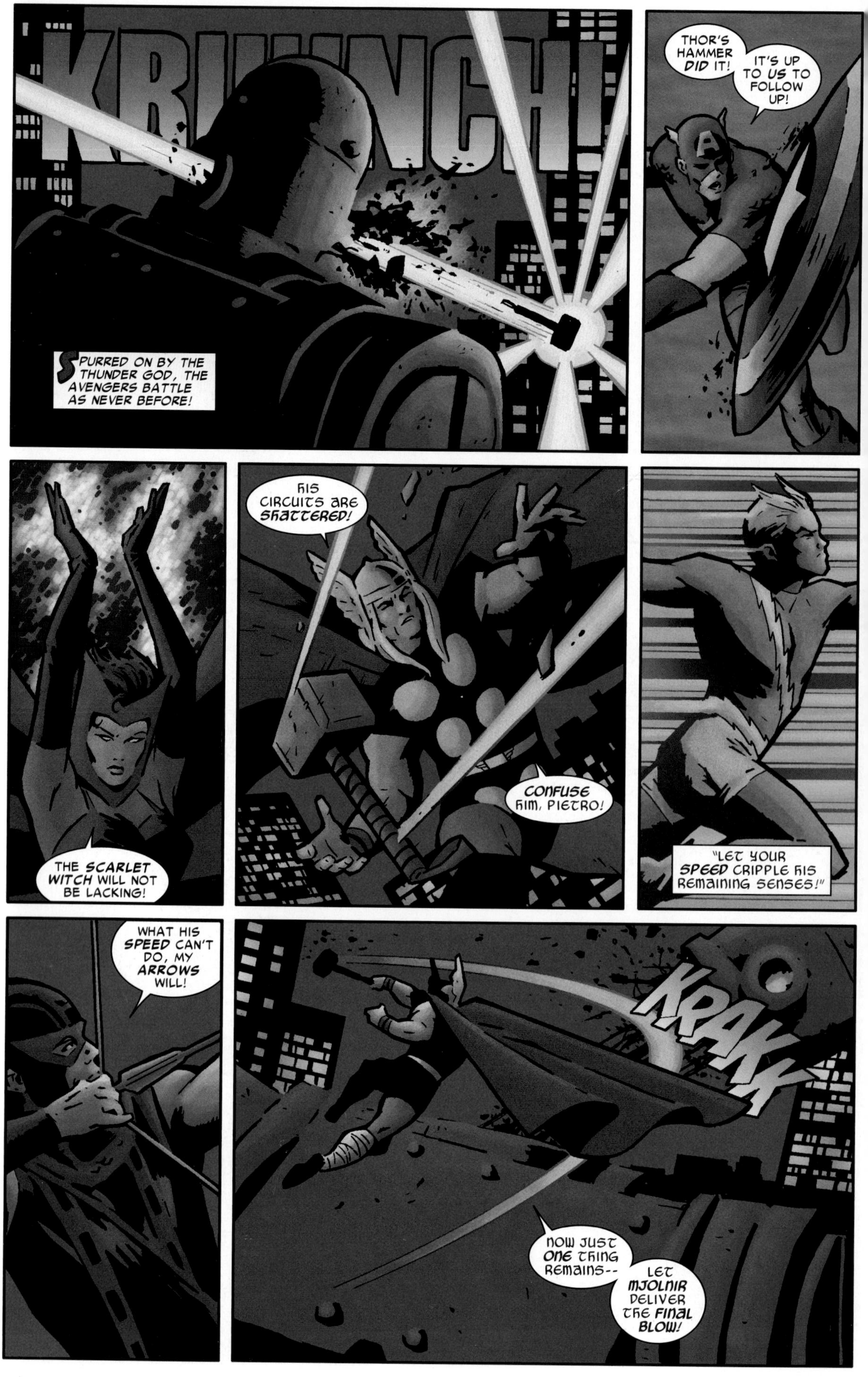
KRUNCH!
SPURRED ON BY THE THUNDER GOD, THE AVENGERS BATTLE AS NEVER BEFORE!
THOR'S HAMMER DID IT!
IT'S UP TO US TO FOLLOW UP!
THE SCARLET WITCH WILL NOT BE LACKING!
HIS CIRCUITS ARE SHATTERED!
CONFUSE HIM, PIETRO!
"LET YOUR SPEED CRIPPLE HIS REMAINING SENSES!"
WHAT HIS SPEED CAN'T DO, MY ARROWS WILL!
KRAKK
NOW JUST ONE THING REMAINS--
LET MJOLNIR DELIVER THE FINAL BLOW!

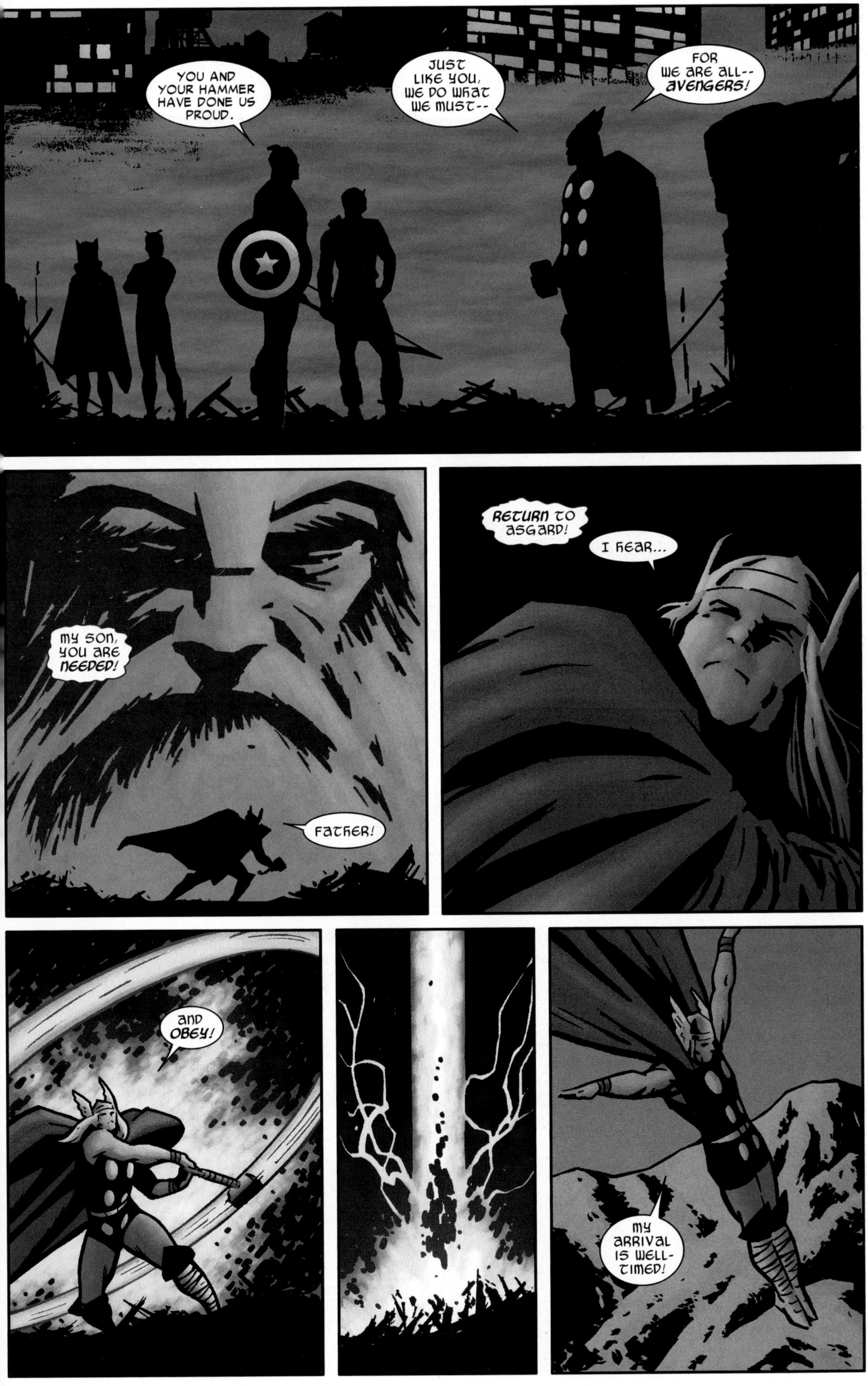
YOU AND YOUR HAMMER HAVE DONE US PROUD.
JUST LIKE YOU, WE DO WHAT WE MUST--
FOR WE ARE ALL-- AVENGERS!
MY SON, YOU ARE NEEDED!
FATHER!
RETURN TO ASGARD!
I HEAR...
AND OBEY!
MY ARRIVAL IS WELL-TIMED!

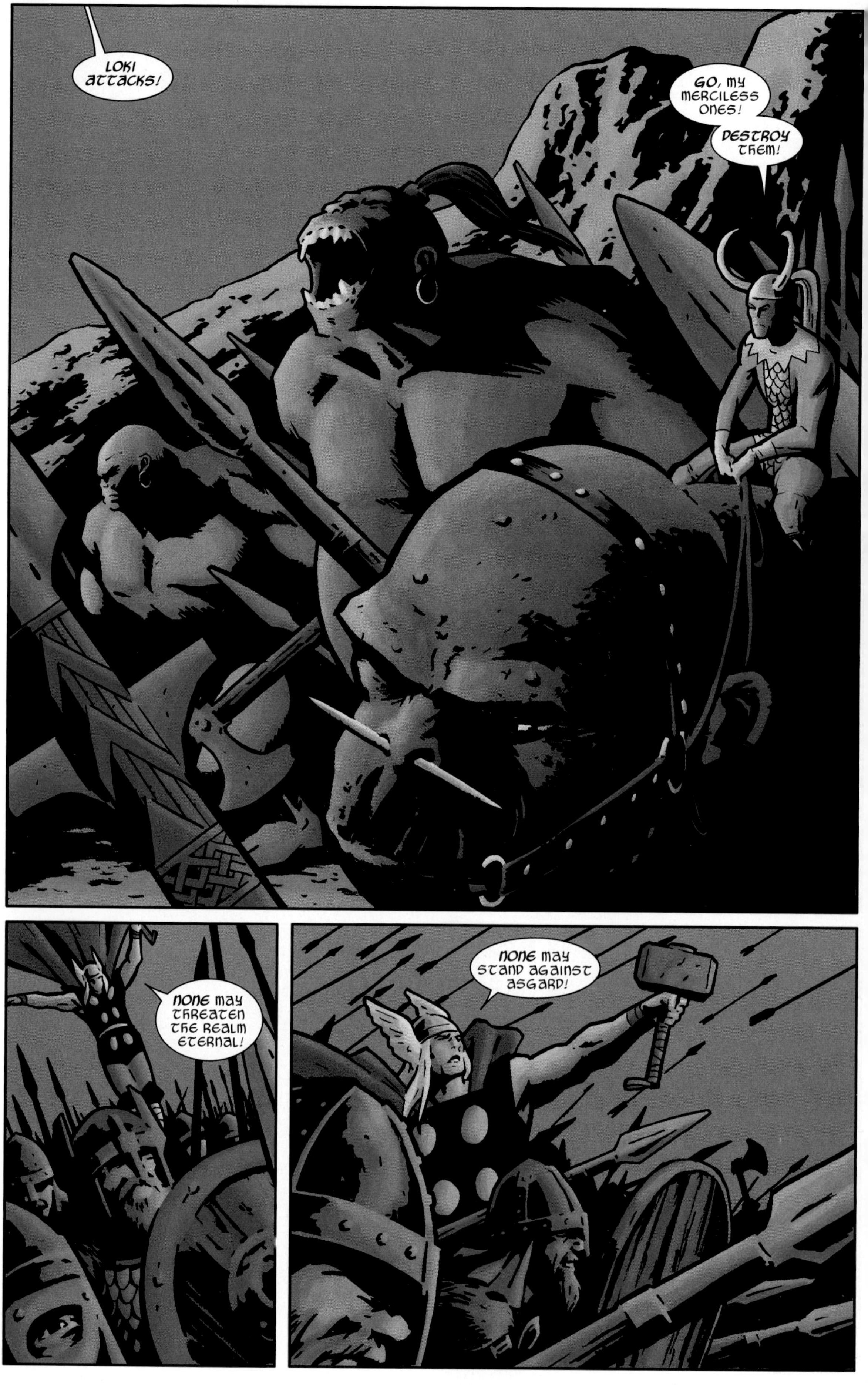
LOKI ATTACKS!
GO, MY MERCILESS ONES!
DESTROY THEM!
NONE MAY THREATEN THE REALM ETERNAL!
NONE MAY STAND AGAINST ASGARD!

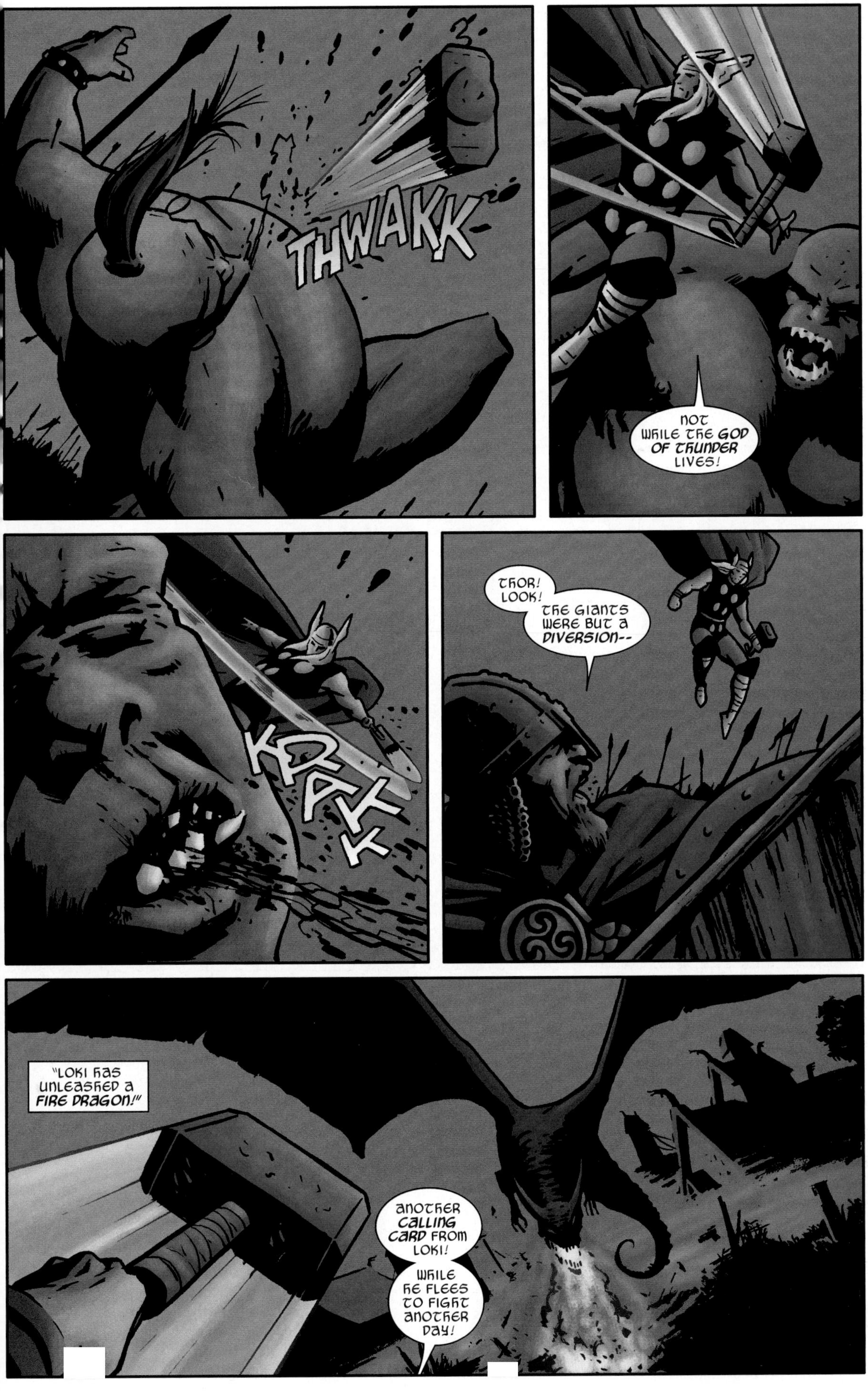
THWAKK
NOT WHILE THE GOD OF THUNDER LIVES!
KRAKK
THOR! LOOK!
THE GIANTS WERE BUT A DIVERSION--
"LOKI HAS UNLEASHED A FIRE DRAGON!"
ANOTHER CALLING CARD FROM LOKI!
WHILE HE FLEES TO FIGHT ANOTHER DAY!

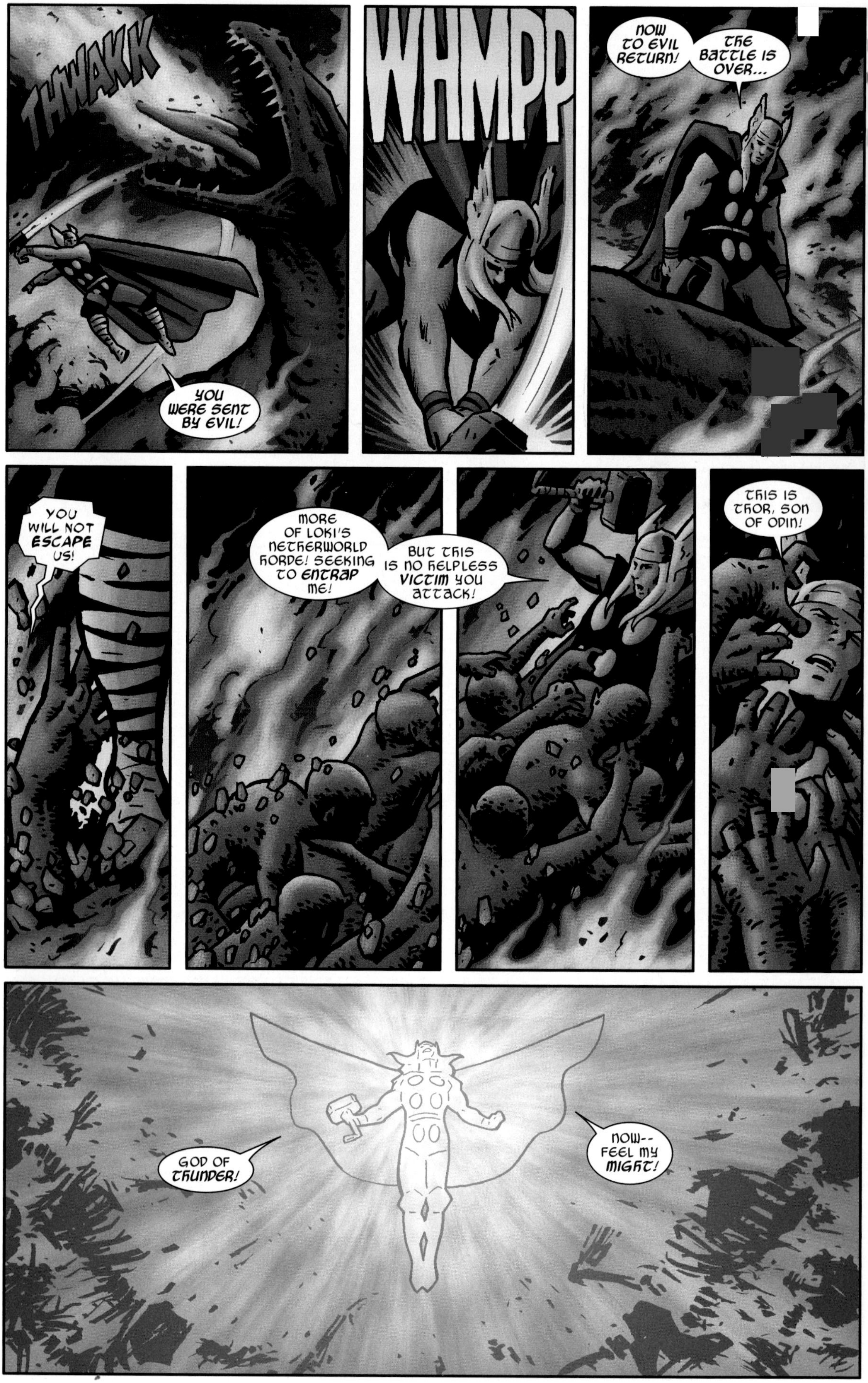
THWAKK
YOU WERE SENT BY EVIL!
WHMPP
NOW TO EVIL RETURN!
THE BATTLE IS OVER...
YOU WILL NOT ESCAPE US!
MORE OF LOKI'S NETHERWORLD HORDE! SEEKING TO ENTRAP ME!
BUT THIS IS NO HELPLESS VICTIM YOU ATTACK!
THIS IS THOR, SON OF ODIN!
GOD OF THUNDER!
NOW-- FEEL MY MIGHT!

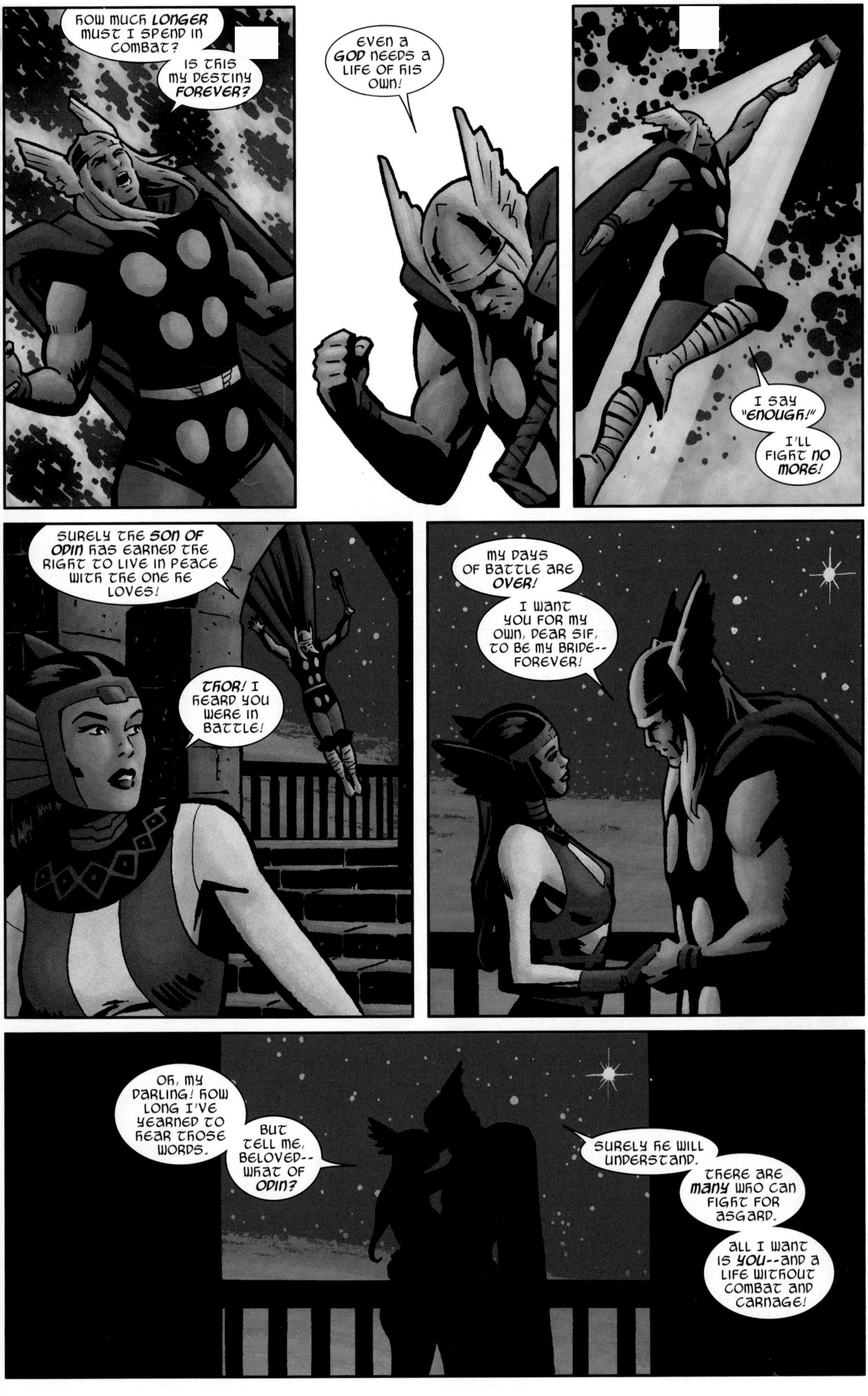
HOW MUCH LONGER MUST I SPEND IN COMBAT?
IS THIS MY DESTINY FOREVER?
EVEN A GOD NEEDS A LIFE OF HIS OWN!
I SAY "ENOUGH!"
I'LL FIGHT NO MORE!
SURELY THE SON OF ODIN HAS EARNED THE RIGHT TO LIVE IN PEACE WITH THE ONE HE LOVES!
THOR! I HEARD YOU WERE IN BATTLE!
MY DAYS OF BATTLE ARE OVER!
I WANT YOU FOR MY OWN, DEAR SIF, TO BE MY BRIDE-- FOREVER!
OH, MY DARLING! HOW LONG I'VE YEARNED TO HEAR THOSE WORDS.
BUT TELL ME, BELOVED-- WHAT OF ODIN?
SURELY HE WILL UNDERSTAND.
THERE ARE MANY WHO CAN FIGHT FOR ASGARD.
ALL I WANT IS YOU--AND A LIFE WITHOUT COMBAT AND CARNAGE!

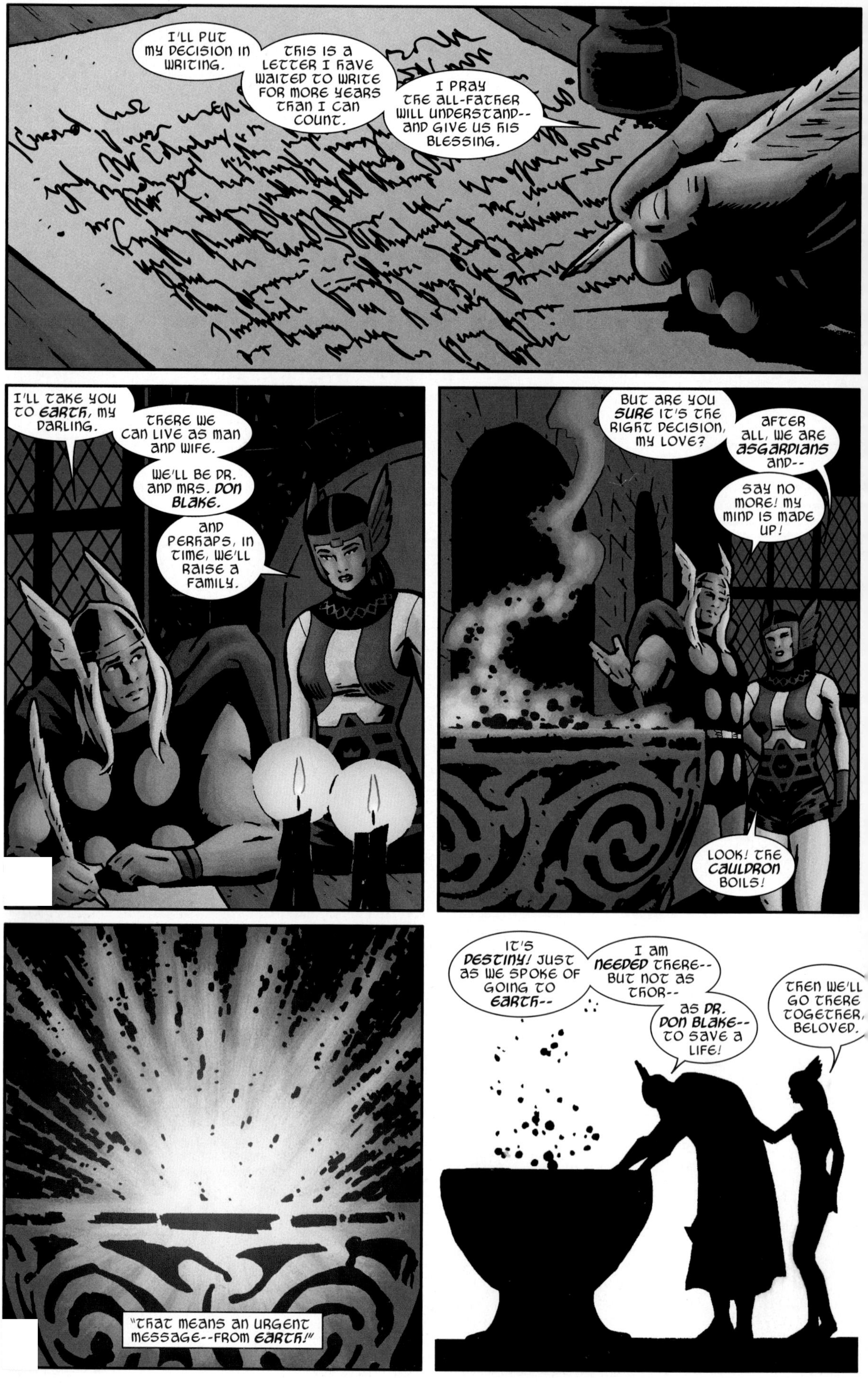

I'LL PUT MY DECISION IN WRITING.
THIS IS A LETTER I HAVE WAITED TO WRITE FOR MORE YEARS THAN I CAN COUNT.
I PRAY THE ALL-FATHER WILL UNDERSTAND-- AND GIVE US HIS BLESSING.
I'LL TAKE YOU TO EARTH, MY DARLING.
THERE WE CAN LIVE AS MAN AND WIFE.
WE'LL BE DR. AND MRS. DON BLAKE.
AND PERHAPS, IN TIME, WE'LL RAISE A FAMILY.
BUT ARE YOU SURE IT'S THE RIGHT DECISION, MY LOVE?
AFTER ALL, WE ARE ASGARDIANS AND--
SAY NO MORE! MY MIND IS MADE UP!
LOOK! THE CAULDRON BOILS!
"THAT MEANS AN URGENT MESSAGE--FROM EARTH!"
IT'S DESTINY! JUST AS WE SPOKE OF GOING TO EARTH--
I AM NEEDED THERE-- BUT NOT AS THOR--
AS DR. DON BLAKE-- TO SAVE A LIFE!
THEN WE'LL GO THERE TOGETHER, BELOVED.

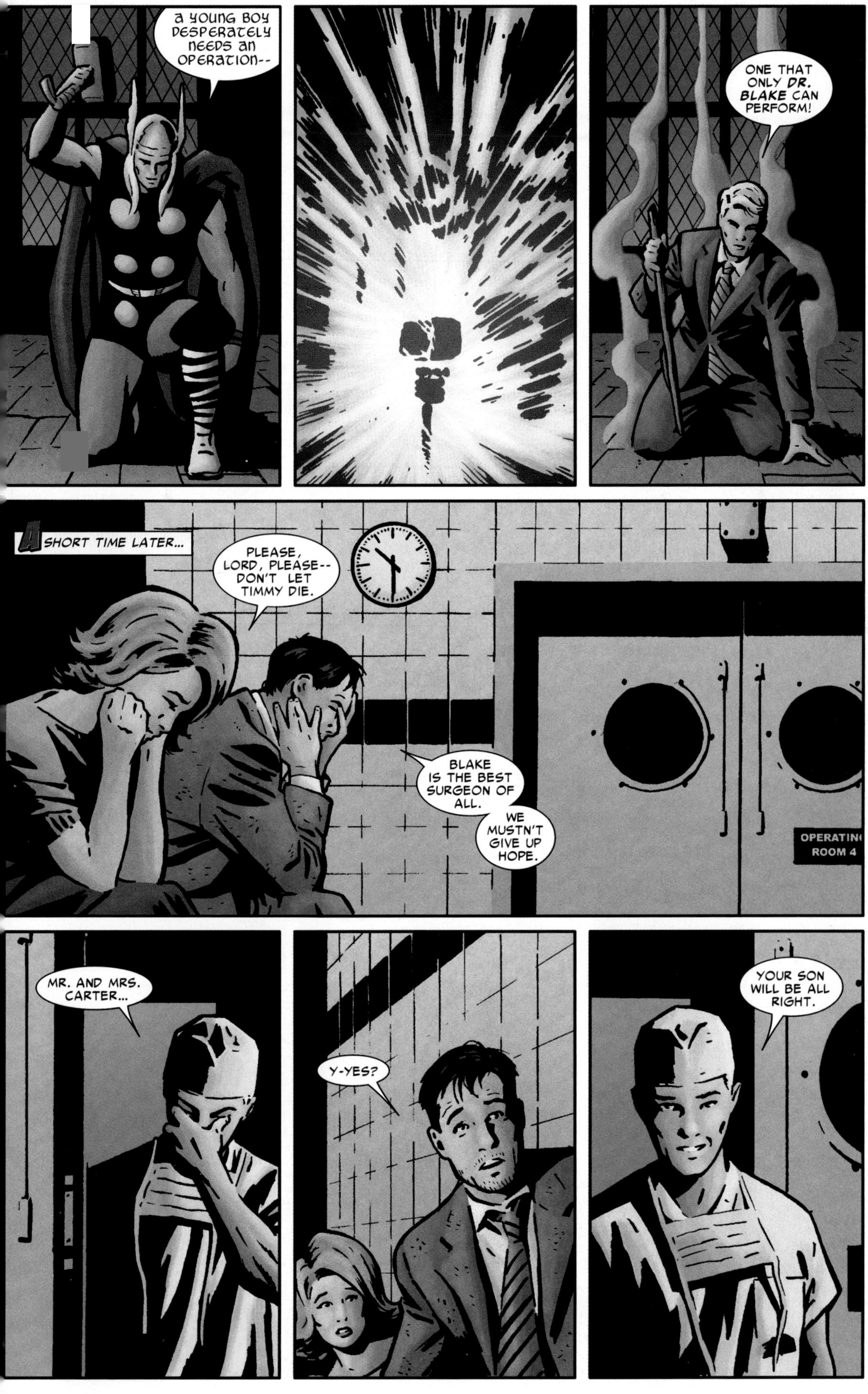

A YOUNG BOY DESPERATELY NEEDS AN OPERATION--
ONE THAT ONLY DR. BLAKE CAN PERFORM!
A SHORT TIME LATER...
PLEASE, LORD, PLEASE--DON'T LET TIMMY DIE.
BLAKE IS THE BEST SURGEON OF ALL.
WE MUSTN'T GIVE UP HOPE.
OPERATING ROOM 4
MR. AND MRS. CARTER...
Y-YES?
YOUR SON WILL BE ALL RIGHT.

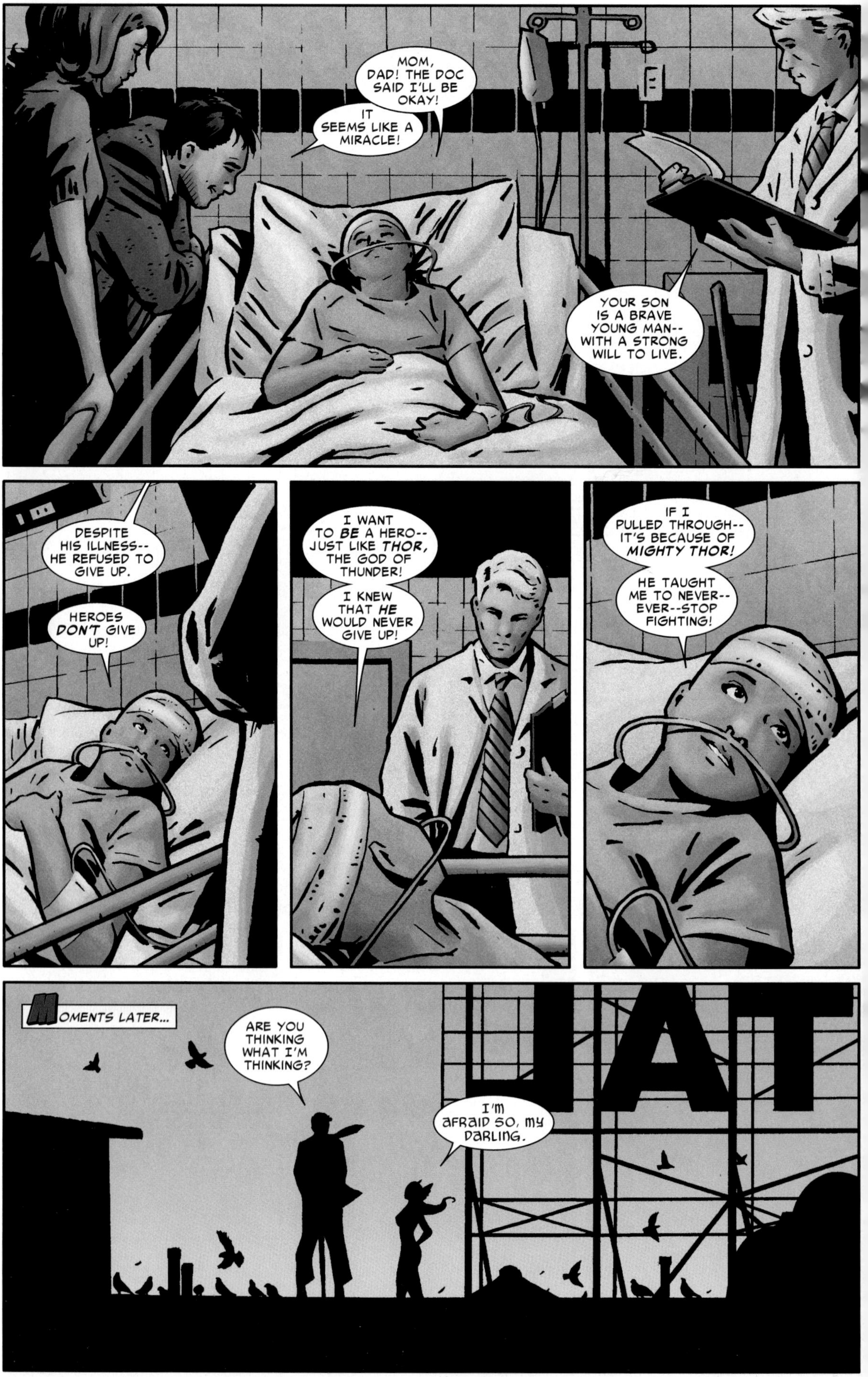
MOM, DAD! THE DOC SAID I'LL BE OKAY!
IT SEEMS LIKE A MIRACLE!
YOUR SON IS A BRAVE YOUNG MAN-- WITH A STRONG WILL TO LIVE.
DESPITE HIS ILLNESS-- HE REFUSED TO GIVE UP.
HEROES DON'T GIVE UP!
I WANT TO BE A HERO-- JUST LIKE THOR, THE GOD OF THUNDER!
I KNEW THAT HE WOULD NEVER GIVE UP!
IF I PULLED THROUGH-- IT'S BECAUSE OF MIGHTY THOR!
HE TAUGHT ME TO NEVER-- EVER--STOP FIGHTING!
MOMENTS LATER...
ARE YOU THINKING WHAT I'M THINKING?
I'M AFRAID SO, MY DARLING.

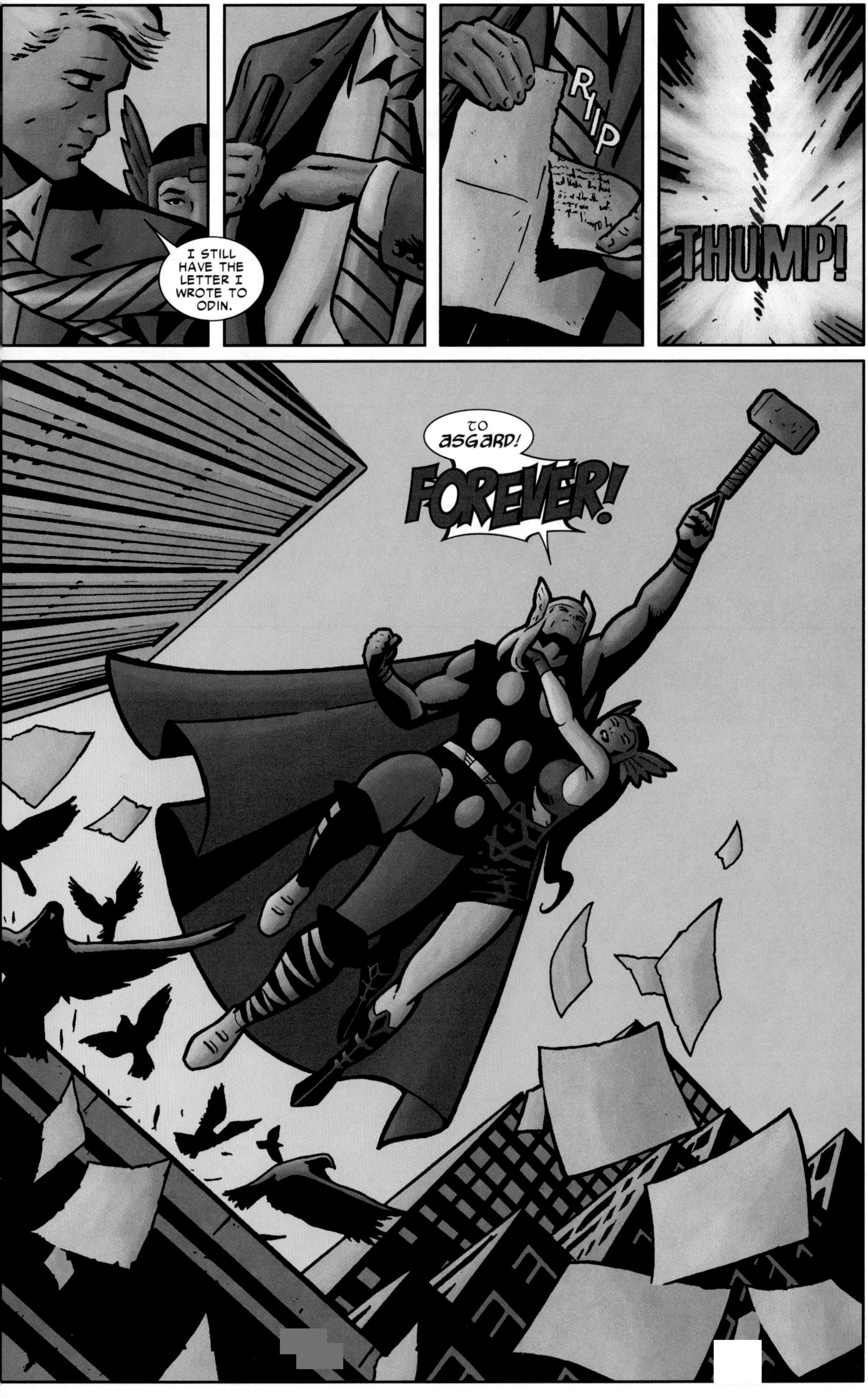
I STILL HAVE THE LETTER I WROTE TO ODIN.
RIP
THUMP!
TO ASGARD!
FOREVER!

The MINI MARVELS present...

WELCOME BACK THOR

by CHRIS GIARRUSSO chrisGcomics.com

ALEJANDRO ARBONA - *Assistant Editor* WARREN SIMONS - *Editor* JOE QUESADA - *Editor In Chief* DAN BUCKLEY - *Publisher*

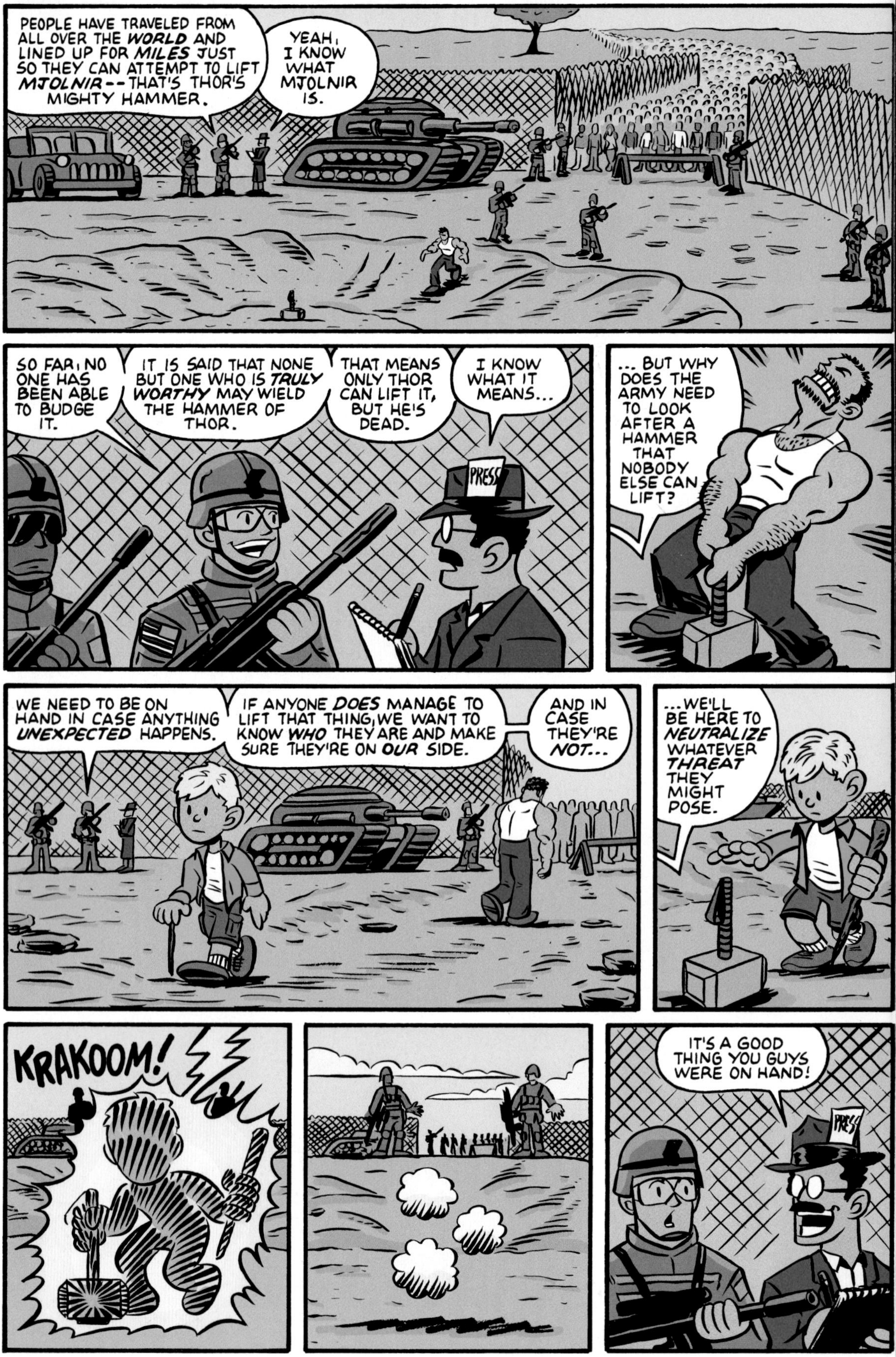

PEOPLE HAVE TRAVELED FROM ALL OVER THE WORLD AND LINED UP FOR MILES JUST SO THEY CAN ATTEMPT TO LIFT MJOLNIR--THAT'S THOR'S MIGHTY HAMMER.
YEAH, I KNOW WHAT MJOLNIR IS.
SO FAR, NO ONE HAS BEEN ABLE TO BUDGE IT.
IT IS SAID THAT NONE BUT ONE WHO IS TRULY WORTHY MAY WIELD THE HAMMER OF THOR.
THAT MEANS ONLY THOR CAN LIFT IT, BUT HE'S DEAD.
I KNOW WHAT IT MEANS...
PRESS
... BUT WHY DOES THE ARMY NEED TO LOOK AFTER A HAMMER THAT NOBODY ELSE CAN LIFT?
WE NEED TO BE ON HAND IN CASE ANYTHING UNEXPECTED HAPPENS.
IF ANYONE DOES MANAGE TO LIFT THAT THING, WE WANT TO KNOW WHO THEY ARE AND MAKE SURE THEY'RE ON OUR SIDE.
AND IN CASE THEY'RE NOT...
...WE'LL BE HERE TO NEUTRALIZE WHATEVER THREAT THEY MIGHT POSE.
KRAKOOM!
IT'S A GOOD THING YOU GUYS WERE ON HAND!
PRESS

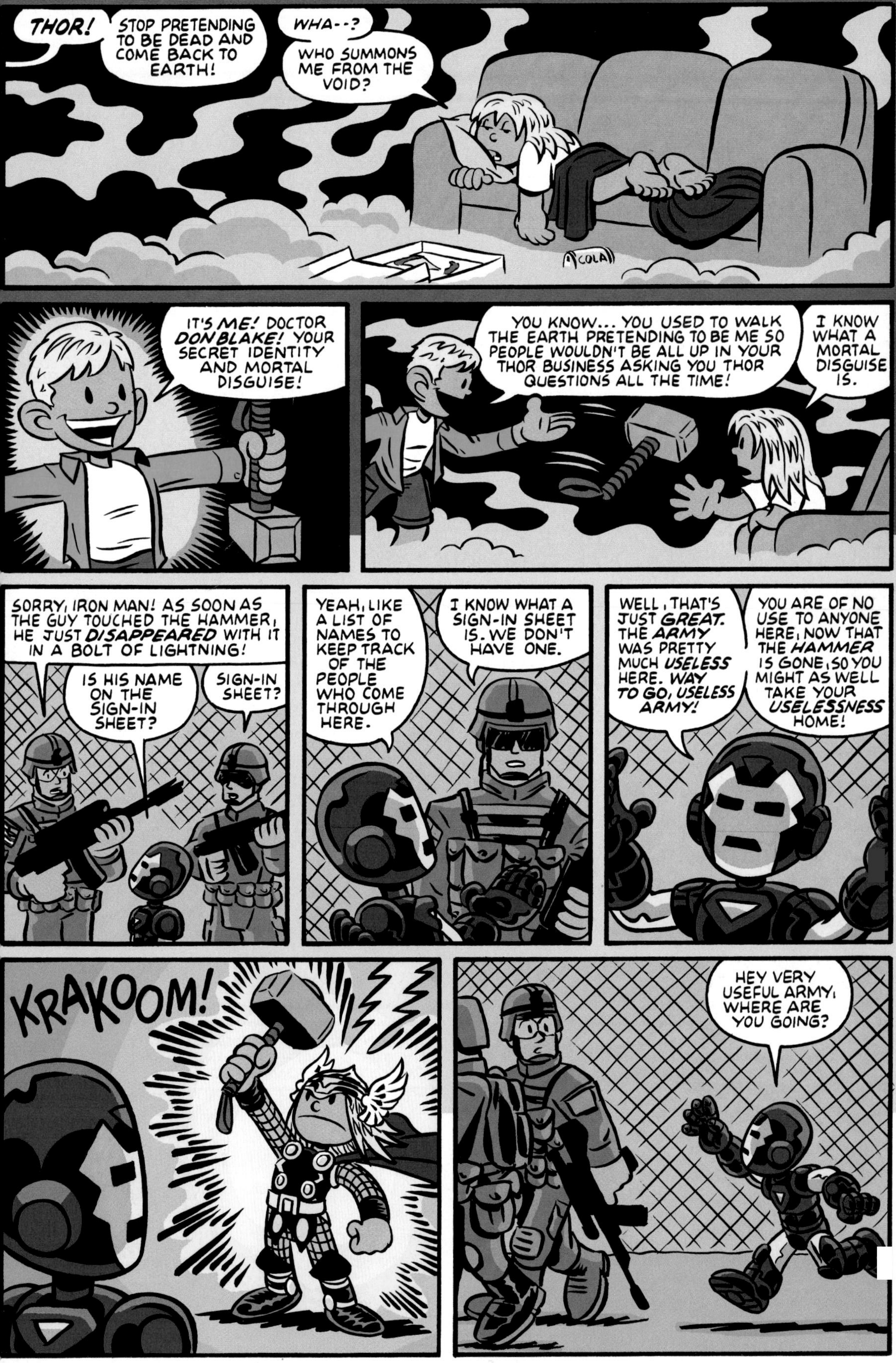
THOR!
STOP PRETENDING TO BE DEAD AND COME BACK TO EARTH!
WHA--?
WHO SUMMONS ME FROM THE VOID?
ACOLA
IT'S ME! DOCTOR DON BLAKE! YOUR SECRET IDENTITY AND MORTAL DISGUISE!
YOU KNOW... YOU USED TO WALK THE EARTH PRETENDING TO BE ME SO PEOPLE WOULDN'T BE ALL UP IN YOUR THOR BUSINESS ASKING YOU THOR QUESTIONS ALL THE TIME!
I KNOW WHAT A MORTAL DISGUISE IS.
SORRY, IRON MAN! AS SOON AS THE GUY TOUCHED THE HAMMER, HE JUST DISAPPEARED WITH IT IN A BOLT OF LIGHTNING!
IS HIS NAME ON THE SIGN-IN SHEET?
SIGN-IN SHEET?
YEAH, LIKE A LIST OF NAMES TO KEEP TRACK OF THE PEOPLE WHO COME THROUGH HERE.
I KNOW WHAT A SIGN-IN SHEET IS. WE DON'T HAVE ONE.
WELL, THAT'S JUST GREAT. THE ARMY WAS PRETTY MUCH USELESS HERE. WAY TO GO, USELESS ARMY!
YOU ARE OF NO USE TO ANYONE HERE, NOW THAT THE HAMMER IS GONE, SO YOU MIGHT AS WELL TAKE YOUR USELESSNESS HOME!
KRAKOOM!
HEY VERY USEFUL ARMY, WHERE ARE YOU GOING?

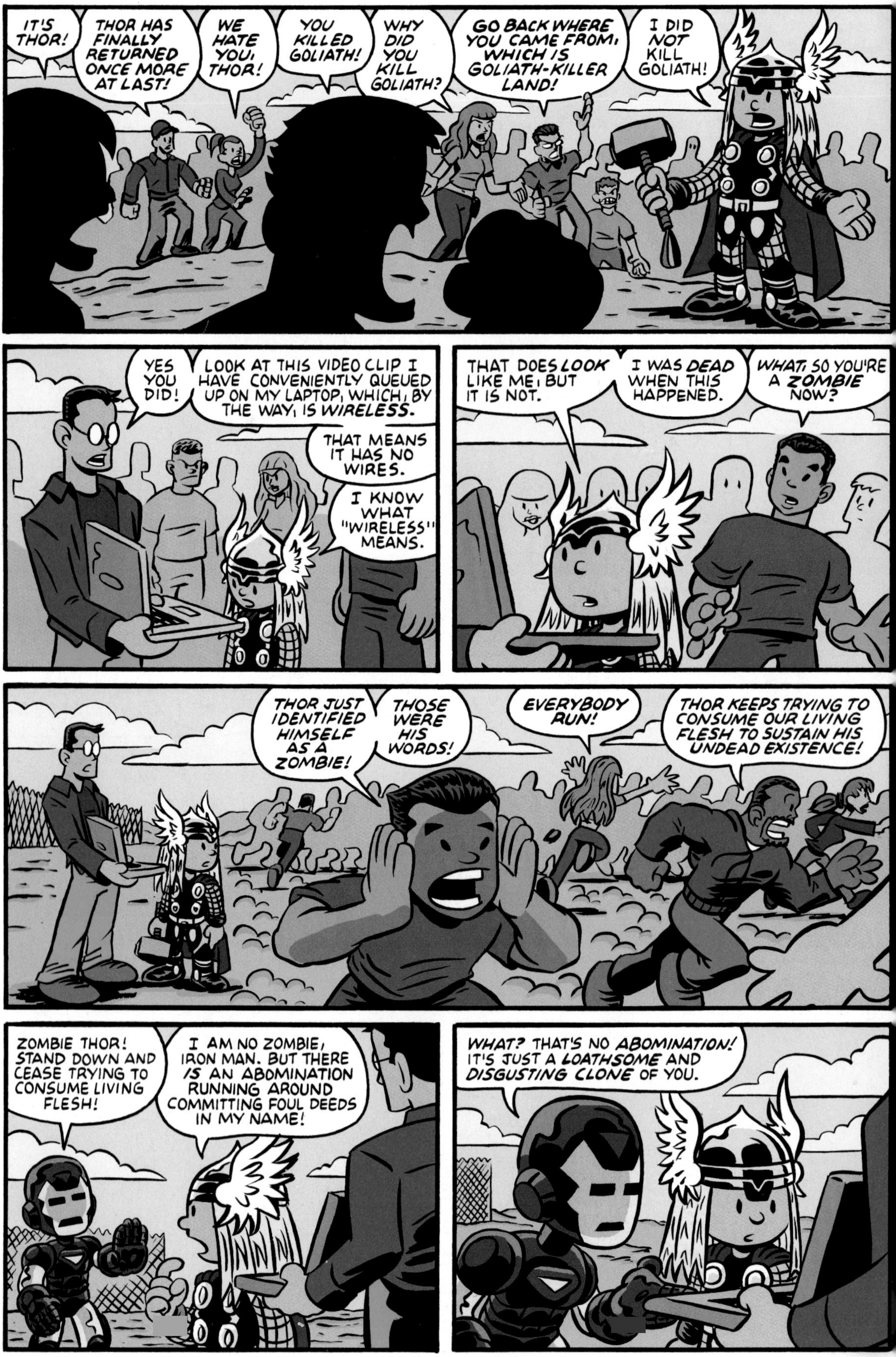
IT'S THOR!
THOR HAS FINALLY RETURNED ONCE MORE AT LAST!
WE HATE YOU, THOR!
YOU KILLED GOLIATH!
WHY DID YOU KILL GOLIATH?
GO BACK WHERE YOU CAME FROM, WHICH IS GOLIATH-KILLER LAND!
I DID NOT KILL GOLIATH!
YES YOU DID!
LOOK AT THIS VIDEO CLIP I HAVE CONVENIENTLY QUEUED UP ON MY LAPTOP, WHICH, BY THE WAY, IS WIRELESS.
THAT MEANS IT HAS NO WIRES.
I KNOW WHAT "WIRELESS" MEANS.
THAT DOES LOOK LIKE ME, BUT IT IS NOT.
I WAS DEAD WHEN THIS HAPPENED.
WHAT, SO YOU'RE A ZOMBIE NOW?
THOR JUST IDENTIFIED HIMSELF AS A ZOMBIE!
THOSE WERE HIS WORDS!
EVERYBODY RUN!
THOR KEEPS TRYING TO CONSUME OUR LIVING FLESH TO SUSTAIN HIS UNDEAD EXISTENCE!
ZOMBIE THOR! STAND DOWN AND CEASE TRYING TO CONSUME LIVING FLESH!
I AM NO ZOMBIE, IRON MAN. BUT THERE IS AN ABOMINATION RUNNING AROUND COMMITTING FOUL DEEDS IN MY NAME!
WHAT? THAT'S NO ABOMINATION! IT'S JUST A LOATHSOME AND DISGUSTING CLONE OF YOU.

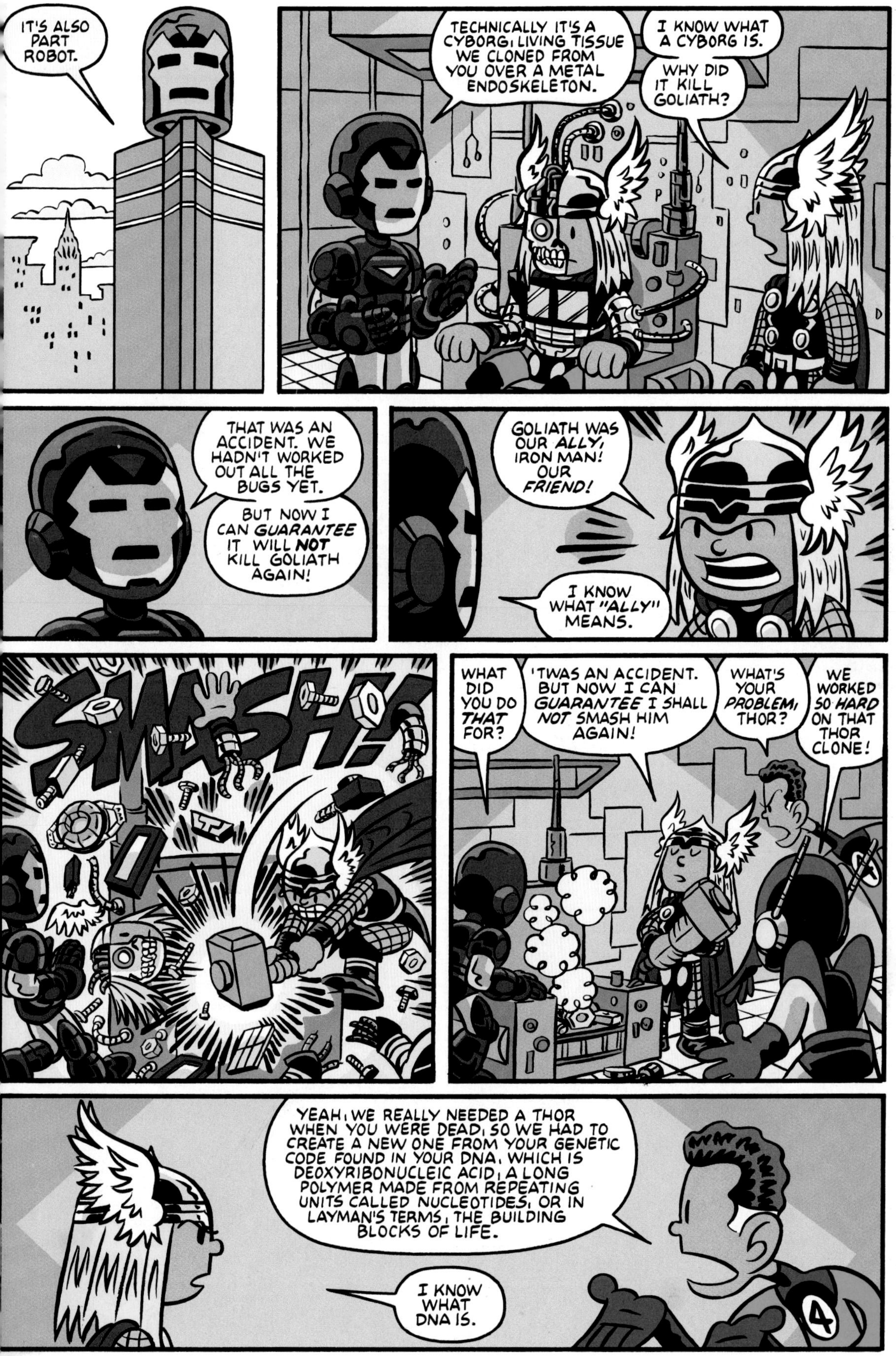
IT'S ALSO PART ROBOT.
TECHNICALLY IT'S A CYBORG: LIVING TISSUE WE CLONED FROM YOU OVER A METAL ENDOSKELETON.
I KNOW WHAT A CYBORG IS.
WHY DID IT KILL GOLIATH?
THAT WAS AN ACCIDENT. WE HADN'T WORKED OUT ALL THE BUGS YET.
BUT NOW I CAN GUARANTEE IT WILL NOT KILL GOLIATH AGAIN!
GOLIATH WAS OUR ALLY, IRON MAN! OUR FRIEND!
I KNOW WHAT "ALLY" MEANS.
SMASH!!
WHAT DID YOU DO THAT FOR?
'TWAS AN ACCIDENT. BUT NOW I CAN GUARANTEE I SHALL NOT SMASH HIM AGAIN!
WHAT'S YOUR PROBLEM, THOR?
WE WORKED SO HARD ON THAT THOR CLONE!
YEAH, WE REALLY NEEDED A THOR WHEN YOU WERE DEAD, SO WE HAD TO CREATE A NEW ONE FROM YOUR GENETIC CODE FOUND IN YOUR DNA, WHICH IS DEOXYRIBONUCLEIC ACID, A LONG POLYMER MADE FROM REPEATING UNITS CALLED NUCLEOTIDES, OR IN LAYMAN'S TERMS, THE BUILDING BLOCKS OF LIFE.
I KNOW WHAT DNA IS.

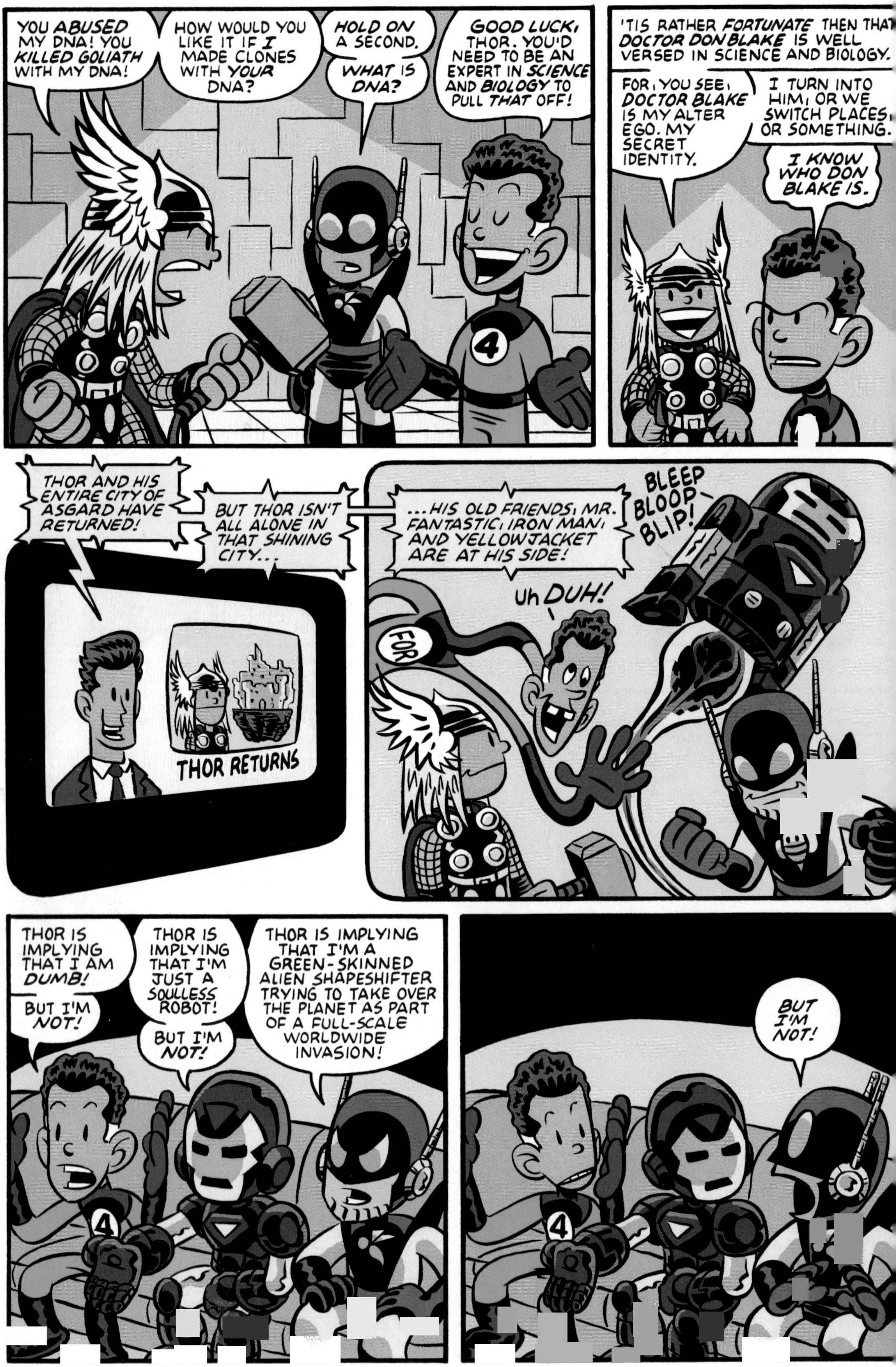

YOU ABUSED MY DNA! YOU KILLED GOLIATH WITH MY DNA!
HOW WOULD YOU LIKE IT IF I MADE CLONES WITH YOUR DNA?
HOLD ON A SECOND.
WHAT IS DNA?
GOOD LUCK, THOR. YOU'D NEED TO BE AN EXPERT IN SCIENCE AND BIOLOGY TO PULL THAT OFF!
'TIS RATHER FORTUNATE THEN THAT DOCTOR DON BLAKE IS WELL VERSED IN SCIENCE AND BIOLOGY.
FOR, YOU SEE, DOCTOR BLAKE IS MY ALTER EGO. MY SECRET IDENTITY.
I TURN INTO HIM, OR WE SWITCH PLACES, OR SOMETHING.
I KNOW WHO DON BLAKE IS.
THOR AND HIS ENTIRE CITY OF ASGARD HAVE RETURNED!
BUT THOR ISN'T ALL ALONE IN THAT SHINING CITY...
THOR RETURNS
...HIS OLD FRIENDS, MR. FANTASTIC, IRON MAN, AND YELLOWJACKET ARE AT HIS SIDE!
BLEEP BLOOP-BLIP!
Uh DUH!
FOR
THOR IS IMPLYING THAT I AM DUMB!
BUT I'M NOT!
THOR IS IMPLYING THAT I'M JUST A SOULLESS ROBOT!
BUT I'M NOT!
THOR IS IMPLYING THAT I'M A GREEN-SKINNED ALIEN SHAPESHIFTER TRYING TO TAKE OVER THE PLANET AS PART OF A FULL-SCALE WORLDWIDE INVASION!
BUT I'M NOT!

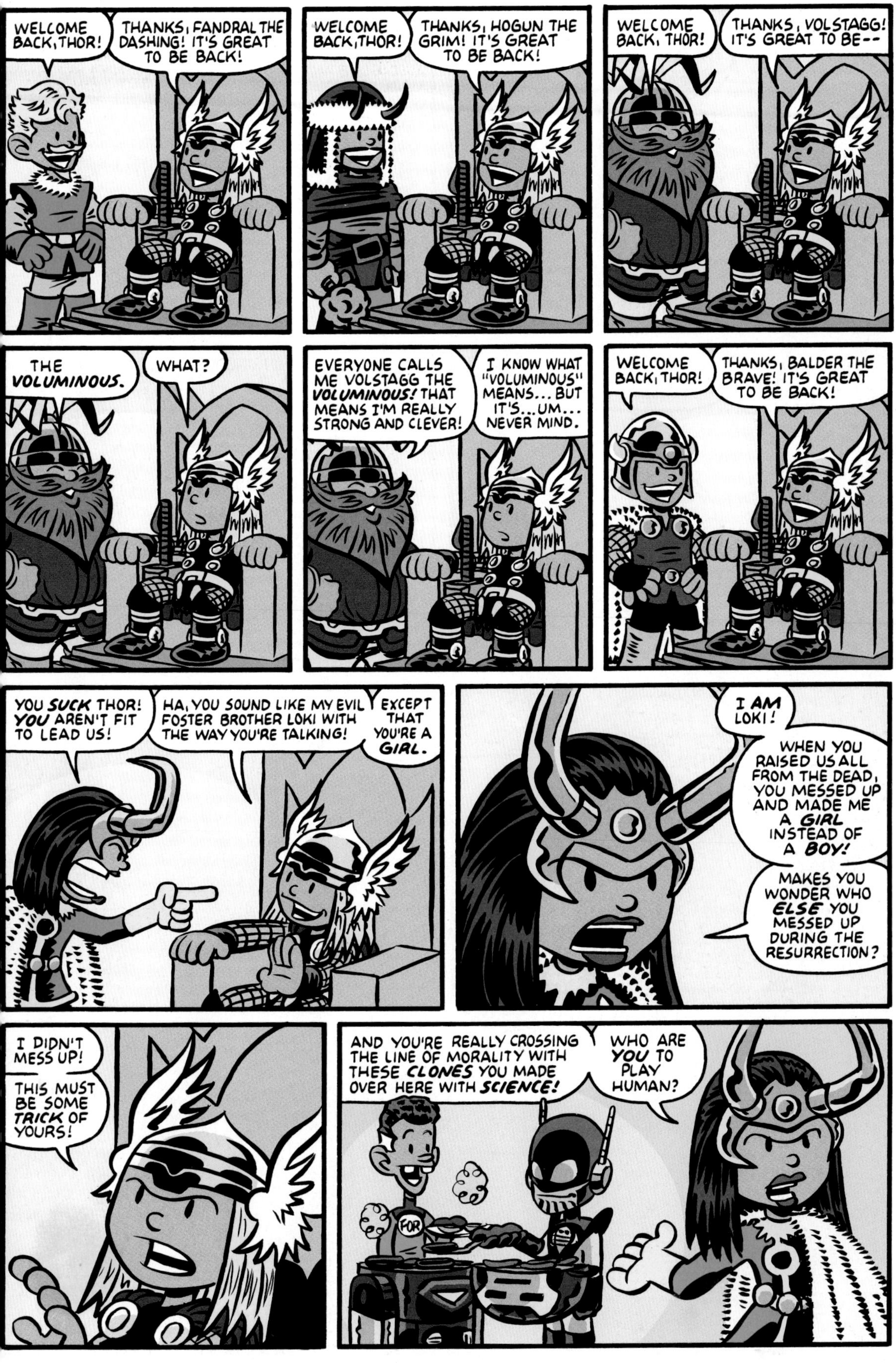

WELCOME BACK, THOR!
THANKS, FANDRAL THE DASHING! IT'S GREAT TO BE BACK!
WELCOME BACK, THOR!
THANKS, HOGUN THE GRIM! IT'S GREAT TO BE BACK!
WELCOME BACK, THOR!
THANKS, VOLSTAGG! IT'S GREAT TO BE--
THE VOLUMINOUS.
WHAT?
EVERYONE CALLS ME VOLSTAGG THE VOLUMINOUS! THAT MEANS I'M REALLY STRONG AND CLEVER!
I KNOW WHAT "VOLUMINOUS" MEANS... BUT IT'S...UM... NEVER MIND.
WELCOME BACK, THOR!
THANKS, BALDER THE BRAVE! IT'S GREAT TO BE BACK!
YOU SUCK THOR! YOU AREN'T FIT TO LEAD US!
HA, YOU SOUND LIKE MY EVIL FOSTER BROTHER LOKI WITH THE WAY YOU'RE TALKING!
EXCEPT THAT YOU'RE A GIRL.
I AM LOKI!
WHEN YOU RAISED US ALL FROM THE DEAD, YOU MESSED UP AND MADE ME A GIRL INSTEAD OF A BOY!
MAKES YOU WONDER WHO ELSE YOU MESSED UP DURING THE RESURRECTION?
I DIDN'T MESS UP!
THIS MUST BE SOME TRICK OF YOURS!
AND YOU'RE REALLY CROSSING THE LINE OF MORALITY WITH THESE CLONES YOU MADE OVER HERE WITH SCIENCE!
WHO ARE YOU TO PLAY HUMAN?
FOR

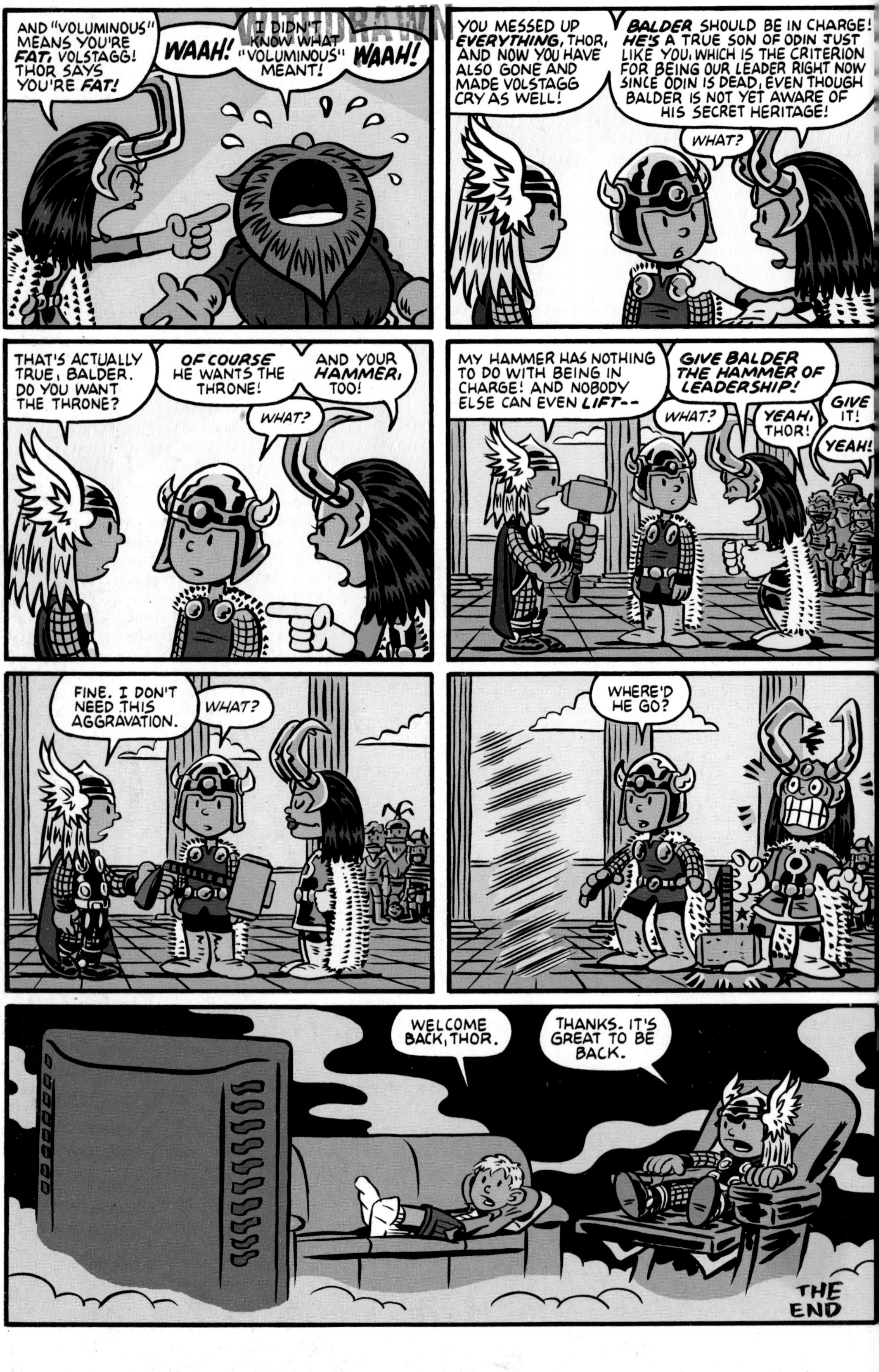
AND "VOLUMINOUS" MEANS YOU'RE FAT, VOLSTAGG! THOR SAYS YOU'RE FAT!
WAAH!
I DIDN'T KNOW WHAT "VOLUMINOUS" MEANT!
WAAH!
YOU MESSED UP EVERYTHING, THOR, AND NOW YOU HAVE ALSO GONE AND MADE VOLSTAGG CRY AS WELL!
BALDER SHOULD BE IN CHARGE! HE'S A TRUE SON OF ODIN JUST LIKE YOU, WHICH IS THE CRITERION FOR BEING OUR LEADER RIGHT NOW SINCE ODIN IS DEAD, EVEN THOUGH BALDER IS NOT YET AWARE OF HIS SECRET HERITAGE!
WHAT?
THAT'S ACTUALLY TRUE, BALDER. DO YOU WANT THE THRONE?
OF COURSE HE WANTS THE THRONE!
AND YOUR HAMMER, TOO!
WHAT?
MY HAMMER HAS NOTHING TO DO WITH BEING IN CHARGE! AND NOBODY ELSE CAN EVEN LIFT--
GIVE BALDER THE HAMMER OF LEADERSHIP!
WHAT?
YEAH, THOR!
GIVE IT!
YEAH!
FINE. I DON'T NEED THIS AGGRAVATION.
WHAT?
WHERE'D HE GO?
WELCOME BACK, THOR.
THANKS. IT'S GREAT TO BE BACK.
THE END